☐ *Mysterious Worlds*

◻ Other Books by DENNIS BARDENS

Mysterious Worlds

A PERSONAL INVESTIGATION OF
THE WEIRD, THE UNCANNY, AND
THE UNEXPLAINED

Dennis Bardens

COWLES BOOK COMPANY, INC.
NEW YORK

COPY 4

For Marie and Peter

☐ Acknowledgments

EVERY author of a factual work of this kind is indebted to many people for help as to sources, for information, and advice. They are so numerous in this instance that it is impossible to mention them all.

Firstly, I must thank Mr. John Cutton, Honorary Secretary of the Society for Psychical Research, and Miss Eleanor O'Keefe, his secretary, for much useful help and advice (adding the necessary rider that the society—a scientific one—holds no corporate view and is not by inference committed to approval or endorsement of anything this book contains). I am grateful, too, to the Parapsychology Foundation of New York for generous support and encouragement.

Mr. Bernard J. Kelly of the Denver *Post,* Colorado, gave invaluable assistance in my experimentation into precognition by making my needs and interests widely known in that vast area, as did Mr. Frank Scott, General Manager of Radio KBON, Omaha, Nebraska. Professor Leo Sprinkle, Ph.D., of the University of Wyoming was good enough to hypnotize a student, *J.S.,* for the purposes of my precognition research; Professor Stanley Krippner, Ph.D., Director of the Dream Laboratory of the Department of Psychology, Maimonides Medical Center, New York, provided valuable information on the subject of dreams.

I also extend my thanks to Mr. Alan H. Wesencraft of the University of London Library and to Miss D. Tindall, Librarian of the Reform Club, for their patient attention to my many and often difficult queries; to Mr. Maurice Barbanell, Editor of *Psychic News* and his staff for their unfailing courtesy and help; to Dr. George Morey, LL.D.; and, finally, to Mrs. G. Phillips and Miss

Dorothy Richardson for their care and kindness in reading and checking the finished manuscript.

To my many correspondents and informants throughout the world I say "Thank you" for all the trouble they have taken to relate their experiences, answer queries, and follow up inquiries.

Dennis Bardens

☐ Contents

☐ Introduction

ONE night in October, 1967, Mrs. Helen Peters of New Jersey awoke from a troubled dream to find herself in tears. Nor did the horror of her nightmare lift with full consciousness, as the terrors of that mental twilight world of sleep so often do. An overwhelming sense of imminent tragedy had gripped her. She was convinced with every instinct that she possessed that the plane in which her husband, Nicholas Peters, was traveling had just crashed.

She telephoned the airline's agent in New York.

"Everything's all right," she was told. But her sense of urgency made itself felt at the other end of the line. "We'll check, just to reassure you, and call you back," the airline official promised.

Within an hour her conviction was proved. The British European Airways Comet carrying sixty-six passengers had crashed off the coast of Cyprus, killing all passengers and crew.

Mrs. Peters was six thousand miles away from her husband at that time. How did she know? Was it coincidence born of anxiety? Was it premonition? Was it telepathy?

In 1968, a bus conductor named Charles Hill moved into a council house in Nottingham with his family. They had waited a long time to qualify for the rent-controlled accommodation, which was a great improvement on their previous home, with better amenities and a much nicer environment.

They had been there only a short time when Mr. Hill suddenly awoke in his upstairs bedroom, early one morning, and saw the figure of a man walking toward the window. He looked rather like a soldier in the French Foreign Legion, Mr. Hill thought, because he was wearing a white cloth over his neck, and a cape. Then he just disappeared. Later, Sandra Hill, the family's elder daughter, glimpsed a similar figure on the stairs in broad daylight.

Both Charles and Sandra Hill were terrified. So terrified, in fact, that the entire family left the house and refused to return there, although this meant abandoning all their belongings and the home they had waited so long to move into.

Could the "sightings" have been hallucinations? Or was there any connection with the fact that a young man had committed suicide, not too many years before, in that upstairs bedroom?

It is now more than thirty years since I made my way to Banbury Castle, in Oxfordshire, to enjoy long chats with J. W. Dunne, who had astounded the scientific world with his book *An Experiment with Time,* in which he propounded the unprecedented and extraordinary theory that our conceptions of time were wrong, that in sleep the mind could travel backward and forward in time once it was freed of the shackles of consciousness.

In order that I might interpret his ideas correctly, I took my typewriter with me and wrote the interview there. It was printed in a Sunday paper, but I well remember the skeptical hilarity of the subeditors as they prepared it for print.

Now we have to revise our ideas about time. In astronomy, for instance, as the Astronomer Royal has said, "there is no such thing as present time." Light takes time to travel. The rays reaching the telescope have been traveling hundreds, often thousands, even millions of years. The astronomers at Mount Palomar, California, and Jodrell Bank in Cheshire are looking back into the past and viewing it as reality, although some of the things they see may have disappeared, and in any case would have changed their form and perhaps their position. In other words, the farther they look out into space, the longer they are moving backward in time. They can see and record what, in many cases, may no longer exist.

In certain circumstances, therefore, one can travel back in time. Can one also travel *forward,* into the future? Yes, says one expert. Anybody traveling faster than light would be outstripping time and would be moving into the future. But how can anybody move into a future that hasn't yet come to pass? Am I to believe that, while I am at home watching my television on Friday night, somebody else could, *in that same instant,* be seeing the world as it would be the day after tomorrow? It sounds like nonsense, but is it? Now that rockets are capable of achieving speeds of thousands of miles an hour, and since we know that friction is not a factor in space, how can we be sure that in future generations speeds greater than that of light will not be reached? And in that case, since men would be able to travel into the future, does this mean that the pattern of events is already laid out—that there is predestination?

I have mentioned only three of the worlds of thought that may justly be termed "mysterious." Such phenomena as telepathy, "hauntings," and the nature of time fascinate as well as tax the imagination. It is not morbid, surely, but a healthy intellectual exercise to seek some explanation, some logic, underlying the mysteries that confound us. In a world that is becoming increasingly standardized and hostile to individuality, it is at least of some comfort to know that there are worlds yet to explore—the worlds of telepathy, premonition, reincarnation, immortality, time, magic, hauntings, and the whole field of subjects covered by the broad term *psychical.*

In recent years psychical phenomena and science have impinged increasingly upon each other. To show an interest in such matters may cause amusement in some circles, but these subjects are no longer the domain of the superstitious, the credulous, the fearful, or the merely romantic. Although, because of the long legacy of struggle by which man has reached his present status, we are all born with a deep-rooted fear of the unknown, with a predisposition to believe in magic, and with certain atavistic instincts (as manifested in wars, persecutions, and crime), the facts of life and death and the workings of the human mind are now objects more of curiosity than of fear. Even the materialistic Soviet Union has assigned a team of experts to explore and, if possible, unravel the secret of the manner in which telepathy comes about, while the United States Air Force is engaged in similar research.

Similarly, we have been regaled for years by a constant spate of reports of unidentified flying objects, known as UFO's or "flying saucers." Are these the result of a sort of mass hysteria, or is there some residue of the unexplained? One cannot prove that little green men are invading us from Mars, but even the long-winded and obscure report on UFO's produced by the University of Colorado for the United States Air Force contains some highly factual accounts which have left the skeptical compilers quite baffled.

However, although the United States Air Force has decided to discontinue its investigations of unidentified flying objects, many organizations interested in these objects are still continuing their own independent studies and research.

It is, therefore, in a spirit of objective investigation but absorbing interest that I have applied myself to this somewhat difficult exploration. As I have explained in my previous work, *Ghosts and Hauntings,* I have for a very long time—for nearly forty years, in fact—been interested in psychical phenomena. I have never felt unduly intimidated by the fact that I am less sustained by academic achievement than some others in the same field.

It is, indeed, impossible for any one person to be a specialist in all the scientific fields covered by psychical research. These include psychiatry (to assess the reliability of informants); mathematics (to estimate the laws of probability and chance as they relate to certain types of spontaneous phenomena, such as precognition); physics (in relation to time, and the possibility of people being able to go backward and forward in time); physiology and medicine (in relation to the weight that may be attached to individual testimonies, remembering the limitations of the senses of sight and hearing); and a great many other specialized fields.

But let it not be thought that every inquirer must be weighed down with degrees as a prerequisite to probing into psychical phenomena. In the past, experts have been very wrong indeed. Specialists are often thinkers in blinkers. Their empirical knowledge is frequently a handicap when they are confronted with facts that do not fit any known pattern; possibilities are dismissed as impossibilities.

It was John Logie Baird (1888–1946), a comparative amateur with many technical limitations, whose imagination paved the way to television. It was Baird who, in 1925, demonstrated a mechanical television system utilizing the Nipkow disk; a few years later, in association with the British Broadcasting Corporation, he transmitted the first pictures. This tenacious Scot had an uphill fight to convince anyone that his dream was either practicable or potentially useful.

Alfred Smee, a member of the Royal Society, solemnly told Victorians that electricity would "forever remain a pretty scientific toy." Smee had, in 1839, introduced useful modifications in the construction of the voltaic cell—but, as his remarks show, he failed to see its immense potentialities.

Sir John Cockcroft, who split the atom in 1932, declared that the discovery could never be put to any commercial use; to try and control the breakup of the atom would be, he declared, rather like "trying to shoot a gnat in the Albert Hall with a bow and arrow." (The point of Sir John's analogy will be appreciated if one remembers that the Albert Hall, in Kensington, London, which will celebrate its centennial in 1971, is in the form of a gigantic ellipse covered by a dome—it is 200 feet long, 160 feet wide, and 140 feet high.)

Since Sir John's remark was made, nuclear power reactors—which, in effect, are carefully controlled explosions—have been built all over the world. Nuclear power has become a reality, harnessed to man's needs and purposes.

Let us, then, avoiding fear and superstition on the one hand and arid skepticism on the other, ask ourselves: Are there ghosts, and if so, what are they? If people really do see and hear them, are these things due to some trick of time or light or the special sensitivity of particular people? Do ghosts have an active intelligence and volition of their own (which would imply some measure of immortality) or are they merely a trace, registered in some way we do not yet understand, of those who once lived but now are dead? Does magic work, and if so, what is it and how and why does it function? Is witchcraft a mad cult or a dynamic and significant expression of some mysterious force? Is telepathy a fact? If so, why does it occur?

I would be rash, indeed, to pretend to offer the reader a definitive answer to all these rhetorical questions. Any one of the subjects covered in this book could, if enlarged upon sufficiently, become a book in itself. In order to fulfill the mandate I have set myself there must inevitably be omission and compression. However, because I am convinced that these fields of thought and activity are important, I shall be satisfied if the reader's curiosity and interest are aroused. I hope to provide him with a greater understanding of the complexity of the problems that others are trying to explore and solve, and to leave him free to pursue on his own account a more detailed appraisal of any particular subject that appeals to him.

Dennis Bardens

Reform Club,
Pall Mall,
London, S.W. 1

☐ 1. Mind to Mind

THE scene is the railroad station in Moscow. The date I do not know, except that it is sometime in the future. How far distant I cannot tell. It may be soon. It may be late.

A young student, clutching his ticket, his international passport, and a cheap fiber suitcase, bundles in the train at the last moment. He takes a corner seat by the window. Opposite him sits a nondescript, middle-aged man, the kind nobody would notice. He is rather good at not being noticed.

Soon the train speeds on its way. The student produces a newspaper and buries his face behind it. He catches sight of an item dealing with a border clash between Russian and Chinese troops. "Perhaps it will do us good to have a little opposition from somebody stronger than ourselves," he thinks to himself. "We're always sneering at imperialists, but what are we, really? What about the way we crushed the Hungarian uprising? What about the way we occupied Czechoslovakia? Perhaps our rulers will now learn for themselves how unpleasant it is to be bullied and threatened by a stronger power. . . ."

Like many students, he sees the monolithic, militaristic state for what it is; he longs for a degree of freedom impossible in a police state.

He puts down his newspaper. He finds himself looking into the business end of the other man's revolver.

"What's this supposed to be?" he demands. "A joke?"

"Do not ask me questions," is the reply. "You are under arrest."

"But this is madness," says the student, the smile freezing on

1

his face and then changing to bewilderment. "What have I done? I don't know you. I haven't said a word."

"You are a traitorous reactionary and dangerous deviationist," snaps the secret-police man. "You were gloating over the news that the treacherous Chinese had perpetrated an unprovoked attack upon our brave Soviet soldiers. You were criticizing our heroic defense of the revolutionary proletariat in Hungary and Czechoslovakia."

"I deny it! You are an *agent provocateur!* What nonsense it is for you to pretend to read my thoughts!"

"Whether you like it or not, we *can* read your thoughts—and as you know well enough, I have just done so. But we're not going to tell traitors how we do it."

This isn't the pessimistic prescience of George Orwell carried to extremes. It is a forecast of what could happen if experiments in telepathy now taking place in the Soviet Union achieve the complete success that their initiators anticipate. *Telepathy* is a word coined toward the end of the last century by Frederick W. H. Myers, M.A., a brilliant classical scholar, a Fellow of Trinity College, Cambridge, and a researcher with both the curiosity and the discipline of the true scientist.

Together with such scholars as Edmund Gurney, a Fellow of Trinity with a special grounding in psychology and medicine, and Frank Podmore, Myers was author of the classic and monumental survey, *Phantasms of the Living,* which riveted the attention of the Victorians on the fact that weird things were happening almost every day which could not be explained by any known scientific standards. The book's careful assembly and thorough documentation of hundreds of cases of phantasms being seen in circumstances where there was a degree of corroboration from others of integrity, intelligence, and with no axes to grind, set a standard which serious psychical researchers have tried ever since—although not always with the same success—to emulate.

With Henry Sidgwick, Professor of Moral Philosophy at Cambridge, and others, Podmore was one of the founders of the Society for Psychical Research in 1882. The society, the first of its kind in the world, was formed for the purpose of investigating paranormal phenomena, collecting evidence by scientific means, and generally bringing intelligence and discipline to bear on matters that hitherto

2

had been a mixture of rumor, folklore, conjecture, and fact. One of the six committees formed by the society had as its object:

> An examination of the nature and extent of any influence which may be exerted by one mind upon another, apart from any generally recognized mode of perception.

In other words, the society was concerned with what we now term telepathy—the transmission of facts, messages, information, and mental images by other than normal or identifiable means.

Since then, thousands of cases have been reported to the society, many of them with a degree of corroboration and proof that establish telepathy as a fact.

Before we consider what the Soviet Union and other countries are doing to unravel the mysteries of telepathy, let me first illustrate what I mean by it.

There are two categories of telepathy—"spontaneous" (unsought, unpremeditated, unexpected) telepathy and "experimental" or contrived telepathy, where by deliberate act and logical routine, thoughts or mental images are transmitted over distances without mechanical aid of any kind. In the latter case, the number of thoughts so received, as well as the degree of their accuracy, gives some indication of whether the receiver, usually called the percipient, has some capacity for getting results that would not occur according to the laws of chance, or be made to occur by mere guesswork.

The spontaneous cases, apart from being less repetitive and boring than the long scientific experiments, illustrate quite well and often dramatically that some factor is often at work that defies all scientific explanation.

There are, for example, the many authenticated cases of apparitions that have appeared at the moment of death. Such instances are to be found in the literature of all countries and from all periods, but, more significantly, are also to be found in the files of the Society for Psychical Research and the American Society for Psychical Research, which was formed later, on the inspiration of its British counterpart.

Certain apparitions suggest strongly that a message has been sent, somehow, by one mind to another. There is the well-known case of the poet John Donne (1572–1631), who accompanied his

3

friend Sir Robert Drewry to the court of Henry IV of France. He had at first refused the invitation because of the pleadings of his wife, who was expecting a child at the time, but finally yielded to his friend's blandishments and left with his wife's reluctant permission.

Travel in those days was a long-winded business. It took nearly three weeks to reach Paris, and there Donne received a shock. He was sitting alone in his room when the phantasm of his wife passed through the room, bearing in her arms a dead child. Nor did it merely happen once. She appeared again and on the second occasion she looked Donne in the face, and then vanished. Seeing his friend so distraught, Sir Robert sent a messenger to England in the expectation that he would return after six weeks with reassuring news. Instead, the messenger returned with the news that, at the time Donne had seen his wife's phantasm in his room, she had been delivered of a still-born child.

There is the case of the poet Goethe (1749–1832) who was taking a walk with a friend one rainy summer evening when he exclaimed to his companion: "If I weren't sure that Frederick is in Frankfurt I'd swear it's him!"

He saw, but his friend did not, the figure of an old friend, in a dressing gown and slippers and nightcap, an odd attire to be wearing on a rainy evening on a public road. The poet was about to challenge the apparition when it vanished.

On returning home, however, Goethe was astonished to find his friend Frederick sitting by his fireside in dressing gown, slippers, and nightcap. Caught in the rain on his way to pay Goethe a surprise visit, he had found him out, discarded his wet clothes, dried out, put on his night attire, and had fallen asleep by the fire. While asleep he dreamed of meeting Goethe and heard him remark, "But why are you dressed in your dressing gown, with your nightcap and your slippers on the public road?"

When a bad epidemic of plague was raging in London, the poet Ben Jonson—I am not implying that poets, as distinct from any other class of person, are particularly prone to these experiences—was staying in the country as a guest of Sir Robert Cotton. While there he had a vision of his eldest son with the mark of a bloody cross upon his forehead. Soon afterward he received a letter informing him of his son's death from the plague.

The ancient world is rich in stories concerning "mind-to-mind" communication, the most impressive being that in which Cicero (106–43 B.C.) describes how two youths journeyed to Megara, one to stay with friends there and the other at an inn. During the night the phantasm of the young man at the inn appeared to his friends, saying he was in dire danger. Next, he appeared to say that he had been murdered by the innkeeper, who planned to smuggle his body through the city gates at dawn, in a dung cart. The friend went to wait at the city gates and when the cart came through, he flung himself upon it, finding the body of his murdered friend there.

Whether that story, assuming it to be true—and Cicero was a reliable historian—could be held to be relevant to telepathy, one cannot, of course, be absolutely certain. Regarding the first appearance of the phantasm, the anxious youth may well have transmitted his thoughts to his friend in the home. But the *second* visitation? If the young man had been murdered, how could he convey mentally what had happened to him?

Perhaps the question is less puzzling now than it might have been years ago, since doctors themselves are not dogmatic on what is or is not the precise moment of death. During a heart transplant a person really "dies" before he lives again. In any case, do all the brain cells die at once? According to some medical authorities, the brain goes on living after heart stoppage for several minutes. It is claimed that sometimes, in the case of children, the brain lives as long as seven or eight minutes, but for most adults the average length of time is four minutes before actual biological death occurs. May it not be that, for some time, almost certainly a short time, some part of the brain continues to work? It is not the case that *all* of the brain must work at once or not at all. In operations such as leucotomy, portions of the brain can be removed without impairment; indeed, the result can be an improvement of the brain that remains.

It must not be thought that accounts of telepathic transmission are mostly unilateral. A great proportion of the cases on record are corroborated by other evidence. There is one occurrence in English judicial history in which telepathy may well have played a part, and in which many witnesses were involved. It is the very strange story of "Booty's ghost" related in Kirby's *Wonderful and*

Eccentric Museum (Vol. II, p. 247), which describes an action for slander of a deceased husband brought by a widow. Consider this quotation from the journal of a Mr. Spinks:

Friday, May 15, 1687—We had the observation of Mr. Booty this day. Captain Barrisby, Captain Bristowe, Captain Brown, I and Mr. Ball, merchant, went on shore in Captain Barnaby's boat to shoot rabbits upon Stromboli [a volcanic island whose volcano was—and still is—active]; and when we had done, we called our men together by us, and about half an hour and fourteen minutes after three in the afternoon, to our great surprise, we all of us saw two men running towards us with such swiftness that no living man could run half so fast as they did run, when all of us heard Captain Barnaby say "Lord Bless Me! the foremost is old Booty, my next door neighbour," but he did not know the other that ran behind; he was in black clothes, and the foremost was in grey. Then Captain Barnaby desired all of us to take an account of the time, and put it down in our pocket-books, and when we got on board we wrote it in our journals; for we saw them into the flames of fire, and there was a great noise which greatly affrighted us all, for we none of us saw or heard the like before. Captain Barnaby said he was certain it was old Booty which he saw running over Stromboli and into the flames of hell.

It is stated that Captain Barnaby told his wife, and she told somebody else, and that it was afterwards told to Mrs. Booty, who arrested Captain Barnaby in a thousand-pound action for what he had said of her husband. Captain Barnaby gave bail to it, and it came on trial in the Court of King's Bench, and they had Mr. Booty's wearing apparel brought into Court, and the sexton of the parish, and the people that were with him when he died; and we swore to our journals, and it came to the same time within two minutes.

Ten of our men swore to the buttons on his coat, and that they were covered with the same sort of cloth his coat was made of, and so it proved.

The jury asked Mr. Spinks if he knew Mr. Booty. He answered, "I never saw him till he ran by me on the burning mountain." The judge said, "Lord, have mercy on me, and grant that

I may never see what you have seen. One, two, or three may be mistaken, but thirty can never be mistaken."

The widow, incidentally, lost her suit.

It must not be supposed that all accounts of telepathy are concerned with tragedy. They are often merely concerned with danger. What makes them particularly interesting is that impressions or images are received with tremendous vividness over great distances. There is something immensely significant about this, something that renders invalid the basic assumption that has dominated so much research—in particular Russian research over the last forty years—namely, that "brain waves" act like radio waves which are picked up by specially sensitive people in circumstances that have yet to be discovered.

For the moment, however, we are considering the nature of what we mean by telepathy, or at least the nature of its spontaneous manifestations. I want to make the point that we are not considering occurrences that can be explained away by mere chance, or that have not withstood the analysis of objective and scientific minds. The experimental aspects of telepathy, and its scientific implications, we will come to later.

I have related in an earlier book of mine (*Ghosts and Hauntings*) how Mrs. Maureen Hayter, wife of Lieutenant-Commander H. M. Hayter, U.S.N., awoke with a shock when her house seemed to shake with a mighty crash one night in November, 1942.

She found nothing amiss when she got out of bed and—having first assured herself that her children were safe—hurried downstairs to investigate. No gale blew. No furniture was disarranged, no doors were open or broken.

Returning to her room, she saw the phantasm of her husband, then serving as Damage Control Officer of the heavy cruiser U.S.S. *New Orleans,* "bathed in a heavy mist." There was an expression about him both sad and protective. At that moment his ship was sunk in the Pacific. Mrs. Hayter was in Minnesota. Assuming that in those last tragic moments Lieutenant-Commander Hayter's thoughts were of his wife—which they certainly would be—his thoughts could not reach her by "brain waves" of electromagnetic origin. They would not and could not, by the laws that govern this particular kind of wave, have spanned such a distance and reached their destination with that degree of intensity. There must, in such instances, be some other means of communication operating, and it is this that scientists are seeking now—a sort of "philosopher's stone" of communications.

My late friend William Oliver Stevens of New York quotes in his excellent book *Unbidden Guests* a case taken from the pages of the *Journal of the American Society for Psychical Research.*

One evening an astronomy instructor, having given a lesson at the Y.M.C.A. in Dallas, Texas, arrived home after midnight. To avoid disturbing his wife, who was asleep, he made his way quietly to his bed, which was placed in front of a double window, with enough space between it and the foot of the bed to allow somebody to pass. He lay on his back quietly, thinking of some of the problems raised during class. Suddenly he felt dizzy, and in a corner of the room saw the seated figures of his mother and younger brother, who lived with his father in Los Angeles. In the same instant the doorknob rattled. He sat up and looked toward it. The door opened, and in walked his father.

"I could see him as plainly and with as much detail as I am seeing the lines on this paper as I write," he later declared.

His father walked across the room and stood opposite his son, who wondered if this surprise visit was another of his father's practical jokes. When he was two feet away, the son was able to look closely at his father's figure and face. He was surprised to see him wearing his usual working clothes, a tan-colored shirt, cap, and trousers. His suspenders were brown and in his pocket were his usual working impedimenta of pencil, fountain pen, and caliper ruler.

It then became clear to the son that this was not a joyful visit. His father's expression was sad. Up to this point neither son nor father had exchanged a word. Then the older man took his son's hand in a strong, determined grasp "much harder than his usual handshake." Still holding the younger man's hand, he shook his head as though the news he brought was too harrowing to express in words. Then he vanished.

As the instructor sat there, astounded and trying to collect his thoughts, the doorbell rang. It proved to be a messenger with a telegram. It read:

DAD DIED AT EIGHT THIRTY. WIRE ANSWER BY WESTERN
UNION CAN YOU COME?

The telegram was dated at Los Angeles, April 20, at 10:08

P.M. and had been received in the Dallas office at 12:13. The instructor's wife, awakened by the doorbell, burst into tears when she saw the telegram, and was distressed and puzzled to see her husband unmoved by the news. He was unmoved because he did not believe the telegram, whose message was, in due course, confirmed.

Later, when he visited his mother, the instructor asked what kind of clothes his father was wearing on the day of his death. His mother took him to the wardrobe after he, without waiting for a reply, had told *her*. There, hanging up, were the tan trousers, with their brown suspenders, and the tan shirt and cap. In the shirt pocket he found, in the same order, the items he had seen—the pencil, the fountain pen, and the caliper ruler. His mother explained that the father had been working all that day on his brother's car—hence the work clothes. When he went to bed he left them lying on the chair. Two hours later he died in bed of a heart attack.

An odd feature of this story is that the father's grip was not cold, as one would expect with a ghostly visitant, but warm and strong—in other words, lifelike. Another interesting point is that the details the instructor gave his wife about his father's clothing were absolutely correct.

A recent example of telepathy is given in the *Journal of the* [British] *Society for Psychical Research* of March, 1968 (pp. 237–9). Briefly summarized, the facts are these:

On October 5, 1965, Mr. William Freed awoke in Wellington, New Zealand, with "a strong feeling that something was wrong with my younger daughter, Anna." He had no reason to be apprehensive about her. His last news of her was that she was enjoying a vacation in the Balearic Islands. But the conviction of impending disaster was so strong that he resolved to telephone his wife in London. She ought to have returned there after taking a vacation in Denmark, but as she had given up her apartment, he telephoned a mutual friend in London, without success. He then called another friend in Paris, who confirmed that his wife had been through Paris on her way to London, but that she did not know Mrs. Freed's address. Twice more he called the London friend. Still very anxious, he telephoned his elder daughter in Brisbane, Australia, who was quite naturally surprised that her father had been making such a series of calls from such a distance—and at such expense—concerning what seemed to her an unreasonable worry.

9

As Mr. Freed was sitting nervously in a chair, in a state of mounting tension, the telephone rang. It was his wife, speaking from New Zealand House in London, to say that the previous evening she had heard that Anna was dangerously ill in Formentera (Balearic Islands) and she needed his urgent intervention through the New Zealand External Affairs Department to arrange her own flight to Majorca, where she was to be met by the British Consul, who would help her on the final stage of the journey.

On Mrs. Freed's arrival at Formentera she found her daughter's condition much improved and shortly afterward was able to bring her back to London. But for several days before that—the material time of Mr. Freed's anxiety and strong premonition—Anna had been very ill.

This is one of those cases where there is ample confirmation from all concerned that the facts are as stated. *Why* did Mr. Freed receive so strong an impression of his daughter's illness, in view of the fact that all previous reports pointed to her being in good health?

Mr. Harvey Matusow, the American journalist and author, made the following statement to me which seems relevant in the context of a discussion on telepathy.

Early in 1966, when he was living in New York, a doctor friend of his invited him to test "the sacred mushroom" (a mushroom which can produce remarkable effects, including "second sight" in certain people). Mr. Matusow agreed. The doctor also said that he and Mr. Matusow would later be joined by some other people who were going to eat some of the mushroom when they left their homes, so that they should be feeling its effects by the time they reached their friends. At this point, to quote Mr. Matusow, the following sequence of events took place:

"Well, at about seven o'clock at night I took the mushroom and a few minutes later the phone rang and it was these three people, who were coming up from downtown. There was Adrian, there was Alan—I forget the other girl's name. They said they were leaving their house near Sixth Avenue and that they had about half a block to walk to the subway. They were leaving, they were just taking their mushroom, and they were coming up on the subway.

"About twenty minutes later I was sitting in my living room west of 93rd Street, and I turned to one of the two doctors who were there—this friend of mine and his associate—and I said 'I'm in a subway train which has just passed under this house. Adrian and Alan are in the train but the girl isn't with them.' They said, 'That's strange, they just called and said that they're leaving.' I repeated, 'But she's not there.' I then went on to describe, *in toto,* the subway car and described the people who were in the car. The train stopped at 96th Street, and I was taking these people into the house. I said that they were walking in a wrong direction on the platform, that they had to turn around and come out on the 96th Street exit. I said that they were walking to 97th Street, which they did.

"I said 'Now they're coming down Central Park West,' and I described them walking down the street. When they got to my house, I said, 'They're entering the elevator downstairs.' I said to one of the doctors, 'Now you stand by the door and I'll tell you when to open it. It will be three seconds before they arrive.'

"As he opened the door and counted to three, they came in."

As anticipated, they confirmed the visual picture he had received of them—their taking the wrong turning in the subway, the girl leaving them because she met an old friend she was anxious to see on the way, the descriptions of the passengers in the subway.

It may be that both hypnotism and the taking of certain drugs heighten the faculty that comes into play where telepathy is involved. The faculty, not having been positively isolated, has been given many names, such as second sight, extrasensory perception (ESP), paranormal cognition (PNC), and, more recently, the Greek letter *psi,* this being considered even more appropriate because its use does not imply acceptance of any final explanation as to the nature of the factor.

The coining of so many words tends to obscure the more interesting aspects of psychical research from the general public, just as the terminology of medicine, psychology, and psychiatry creates a mystique that separates and, perhaps, is intended to isolate the sacred profession from the profane public. For my part and for the sake of simplicity, I propose to use the old word, *telepathy,* to identify mind-to-mind transmission of thoughts and images. But telepathy may well be involved when, as in the case of Goethe or Donne or some of the other cases mentioned, a visual image, or hallucination, or phantasm is seen. So much for "spontaneous" telepathy. Now for experimental telepathy.

11

☐ 2. The Race to Win Your Mind

FOR the ordinary person, the background research into the nature of telepathy and how, if ever, it can be made to function at will, is a somewhat monotonous business. Though it is no fault of the specialists, the fact remains that the more scientifically controlled experiments into telepathy become, the greater the cramming of the theses and reports with technical terms, tables, graphs, analyses, and arguments. In short, even specialists find these experiments tremendously demanding because in testing for manifestations of telepathic capacity under controlled conditions, mathematical precision and patience are required. It takes a very great deal of work to establish a very little fact. This is true of most sciences, but especially true of all paranormal phenomena, and in particular of telepathy, which impinges on so many related sciences.

It is not surprising, therefore, that current researches into telepathy fail to interest, far less excite, the man in the street. He is vaguely bored by the subject anyway, and skeptical of the terminology, which sounds pompous to him; he remembers that somebody once said that solemnity is a garment often worn to hide defects of the mind. He will be attracted by any account of a spontaneous example of telepathy, but the serious and dedicated experimenters in the field turn him off.

However, if the researchers succeed in their attempt to isolate, identify, and apply the secrets underlying telepathy, they will have revolutionized the lives of all of us—and not necessarily for the

12

better. The governments of the world—most of which are dictatorships or near-dictatorships—will have at their disposal a terrifying new weapon by which to influence the popular masses and hold them in subjection. It is no consolation to know that terrifying weapons already exist, and that this new one will be just another in a diverse, lethal armory of horror.

The cobalt bomb and chemical and biological weapons capable of decimating mankind, animal life, and vegetation on a global scale are horrible enough; but even to the persecuted, the imprisoned, and the condemned there has remained one forlorn but dignified bastion of privacy—the mind.

It is true that brain-washing techniques, as practiced by most secret police (and some non-secret police and security forces) and perfected by the Russians and Chinese, constitute a grievous intrusion on human dignity and the privacy of one's thoughts. But even under the worst treatment people often *thought* what they liked, even if they did not show it. That last privilege may go, too.

Accordingly, even if we are not romantics with a predisposition to the mystical, it is imperative that we gain some knowledge about telepathy.

The original researchers into the phenomenon were simply men dedicated unselfishly to the pursuit of truth. Although the manifestations of telepathy have been noted for centuries, they were not identified as such. In other words, explanations other than mind-to-mind communication were adduced. The appearance of phantasms of the living, as the earliest founders of the Society for Psychical Research well realized, might well, in some instances, be telepathy at work. Equally, if theories about "astral travel" (wherein a person's body remains in one place but some other comparable and related semblance of him appears elsewhere, the two being linked by a duality of consciousness) have a basis in fact—something we shall consider later—an element of telepathy may be said to operate in such cases as well.

In any event, telepathy has been happening for thousands of years, but only in the last century have serious efforts been launched to discover its nature.

In 1871, attempts to transmit thoughts were made by the Rev. P. H. and Mrs. Newnham. Over a period of eight months they demonstrated that some factor other than the laws of chance was in operation. The degree of success in identifying the thoughts of the sender or "agent" could not be accounted for by any known laws of logic and science. A few years later, Professor W. F. Barrett told the British Association for the Advancement of Science that telepathy was a fact—and important enough to justify serious and sustained investigation.

From the inception of the Society for Psychical Research pioneering work—expensive in time and money, exhausting in terms of thought and patience—was conducted by its members. Among them they evolved a language of clear definition by which to describe various aspects of the problem, so that those cooperating would not use different words to describe the same thing, and so mislead and confuse each other. Thus the sender of a telepathic thought was designated the "agent" and the receiver the "percipient."

The experiments are too numerous and too long to summarize. The volumes of *Proceedings of the Society for Psychical Research* contain an impressive array of facts. Volume XXIX describes the lengthy series of experiments carried out by Professor Gilbert Murray in conjunction with his daughters, Mrs. Arnold Toynbee, Miss Agnes Murray, and other members of his family. The experiments ranged over a period of fourteen years (1910–24) and achieved results that removed forever any suspicion that thought transference was merely a parlor game practiced by a number of rather nutty people.

Professor Murray described his procedure as follows:

> I go out of the room and, of course, out of earshot. Someone who is in the room, generally my eldest daughter, thinks of a scene or an incident or anything she likes, and says it aloud. It is written down, and I am called. I come in, usually take my daughter's hand, and then, if I have luck, describe in detail what she has thought of.
>
> The least disturbance of our customary method, change of time or place, presence of strangers, controversy, and especially noise, is apt to make things go wrong. I become myself somewhat over-sensitive and irritable, though not, I believe, to a noticeable degree. When I am getting at the thing which I wish to discover, the only effort I make is to achieve a sort of attention of a quite general kind. The thing may come through practically any sense channel, or it may discover a road of its own, a chain of reasoning or

association which, as far as I can remember, never coincides with any similar chain in the mind of anyone present, but is invented much as a hallucination is invented, for the purpose of the moment.

Anyone with any doubts about the integrity of the Professor or the validity of his methods and reasoning should refer to the records of the experiments, surely the most thorough, extraordinary, and significant ever attempted, whose impact on the shape of things to come may prove shattering compared with the localized and limited interest they aroused at the time. A mere extract illustrates the amazing degree of accuracy which was achieved:

1. *Mrs. Arnold Toynbee* (agent): "Lord Jim being tried at Aden in Conrad's book. The scene is the Law Court."
   Professor Murray: "No, not a glimmer."
2. *Mrs. Arnold Toynbee* (agent): "Mr. Fisher and Mr. B. drinking beer in a café in Berlin."
   Professor Murray: "It's got something to do with a public-house—no, it's beer. It's Fisher and somebody drinking beer—somebody who has nothing to do with Fisher. I can't be at all sure—I should think little B."
3. *Mrs. Arnold Toynbee* (agent): "Savonarola having the pictures burnt in Florence and standing up and a crowd around."
   Professor Murray: "It's Italian—I think it's something in a book. Well, this is the merest guess and may have something to do with the spark that came out of the fire —I get a smell of burning, the smell of a bonfire—I get Savonarola burning the pictures in Florence."
4. *Mrs. Arnold Toynbee* (agent): "I think of a scene in a Strindberg play—two people sitting in a round tower and the man has a fainting fit and the wife hopes he is dead."
   Professor Murray: "This is a book and a book I haven't read. No—not Russian—not Italian. It's somebody lying in a faint. It's very horrible. I think somebody is fainting and his wife or some woman is hoping he is dead. It can't be Maeterlinck—I think I have read them all— oh! it's Strindberg. . . ."
   Mrs. Arnold Toynbee (agent): "Can you get the place?"
   Professor Murray: "I thought of them in a great round tower. That was why I thought of Maeterlinck."

When one considers the immense range of literature (there are more than 6 million books in the British Museum library alone) and the immense number of thoughts that might be recalled from even a single volume, and the fact that the agent wasn't committed to thinking merely of literary extracts (many of the thoughts had no relation to books or plays at all but to home-made mental imagery connected with people, such as "Mother hitting the purser with a skipping rope"), coincidence could not account for so many of the Professor's spot-on "guesses."

During the first series of 505 experiments conducted between 1910 and 1915, 33 percent were successful, 28 percent partly successful, and 39 percent were failures. Between 1916 and 1924 a further series of 295 long experiments was held in which the percentages of successes was 36, the partial successes 23 percent, and the failures 41 percent. The mathematical odds against such a degree of success are astronomical.

At about the same time Dr. Paul Joire, Professor at the Psycho-Physiological Institute of France, and President of the Société Universelle D'Etudes Psychiques, was conducting experiments into telepathy, a term he accepted from W. H. Myers, and defined the phenomena he was investigating as *"the knowledge which a subject (called a percipient) receives of a fact concerning another subject, whom we call the agent, and which takes place at a distance, outside the range of the normal senses, and without this fact being able to come to his knowledge by the normal operation of his senses or by any known means."*

Dr. Joire's definition is good enough as far as it goes; it is incomplete, however, because it appears to exclude many "visitations at the moment of death," which may well be due to some telepathic link. Not merely facts, but visual impressions, often in considerable detail, have been transmitted by thought transference. But it is only in his definition that Dr. Joire falls short; his investigations did, in fact, cover many dramatic cases of visual scenes being transmitted, and of the phantasm being seen by a percipient at the moment of death of some person they knew. In fact, he declared that "in the majority of cases the agent is at the point of death at the moment when the telepathic communication takes place."

Sometimes the agent is simply *near* death, or has suffered some serious accident. The fact that mental images are, so to speak,

16

"projected" to some friend or relative far away, at a time when the agent is often unconscious, may be significant in considering the role played by hypnotism in relation to telepathy. It has been found that extrasensory perception is heightened and sharpened in a hypnotic state, when, of course, the conscious mind is held in suspense and the subconscious mind—the invisible but imperious master whose power and foibles were exposed by psychologists such as Freud—is active and receptive.

Concrete evidence of the existence of telepathy was also provided by a census of hallucinations, initiated at the Congress of Experimental Psychology in 1889, under the general direction of Professor Henry Sidgwick. Of the 17,000 people who replied to a questionnaire, 1,684 claimed to have experienced an hallucination. Analysis of those 1,684 cases, however, revealed an even more startling fact. In 350 of them the apparition was recognized, and 30 of the 350 recognized apparitions appeared at the moment of death. The committee concluded that there existed between the dying persons and those who saw their apparitions some connection that was not due to chance alone. What could the link be? On the face of it, there being no prior knowledge in all these cases, and no apprehension on the part of the percipients, the link could be only a mental one.

I do not at this stage want to get involved in the pros and cons, methods, possibilities, or implications of hypnotism, but it is necessary at this point to state that further conclusive evidence of the existence of telepathy was produced by successful experiments in hypnotizing at a distance. A Dr. Janet, in the course of twenty-five experiments, hynotized nineteen people—a degree of success that showed beyond question that hypnotic suggestions, normally heard by the subject at close proximity, were being conveyed by means other than sound. In every such case the hypnotic trance either coincided with the making of the mental suggestions by the hypnotist, or followed immediately afterward.

During the early days of the Society for Psychical Research, much experiment in telepathy was initiated also in Germany. One such experimenter was Dr. Albert von Schrenck-Notzing, who had taken his medical degree at the University of Munich and studied hypnotism and related subjects with Sigmund Freud in Nancy. As early as 1887 Dr. Schrenck-Notzing found that a subject whom he described as Lina carried out instructions conveyed to her by telepathy while she was in a state of hypnosis. Useful experiments were also conducted by a German parapsychologist, Dr. Gerda Walther, who worked with Schrenck-Notzing during the latter years of his life and, on the centennial of his birth, published an invaluable summary of his lifelong researches into telepathy and other parapsychological subjects under the title *Grundfragen der Parapsychologie* (Kohlhammer, 1962).

Two other prominent people working in this area of study and experiment were the English researchers G. N. M. Tyrrell and Whateley Carington. Choosing subjects for transmission at random, they would pin the drawings of the objects up on the wall and ask two hundred and fifty percipients to draw them.

In the twenties the famous American novelist Upton Sinclair conducted a long series of experiments in mental transmission which he embodied in his book *Mental Radio*. It came as a shock to some of his friends that this writer, whose factual and vitriolic pen had focused public attention on many public scandals and social evils, should interest himself in a subject so remote and seemingly unrelated. But for Sinclair there was no doubt whatever. Telepathy, he declared more than forty years ago, was a fact.

The tests carried out by Dr. J. B. Rhine at Duke University in Durham, North Carolina, from the early twenties onward, have now become part of history. Like the pioneering work of Myers, they will always be remembered as having established a landmark in telepathic research.

Rhine designed a deck of cards, called Zener cards, on which there were five different designs—square, circle, wavy lines, cross, and star—there being twenty-five cards in each deck. This introduced a new note of simplicity into the process of testing people for telepathic ability. Out of view and out of the hearing of the percipient, the agent would select a card, look at it, and put it down. The percipient would try to state what card it was.

Obviously the cards were taken at random. Now here the laws of probability make the chances of guessing the card correctly one in five. Thus, in a hundred-card selection, one could expect twenty guesses to be correct. The chances of deviation being statistically estimated at one in one hundred and fifty, it was obvious when one of Dr. Rhine's collaborators achieved a success of 33.6 percent that some other factor was involved; the odds against such a degree of success are enormous. Dr. Rhine's books, *Extra-Sensory Per-*

ception (1934), *New Frontiers of the Mind* (1938), and *Extra-Sensory Perception after Sixty Years* (1940), are essential reading for anyone who has a serious interest in telepathy.

The Soviet Union is not, as it often claims to be, first in the field of research insofar as telepathy is concerned, even though it can fairly claim to be the first country in the world to have financed and encouraged an official program of psychical research, with particular emphasis on telepathy.

Before World War I there were a few scientists in Czarist Russia who were interested in and puzzled by reports of telepathic experiments received from the West. The trouble in those days was that the mental climate was excessively superstitious; a dark medieval atmosphere of credulity and fear overhung the court— hence the spectacular success of Rasputin—and the phenomenon of telepathy was not examined in the objective spirit necessary to research. The First World War was, of course, no climate in which such research would flourish, and in the upheaval of the Bolshevik Revolution, when hatred of religion and anything smacking of superstition or mysticism was raised to fever point, the subject was forgotten.

The pioneers in the Russian contribution to parapsychological research, particularly in telepathy, were the famous physiologist V. M. Bechterov, the academician Alexander Leontovitch, Bernard Kazhinsky, an engineer, and Professor Leonid Vasiliev.

Bechterev studied thought transference between dogs at the Institute for Brain Research in Leningrad. His hunch that dogs possessed certain faculties of extrasensory perception was confirmed by a famous circus promoter, Durov, who believed that the supersonic whistle signals which he gave to the animals (signals imperceptible to the human ear) could not in themselves account for his phenomenal success in handling a great variety of animals, domesticated and wild.

Bechterev's researches satisfied him that the signals alone, and training alone, could not account for the extraordinary understanding between man and animal. Bechterev published his findings in various papers. In due course other Russian scientists pursued the same line of study with dogs. The findings of the scientists A. G. Ivanov-Smolensky and P. Fleksor, to name but two, suggest that there is more to the happy man-and-dog relationship than meets the eye. It is probable, if you have a dog, that he knows more

19

about you than you do about him. He can pick up your thoughts, at least to some degree.

Russia's first real step in what we may call the thought race (and it *is* very much a race, for the stakes are large) was in 1922, when Bechterev, then chief of the Institute for Brain Research in Leningrad, formed a team of experts that comprised psychologists, medical hypnotists, physiologists, physicists, and a philosopher. Telepathy, they decided, was important enough to justify research and inquiry, and this was the main theme of a report submitted to the Second All-Russian Congress on Psychoneurology held in Leningrad in 1924.

It was at this conference that a Dr. Konstantin Platonov astonished the delegates and scientists by hypnotizing an ex-patient by telepathic means—e.g., by suggestions made out of his sight and out of his hearing. Dr. Platonov has been pursuing his work on medical hypnosis and the value of suggestion in healing ever since, and has embodied his researches in a valuable book.

As a result of the congress, a department covering such sub jects as hypnotism, neurology, and biophysics was created as an offshoot of the Institute for Brain Research, and two years later papers were prepared describing some of the researches carried out. One, by Leonid Vasiliev—a name of considerable importance in telepathy—was entitled "The Biophysical Foundations of Direct Thought Transmission."

It is possible for the greatest enthusiast to take a wrong path. It is also a fact that no academic worker or intellectual can fail to be conditioned, to some extent, by the prevailing social, educational, and intellectual climate in which he is forced to live. We can, therefore, understand why Vasiliev talked of a "materialistic approach" to the problem of telepathy. Materialism was a magic word, implying a brutal and final repudiation of the spiritual and metaphysical, and it is probable that if he had not made his researches sound as though they were in step with Communist ideology, his academic career and his researches would have come to an abrupt end.

In other words, Vasiliev looked first for a *physical* explanation of telepathy. But as thought was known to involve the generation of mild electrical impulses, of the sort that are registered by hospitals on the encephalograph, we can scarcely blame Vasiliev for believing, or strongly suspecting, that the answer might lie in the transmission of brain waves. Western scientists had demonstrated that subjects could be hypnotized at a distance, nearly forty years before the demonstration at the Leningrad conference in 1924. Many contemporaries of Vasiliev, notably the Italian expert on the paranormal—Dr. F. Cazzamaralli—believed that these alleged brain waves must be the explanation of telepathy. The thoughts in a person's mind must be conveyed by electromagnetic waves to the mind of another, and by some means received and interpreted.

Bechterev's team was greatly enlarged in 1926, but when he died six years later his successor, Professor Ossipov, was opposed to using any hypothesis other than a purely physical one as a working basis for research into such matters. The search for the electromagnetic impulses continued—and ended in failure. For Vasiliev found, over many years of experiments, that when "screening" was employed (devices for preventing the transmission of electromagnetic impulses), his success in conveying commands to subjects at a distance was just as great as when there was no such screening. In transmitting mental instructions to patients to go to sleep, or to wake up, he found they did go to sleep, and did wake up, as instructed by telepathy, *but irrespective of whether there was screening or not.*

So there it was. The human being did not carry a radio transmitter in his head. Nor was the human being a radio receiver, either. Yet people could receive commands over huge distances, be made to envisage objects that were miles away. How? Why?

One basic fact should have warned the team that they were on the wrong track. Telepathy is unaffected by distance. The intensity of electromagnetic waves diminishes in inverse proportion to the square of the distance; in simpler language, the farther such an impulse has to travel, the fainter it becomes. But the Russians held to the erroneous electromagnetic theory even up to 1966, when Dr. Asratjan, Director of Moscow's Institute of Higher Nervous Activity, told an English visitor that experiments had shown that telepathy is due to the utilization of electromagnetic radiation from the brain. This shows a certain confusion and a lack of cohesion in the Soviet researches.

Vasiliev was a brilliant and dedicated scientist, and the mere fact that he did not achieve his ambition (he died in 1966) does not diminish the importance of his patient research. The mere elimination of wrong ideas in the course of the search for truth narrows the field of inquiry, or at least diverts energy and effort into more worthwhile channels, making the discovery of the truth more likely. Vasiliev carried out tests to determine whether the answer could be found in some sort of X ray, the infrared rays, or the long, alternating rays of the kind emitted by an electrical generator.

In recent years the search for the secret underlying telepathy has become a high priority with the major powers. With respect to China, we know virtually nothing about its attitude toward such problems. However, there has been no hint that the Chinese are interested in what are broadly called the paranormal subjects, including telepathy. The Soviet Union certainly is, and has more than one hundred specialists of various kinds—brain physiologists, physicists, doctors, electronic engineers, mathematicians, and others—working on telepathy projects, centered mainly in Leningrad and Moscow.

Russian determination to be first in the thought race began in 1959. There were unconfirmed reports in the press at that time that the United States had conducted experiments in telepathy on board the nuclear submarine *Nautilus*. The experiments, it was alleged, entailed sending thought messages not only through lead screening, but through many fathoms of sea water. They were said to have been conducted under the supervision of experts from the Westinghouse Electric Corporation of America. No official statement of results was ever issued, but published accounts freely mentioned 75 percent success with messages transmitted.

A detailed and allegedly accurate account of these experiments appeared in a French scientific magazine, which a correspondent in Paris forwarded to Professor Leonid Vasiliev in Moscow.

To say that the news, which was taken literally, caused consternation in Moscow is to put it mildly. At once *carte blanche* was given to Vasiliev and his team. Telepathy was no longer considered a remote subject. If it could be applied, which would certainly happen once its principles of operation were fully understood, it would be invaluable in space communication—superior to microwaves, better than laser beams. With it, one could implant defeatist ideas in the minds of an enemy army. A spy able to read thoughts would be virtually unbeatable and uncatchable. In brief, applied

22

telepathy would be a formidable military weapon, as well as a means of enforcing complete mind control of the masses.

In fact, there is reason to think that the Russian view of the American experiments was greatly exaggerated. In his book *The Transmission of Mental Images,* Vasiliev admitted quite frankly that it was the *Nautilus* experiments that gave further impetus to the Russian telepathy program. But he accepted uncritically the published and unconfirmed versions of how the experiments were carried out and the success they were supposed to have achieved.

"This experiment showed," he said, "that telepathic information can be transmitted without loss through a thickness of sea water and through the sealed metal covering of a submarine—that is, through substances which greatly interfere with radio communication."

Since 1959 it has been Soviet policy to keep abreast of researches in other countries. It is a safe assumption that their intelligence service would not neglect to collect information on this subject as on any other topic of military importance. Dr. J. Gaither Pratt, Assistant Professor at Virginia University, noted during his visit to Leningrad in 1962 that "their manner of speaking (e.g., of workers in the field of telepathic research in the West) reflected a knowledge of details and an intimacy such as one would normally expect only after long personal acquaintance."

When Anthony Cornell of the Cambridge University Society for Psychical Research visited the U.S.S.R. in 1963 he met Professor Vasiliev and suggested that it would be an interesting and useful thing for them to conduct a telepathic experiment between Cambridge and Leningrad. At the time Vasiliev thought it a good idea. Teams in Leningrad and Cambridge were to have been shown various objects, and try to guess what the other had.

Having virtually accepted the invitation, Vasiliev later rejected it as "not opportune." One consideration may have been that the Russians were reluctant to abandon their theory of electromagnetic radiation. The experiment, which was very detailed in its planning, was designed to test that theory, which the Cambridge team did not accept. Since the strength of telepathic signals, according to the Russian theory, should have fallen off with distance, any spectacular success by the English team would have caused consternation. The experiment was probably abandoned by the Russians under political pressure.

The importance of telepathy was underlined by Dr. Eugene Konecci, one of America's top space medical experts, at the International Space Conference held in Paris in 1963. Mentioning that both Russia and the United States had given telepathy top priority, he pointed out that American spacecraft had found a region between the moon and the earth where their respective gravities negated each other. Because it was believed that brain waves between humans were adversely affected by gravity, it was thought that an astronaut in this belt of nongravity might be able to pick up the thought waves of people on earth. As to the Soviet experiments—"If the results of conducted experiments are half as good as the Soviets claim, then they may be the first to put a human thought in orbit or achieve mind-to-mind communication with humans on the moon," Konecci declared.

"If the results are . . . half as good as the Soviets claim. . . ."
What *do* the Soviets claim?

There have been numerous experiments in long-range telepathy in the Soviet Union in recent years. An intensive experiment in the transmission of images was carried out in 1966, the sessions taking place between April 19 and April 27, with the agent located in Moscow and the percipient in Novosibirsk. Two types of experiment were tried, those with Zener cards (the patterned cards with five simple and distinctive designs) and those with objects. A high degree of success, exceeding the laws of probability, was achieved, it was reported, with the Zener cards.

In the twenty-five Moscow-Novosibirsk experiments in the telepathic transmission of Zener cards over a distance of 3,000 kilometers, 48 percent success was said to have been achieved. In the transmission of thoughts concerning articles between Moscow and Tomsk, a distance of 4,000 kilometers, 100 percent success was claimed. For transmissions over these distances such total success would constitute a breakthrough in deliberate transmission, even if it left the true nature of the telepathic impulse a mystery and its application in any circumstances, for the moment, impossible.

In the transmission of suggestions of images over short distances (of five kilometers) in Moscow, 80 percent success was claimed.

These experiments were held under entirely Russian supervision. There was, obviously, no checking for standards and accuracy by independent and qualified witnesses or collaborators from

24

other countries. This lack of active cooperation in telepathic experiments is no fault of Western enthusiasts, who have tried without success to get the Russians to collaborate with their own experts in the sending of mind-to-mind messages.

There is, of course, another vital consideration, from the Russian point of view. What has the oligarchic, dictatorial, military setup—with its obsessive security complex and almost xenophobic isolation—to gain by instituting telepathic links with other countries? To have citizens sending out thought waves to collaborators abroad is a nightmare to the security forces of almost any country.

All countries, without exception, apply a postal censorship as and when it suits them. In the case of Communist countries the censorship is total insofar as foreign mail is concerned. All countries, including the Western powers, maintain a monopoly of radio communication, in the sense that ultimate control of the right to broadcast lies in government hands. No person in Britain, for instance, can broadcast without a license. If the technique of what Upton Sinclair called mental radio became general knowledge, it is certain that any state, including Britain and America, would seek to confine its use to authorized purposes. It is possible, however, that if the technique did become common property, it might prove technically impossible to detect or limit its use by individuals. We may, therefore, safely assume that if Russia does discover how to apply telepathy at will, the secret will be zealously guarded.

But not, as I say, merely Russia. The United States Air Force has for some years been studying telepathy and experimenting with it at Hanscom Field, Bedford, Massachusetts, and has even designed a special computer, VERITAC, to coordinate, analyze, and speed up the business of telepathic guesses and other data. It is significant that these researches come under the umbrella of the aerospace authorities. They, too, would find a technique of mind-to-mind communication invaluable in their space projects. It would indeed be a wonderfully convenient thing if Americans on the moon could communicate with their colleagues on earth, and in turn receive instructions and information from them, without relying upon apparatus that might fail them at a vital moment.

For my part, I view the possibility with profound pessimism. No country is so civilized as to be trusted with a means of communication that would invade the last refuge of personal privacy.

☐ 3. The Mystery of Dreams

IN 1927 Baron Charles de Richter was on his way by train from Deauville to Nice. The train weaved its rhythmic way through beautiful scenery, and the Baron, settling back in his comfortable seat, was relaxed though pleasantly expectant.

He was on his way to see an old friend, a fascinating personality whose *joie de vivre* was a sort of psychic sunshine that warmed and enlivened everyone who came into the orbit of her impassioned presence; he was making the journey to see once again that world-famous dancer, Isadora Duncan.

"Mind you come and see me when you arrive!" had been her parting words to him. He had promised that he would.

There is something slightly hypnotic about the rhythmic jogging of a railroad car. The Baron slipped into that pleasant hypnagogic state where one is neither awake nor asleep. Then, strangely, a sentence began to repeat itself insistently in his mind, keeping time with the movement of the car wheels: *I have a rendezvous with death.*

I have a rendezvous with death
At some disputed barricade.

"What a curious thing," the Baron thought. "Where have the words come from? Am I getting morbid or something? And it's such a happy day. I'm looking forward to seeing Isadora again so much."

It was a sort of dream in mental sound. Tragically, it came true. When he reached Nice a distraught friend imparted to him the terrible news that Isadora, while trying out a new car, had had her Spanish shawl caught in one of the wheels and had been strangled to death—at the same time as that line, *I have a rendezvous with death,* was echoing through the Baron's mind.

In the early hours of a July morning in 1909 a small boy lay sleeping in his home in the lonely Shetland Islands. He awoke at the climax of a strange and alarming nightmare and fled to his parents' bedroom for comfort. He had, in his dream, been playing at a place where everything seemed white. There was a large building. Suddenly a machine loomed in the sky, landed like a bird near him, and a man "in funny clothes" tried to speak to him and his friend. They couldn't understand him. He couldn't understand them.

The boy's dream coincided both in day and hour with the arrival at Dover of Louis Blériot, the French aviator and inventor, who had just flown the English Channel. (Blériot was the first to accomplish this feat in a heavier-than-air machine.) The boy had dreamed of the event itself as well as the time and place of occurrence.

During World War II, Mrs. W. M. Stoney of Canonbury, London, received a telegram informing her that her son was coming home on leave and would be arriving at Charing Cross station the following evening. That night she had a dream in which she could see clearly the interior of Waterloo station and her son emerging from a telephone booth carrying all his belongings. Because the dream was so vivid, she did not go to Charing Cross, as advised in the telegram, but to Waterloo instead. There she found her son—coming out of a telephone booth with all his kit.

Let us now go back in time a little (actually eighty-seven years is not really such a long interval, if we can rid ourselves of the habit of judging time in terms of our own short lives). In considering dreams chronology carries little import, in the sense that the nature of human beings has not changed fundamentally, and there is no reason why the natural laws underlying and permeating the universe should have altered either. The mechanics of dreaming were no different thousands of years ago.

The following remarkable story appears in *Phantasms of the Living* by Gurney, Podmore, and Myers, who investigated the account and received ample corroboration of the facts from others to whom the tale was confided at the time:

1883

In the month of April, 1876, I dreamt that an invalid, Mary Scaffull, widow, an inmate of Johnson's Hospital, Commercial Road, Hereford (and whose husband had been an officer in the gaol of which I was Governor), was crying out for water; it appeared to have been a long dream, and the cry seemed to be kept up for a long time. When I was sitting with my family the next morning, I asked my wife when she had seen Mrs. Scaffull last: she replied, "Some nine days ago. I took her a rice pudding: I could not get into the house, the door being locked. I therefore had to leave it at her sister's, who was living in the neighborhood, with a request that when she went to see her she would take it to her; the dish has been returned, therefore I assume she had the contents. Why, what is the matter? You seem so troubled about her?" I then told her my dream and said, "I have determined to go after breakfast and see what state she is in." She answered, "I am glad to hear you say so."

As I approached the house I could hear a cry of distress proceeding from some one of the inmates of the hospital. I put my finger on the latch of the door of the room occupied by Mrs. Scaffull, when I heard the following supplication proceed from her in the most distressing tone: "Will some kind Christian friend give me water?"

I took a jug from her lower room, went to the pump and filled it, and then took it with all haste to her bedside. When she saw me there with the water, she said, "Oh, Mr. Gouldrick, the Lord has sent you here, God Almighty bless you for bringing me this water." She then drank copiously of it and said, "It's the sweetest water I ever tasted all my life long." She died the same week, at the age of 77 years.

George Gouldrick.

A feature of this account is that the neighbors, apparently, did not heed the pitiful cries of the old woman, although they must have heard them. Mr. Gouldrick's daughter, corroborating the account, said:

I was present at the breakfast table when my father related his dream. I remember all that happened, and can therefore corroborate all he has written. My mother has since died. She was present, also, and we expressed our astonishment when he returned home and told us what had happened. The only reason that I am aware of that the neighbors (who heard all) did not attend to Mrs. Scaffull's cry, was that she was in receipt of 7s. per week, more than they were, and that caused an ill-feeling towards her.

Hannah Gouldrick. December 11, 1883.

The strange ways in which dreams sometimes jump ahead of present time are illustrated by many accounts given to me by people living in all parts of the world.

Take, for instance, the experience of Mrs. Klaire L. Martin of Mayfield Road, Chardon, Ohio:

"I dreamed of a small plane taking off and upon doing so it crashed into high power lines and exploded. The people in the plane I dreamed of were my mother and brother. This woke me in quite a fright and in near tears. I explained to my husband the dream I was having. . . ."

Mrs. Martin's dream occurred on the night of Saturday, September 9, 1966.

A local plane crash similar in many significant respects happened the following night—on Sunday, September 10, 1966, at Chagrin Falls Airport. Alvin Sheer, owner of the land on which the plane crashed, was walking toward his house from a barn when, as he approached the corner of the house, he heard the wires that held the airport marking balloons snap.

Later he said, "I then heard a second snap as the plane hit the power cables. I grabbed a fire extinguisher and ran toward the plane but before I got there the plane burst into flames. . . ."

The general facts of Mrs. Martin's dream were correct. But her mother and brother were not passengers. And the plane crashed not on takeoff but on landing. Four people were killed. Even so, the vividness of the dream, its nearness to the actual event, and the fact that the plane hitting the power cable was specifically dreamed about and mentioned to her husband before the event, give this dream a precognitive element.

A forty-eight-year old artist, Dilip Roy, of Panditiya Road, Calcutta, India, has described to me a strange dream which he had about ten years ago and how it presaged an actual event:

29

I had a dream about my youngest sister (I have four of them) and I distinctly remember the dream even now. I saw in that dream my youngest sister was running beside a railway track, and I was following her with break-neck speed to catch her up to warn her about the oncoming train. She tripped and fell beside the railway track (not on it) and I felt a sigh of relief, but she started bleeding profusely.

With lightning steps I reached her and lifted her from the ground. . . . I found that she was bleeding from her mouth. Next morning on awakening I wrote the dream in all its details and kept it in order to testify whether there was any scientific explanation or any bearing of my dream on reality.

Within a fortnight of this dream my youngest sister, who was otherwise healthy, started bleeding profusely one night; it oozed from her mouth and would not stop. The doctor was called the next day and she was treated for hemophilia.

Dilip Roy, a graduate of Calcutta University and a poet as well as an artist, had this to say to me about psychic knowledge:

By psychic knowledge, I would like to differentiate between ordinary superstitions, hearsay, myths, or even religious faith or belief. I believe it is possible to train the mind in such a way as to be able to realize such aspects of reality which are not yet grasped by our educational systems. It is more like the metaphysician or the poet who, observing nature and things around them, could perceive more of truth than the ordinary . . . some people are endowed with some inborn gift by which they can grasp more of reality. As Banquo demands of the witches [in Shakespeare's *Macbeth*] that they predict the future, asking, "Look into the seeds of time, and say which grains will grow, and which will not," psychic research of today, with this attitude of mind, can be of great benefit to us.

Between close friends dreams often play an important part. Mrs. Joe McDonald, a thirty-three-year-old art teacher of Moore Road, Avon Lake, Ohio, told me the following story:

When I was a girl my best friend was Robbie Jo Parke, a budding artist. We were very close during high school and attended college together. Then our ways parted, she going on to further degrees in art while I married, moved away, and reared a family. I have not seen her since 1954. As friends will do, we had lost contact, ceased correspondence, and I had no idea where she had gone and what she was doing.

In 1963 I began to dream of her nightly. No matter what I dreamed, she was always somehow involved. It was almost as if her spirit came and stood beside my bed.

Finally this began to puzzle and concern me, so I wrote her a short note asking after her. I addressed this to her home town, Lynn Grove, Kentucky, explaining, rather embarrassed, about my dreams. The letter was forwarded and within a short time I received a reply: She was in a hospital and had been deathly ill.

Once again the friends lost touch, for three years. Miss **Parke** resumed her teaching work while her very good friends, **the** McDonalds, moved from Illinois to Ohio. Then the dreams started up again, persistent and consistent. Once again Mrs. McDonald felt impelled to write, again to Kentucky. This time her friend's reply was in a shaky, almost illegible hand. She had been gravely ill, had undergone a difficult lung operation, and barely pulled through. "She was almost frightened," says Mrs. McDonald, "by my premonition."

I have Robbie Jo Parke's letter to Mrs. McDonald. It is dated October 15, 1965:

Amazing! I received your letter in the hospital and my hands are still a little shaky. When I get better I intend to send a photostat of your letter along with an explanation to Duke University if it is all right with you. Your letter was not only timely and unique—I'd say it was quite out of the ordinary —and I've been forcing these men of science around here to take a look at it!

Some dreams occur long before the event they foretell. Mrs. H. M. Knulst of Railway Parade, East Malvern, Victoria, Australia, relates the following:

When I was a girl of twelve I dreamed one night that I was walking along a row of houses with my mother. The moon was full. Suddenly she said, "Look through the window of this house." When I did and saw my father lying on a bier covered by a white sheet, and realized he was dead, my mother looked gravely at me and said, "Can you understand that it is father who is lying there? It seems so unreal."

Twenty-three years later my father was very ill (cancer) and my mother expected his passing every day. Then I told her that I knew there would be a few more days for him to live because the moon was not yet full. He passed away one day before the moon was full.

I visited my mother the next day (full moon). We stood together in the room where his body lay in the coffin and mother said: "Can you understand that it is father who is lying there? It seems so unreal."

In dreams you often comprehend things which you do not actually see. Mrs. Knulst knew that her father was dead although he was covered by a sheet. She knew it was full moon although in her dream she could not see the moon. For her, this childhood dream was uncannily and unhappily prophetic.

"Key" phrases in dreams often occur in considerable detail. Mr. Altaf Husain Kakkezai, Advocate of the High Court of West Pakistan, recently told me about a strange dream he experienced as a youth of seventeen. He had found that dream and subsequent reality tallied to such a degree that, as he put it, "I really became afraid."

"The most important and inexplicable dream," he told me, "was about the death of my youngest uncle. This is what I dreamed.

"I was back from the school and was having my lunch, at noon. I have forgotten the dish but I was definitely seeing mangoes and musk melon placed before me. Suddenly I looked in front and read a line in Urdu (our language) written with a piece of chalk on a wooden 'basta' (sort of door) which would mean in English 'Priest, Read Quickly.' (These words were written by my elder brother as a child when mullahs used to come to our house for the recitation of the holy Koran. Somehow the sun or water did not reach these written words and they were there for years.) Suddenly it occurred to me that I could not look at those words for long because I was having an inflammation of the eyes.

"I turned my eyes and looked towards my right. I saw my youngest uncle lying on a bed, thin and very pale in the face. I also saw my father sitting in a chair near my uncle's bed. I thought in the dream that my uncle would die. I had just finished the main dish when I heard my father say, 'Son, mangoes and musk melon are both *garam* [heat-producing]. Eat either mangoes or musk melon.' Here the dream ended.

"My uncle was in perfect health in those days. He was a huge man, very strong, like a bull. He became sick after four or five months of my having the dream but did not die until a year after my dream. My uncle was not living in our house in the city but at a distance of about three miles in the Peshawar Cantonment. When he became too ill (he was a bachelor), he came to our house at my father's request.

"During this period my eyes became inflamed. . . . One noon when I was having my lunch I looked in front of me and saw the writing on the same wooden frame. My eyes burned and I realized that they were inflamed. I started remembering the dream and it surprised me that I was having one and the same experience twice. I became apprehensive and was awaiting the missing links.

"I looked to my right and saw my uncle lying ill on the bed and, of course, there was my father sitting in a chair near my uncle. My heart started throbbing. I looked down in front of me and there was the same dish of food along with mangoes and musk melon.

"Now I remembered the whole dream and was wondering whether my father would say 'Son, mangoes and musk melon are both *garam*. Eat either mangoes or musk melon.' I started trembling with fear when, at once, my father said those very words. It was a repetition of a scene seen in a dream, a complete copy."

Mr. Kakkezai had his dream in 1949 when he was a student at the Government Special High School in Peshawar.

The phrase "for whom the bell tolls" has special significance for Mrs. Lyndsay Boles, a high school teacher of fine arts in Melbourne, Australia:

> I awoke one morning and said to my husband, "I do hope Mr. Wills is all right. I dreamed *the bells are tolling for Mr. Wills.*"
>
> I had dreamed that I saw a small church with a hedge and as I saw it a voice said to me, "The bells are tolling for Mr. Wills." With that, I awoke.
>
> When I arrived at work, I told a girl in my office of my dream, and that I hoped Mr. Wills was all right. Almost an hour or so later that morning Mr. Wills visited our office and I looked up to see him standing in the doorway.

I called out cheerfully to him: "Oh, Mr. Wills. I'm so glad to see you. I dreamed the bells were tolling for Mr. Wills!" He looked at me strangely and said "You are quite right, my dear. They are. I called in to tell you my mother has died." Then I noticed that he wore a black suit and a black tie.

Mrs. M. D. Cooper of King's Cross Road, King's Cross, New South Wales, who writes for television, radio, and magazines under the name of Marien Dreyer, often has dreams that come true:

In mid-August, 1939, I returned to Melbourne and married. Subsequently I went back to Victoria Barracks, Melbourne (Army H.Q. for the State) and as I'd had previous experience in working for the Army I was put in the decoding section of Intelligence. Just prior to that September weekend I had an odd dream, wherein I took a tram and went to a suburb I didn't know. (Melbourne is a sprawly place and most of my friends lived in northern and western suburbs. This one was northeastern, as it turned out.)

The tram suddenly turned a corner around a picture theatre, went past the theatre and along a second side of what was a fairly large square with a small park in the centre, then along a tree-lined street and stopped at a cluster of low, grey buildings . . . the place was utterly strange to me.

The week following the declaration of war, I was transferred from coding to the Fourth Division H.Q., told which tram to get, so picked up my bits and pieces and caught the right tram. I was reading, looked up to see if I was near the right street, in time to find the tram was rounding the corner by a picture theatre, went past it, around the second side of the square as I'd seen it in the dream, then along a tree-lined street to the cluster of grey buildings—which is where I got off. It was the drill hall in which the Fourth Division H.Q. was set.

Dreams as a revelation of useful information are by no means uncommon. For such a dream, Mrs. Thora B. Filkins, of Colony Drive, Cleveland, Ohio, has reason to be grateful. She writes:

When I was eighteen, and a senior in high school in New York, I was out of school for a time due to illness. I worried about passing my Senior Regents' Exams, in order to graduate, particularly history. The night before I was to take the examination, I clearly saw the Regents' paper—and memorized in my sleep each question, word for word. Needless to say, I looked up every answer the next morning, and even told some of my friends, who laughed at me, because these particular Regents' examinations were prepared at a central headquarters of the Educational Department of New York State. Even our local teachers had no idea of what might be included in the questions until the sealed envelope was opened in the presence of the class.

The amazing part of this true story is that not only was the paper exactly as I had seen it in my dream, but the fact that I had been able to completely memorize the entire test—an almost unbelievable feat—I got a mark of 96 out of 100, top mark of the class. The question is—did I cheat?

I was able to assure Mrs. Filkins that in my view she did not cheat. For, as the famous British comedian George Formby used to sing, "You Can't Stop Me from Dreaming."

And yet, what is a dream? Why do we dream? How is it that past, present, and future seem to become chaotically mixed in our flow of thought and inner imagery?

But before we dream, we sleep. Like so many terms in common use, "sleep" is a word you and I use without being sure what it means.

You slip between the sheets with a feeling of thankfulness. You reach over to the reading lamp and switch it off. You may or may not close your eyes. If you are not ill, in pain, or acutely worried, you will lie still. Your heart beats less rapidly. Your pulse settles to a slower rhythm. Your breathing slows down. The alpha rhythms of the brain (minute electrical impulses such as are recorded by the electroencephalograph) lose their accustomed pattern—a pattern that is unique for every individual in the world; the impulses subside to a slower, more even rhythm.

If your eyes hadn't closed up to this point, they close now. The brain becomes less active, but the meager light that can still filter through your eyelids is a sort of protective warning system. A burglar's flashlight beam or flames from a fire will probably send a message to the brain and wake you up. The hearing, although partly in suspense, is not wholly dormant. Any unfamiliar noise will probably awaken you instantly. If you sleep by a railroad track the accustomed thunder of passing trains will not affect you; the click of a latch or a turning doorknob probably will.

From the foregoing it is easy to realize that when we sleep we are not unconscious. One shifts in bed to assume a more relaxed position; any tension that assails the muscles is conveyed to the brain and appropriate remedial action is transmitted to the muscles from the brain automatically, without awakening the sleeper. The muscles are capable of this effort, although the reduced intake of oxygen due to more even breathing has, in turn, reduced the supply of fuel going to the muscles.

Where do dreams originate? Professor Wilder Penfield, a Canadian brain surgeon, believes that the temporal lobes—those patches of brain just above the ears—are the site of the strange fantasies that pursue us in sleep. But the brain is not neatly departmentalized like those white china heads, partitioned and numbered into alleged sections of function, so beloved by the phrenologists. The brain is an entity, like the body itself, even though certain functions may have a particular location.

We know, of course, that the brain has an immense storehouse of memory, much of it suppressed, according to psychologists, but often affecting human behavior through the conscious mind. That these "secret store" memories exist is easily proved under hypnosis, when a patient (or subject) can be regressed back to any age and come up with startling, detailed memories. Patients being operated upon under local anesthetic have found, when areas were touched by a needle, that they were listening once again to orchestras playing, long-dead relatives conversing, and similar experiences. The impression is as real as when these things actually happened.

In dreams memories are unleashed, but in disguised form, being often mixed with contemporary thoughts and even glimpses of the future. Past, present, and future jumble together; these are impressions of other-dimensional movement such as floating in air or moving forward or backward at incredible speed; objects change form; logic as we know it is abandoned. It is as if past, present, and future, usually separated by bolted doors, were suddenly commingled by the unlocking of every door at once, so that you can not only wander at will but actually seem to be in several rooms at once, the imagery being mixed.

36

But it isn't all chaos. It merely seems to be. Knowledge uncomprehended by, or not available to, the conscious mind can be imparted in dreams, later remembered and its usefulness and authenticity proved. Glimpses of the future have come to pass.

How can this be? It appears to be contrary to all common sense. How could a bell be heard to ring before it is actually rung? How can the flame of a candle be seen before it is lighted? We know there is cause, followed by effect. But in dreams the effect is sometimes known before the cause. We assume that reality can only exist up to the present moment, of which we are aware; that it is natural to look backward in time, our past experiences seeming very real to us. The present is real, too, because our faculties and sensibilities confirm it. But the future? How could anybody receive knowledge of future events—things that haven't happened—in the course of dreaming?

At this point we must ask ourselves: Are we right about time? Is it the rigid dimension we suppose it to be, something we can travel back along, but never forward? This question takes me back many years, to before World War II, when I discussed these matters with the late J. W. Dunne, the man who experimented with time, a scientist who designed the first British military airplane, who was grounded in mathematics, understood the discipline of logical deduction after painstaking experiment, and came up with revolutionary ideas about time that emerged from an analysis of his dreams.

Dunne was a man of great modesty, charm, and integrity. This does not confirm the validity of his beliefs and findings, of course, but in matters of research it is a good starting point. Furthermore, his whole training and disposition were such as to inculcate a respect for facts, truth, and logic. He had no predilection for the psychical or mystical. His curiosity was aroused by the fact that he was continually finding himself out of step with time. He was constantly discovering that he was conscious of things before they happened. The extent of his knowledge was not such as to be explained by the ordinary laws of chance. And this revelation, if we may use the word for want of a better, came to him in the course of his dreams.

One story will illustrate his point and mine. He dreamed he was standing on a footpath flanked on his left by some sort of railing, beyond which was a deep gulf filled with fog.

"Overhead, I had the impression of an awning. But this was not clearly seen, for the fog partly hid everything except three or four yards of planking ahead of me with its attendant portion of railing or gulf. Suddenly I noticed, projecting upward from somewhere far down in the gulf, an immensely long, thin, shadowy thing like a gigantic lathe. It reached above the plankway, and was slanted so that it would, had the upper end been visible through the fog, have impinged upon the awning. As I stared at it, it began to wave slowly up and down, brushing the railing. . . ."

What Dunne viewed in his dream was, as he realized, a long water jet from a fire engine that was playing a jet against that part of the structure on which he stood. Through the smoke he saw people dropping in heaps. The air was filled with the cries of suffocating people and the noxious stench of thick black smoke.

The following day Dunne read that there had been a big fire at a rubber factory. What was certain was that the conflagration gave off vile, suffocating fumes, that a large number of girls had made their way out on a balcony, which could not for the time being be reached by the firemen's ladders. While awaiting longer ladders, firemen played jets of water on the balcony to prevent it from catching fire. Then came a calamitous climax. A factory window broke behind the balcony, releasing dense smoke and fumes so horrible that, although they were standing in the open air, the girls were suffocated.

To dream of a fire is not unusual. To dream of a fire and then to read that one has occurred is also not a particularly remarkable coincidence, because millions of dreams are experienced every night. What made Dunne's dream in this instance so extraordinary was the unusual character of the blaze. The amount of detail seen by Dunne in his dream went far beyond coincidence.

Then came a dream that ruled out for him delusion, telepathy, or any mystical explanation, leading him to question our fundamental attitude toward time.

It happened when he was staying at a hotel on the edge of the Aachensee in Austria. He dreamed that he was walking down a pathway between two fields, separated from him on each side by iron railings more than eight feet high. He became suddenly conscious of the strange behavior of a horse in the field on his left. The animal had apparently gone mad and was tearing about, kicking and plunging "in a most frenzied fashion."

In his dream he acted as most of us would have done in similar circumstances—looked back and forward along the railings to insure that there was no opening through which the crazed animal could escape onto the footpath. Seeing none, he continued on his way until he was startled by the furious clatter of hooves behind him. The horse *had* escaped, and it *was* running after him. Dunne ran desperately along the path toward a flight of wooden stairs he glimpsed in the distance. He was unable to reach them, however, before he awoke—thankfully—although he was bathed in a sweat of fear.

The next day he went fishing with his brother down the little river nearby. He was absorbed in his angling when his brother called out, "Look at that horse!"

Across the river were two fields, with a fenced pathway running between them. At the end of the pathway were some wooden steps leading to a bridge that crossed the river. Unlike the railings he had seen in his dream, these were no more than four or five feet tall, while the fields were smaller. The horse, too, was smaller, though it was rampaging in the field just as in the dream.

Dunne told his brother of his curious dream. He noted that if he were taking the path as in the dream, the horse they now saw would be on his right and not the other side, as he had dreamed. Nevertheless, its strange behavior was the same. Thankfully, having looked around for any opening in the fence, he told his brother, "At any rate, *this* horse cannot get out."

He spoke rather too soon. Within seconds the horse had managed to get through or over the railings and was thundering down the path toward the wooden steps. It swerved past the steps and plunged into the river swimming straight toward the brothers.

Having no other recourse, the two raced back about thirty yards, picked up some stones, and awaited the horse, which, on reaching the bank, faced them, snorted—then galloped off down a road, away from them.

This set Dunne to thinking furiously. The dreams he had experienced were normal enough, if they had occurred *after* the event. But they were displaced in time.

In the silence of his dungeonlike study at Banbury Castle, Dunne spent considerable time explaining to me the significance of his experiments. He told me he had made a habit of recording his dreams, and concluded that dreams were so frequently prophetic that our ideas about time were wrong. In sleep, particularly, the mind, untrammeled by the limitations of consciousness, traveled freely backward and forward along the dimension of time. Furthermore, he believed that time itself moved in another dimension of time.

For a fuller exposition of his theory of time, anyone interested would be well advised to read *An Experiment with Time*. It is a complex theory to follow, especially on the mathematical side.

Dunne remained convinced that dreams could be precognitive, that the door to the future was not closed to humans. In this sense he came nearer to offering proof of immortality than any other man of our century, for if there are several kinds of time, nothing dies and nothing disappears.

I asked him for some simple analogy that could make his idea of time clear to myself and to others.

"See this," he said, picking up a piece of paper and holding it edge upward. "This line here (indicating the edge of the paper) is how people regard time—a straight line, neatly divided into past, present, and future." He put his finger at one end of the line. "This finger is me. It is the present. Life for me is in the present. And life for me, my present, starts at this point in time, when I am born, even though time—this edge of the paper—stretches backward and forward into infinity.

"Now the present moves (he slid his finger along the edge) and I am getting older. The expanse of the past grows, and I can look back on it. I think that's all time is—yesterday, today, and tomorrow. Until I reach the end, which is death (his finger now had reached the end of the edge of the paper), at which point we find this isn't the only time. Time itself is moving (at this point he moved the whole paper up in the air), time moving in time."

If Dunne was right, if time is not a simple line, a straight dimension, but is moving in another sort of time, all human experiences cannot be the transient thing we imagine them to be, but are swept sideways, so to speak, in an ever-flowing river. Death, in such a case, would not be the end of the road. At the point at which you die, you find yourself moving in a totally different dimension. Or, as Dunne explained in his references to his idea of serial time:

1. Serialism discloses the existence of a reasonable kind of

"soul"—an individual soul that has a definite beginning in absolute time, a soul whose immortality, being in other dimensions of time, does not clash with the obvious ending of the individual in the physiologist's time dimension.

2. It shows that the nature of this soul and of its mental development provides us with a satisfactory answer to the "why" of evolution, of birth, of pain, of sleep, of death.

In his view, Dunne's theory upheld the idea of something very much approaching popular conceptions of God: "It discloses the existence of a superlative general observer, the fount of all that self-consciousness, intention, and intervention which underlies mere mechanical thinking."

Dunne followed up his first work, *An Experiment with Time,* with two supplementary works, *The Serial Universe* and *Nothing Dies.* They are important and unique books, although it is probable that he made his theory "explain" too much. He felt that his time theory made logical the old conceptions of God, immortality, telepathy, and dreams. J. B. Priestley, who has drawn inspiration for books and plays from Dunne's theories, described him as "one of the boldest and most original thinkers of this age." This, I think, is true. Unlike Freud, who read into every dream some form of sexual desire or frustration, Dunne revealed what in the ancient world was taken wholly for granted—that dreams are frequently prophetic, and that they can often contain profound truths.

In the ancient world, when distractions were neither as numerous nor as intrusive as in modern times, the importance of dreams was fully realized, and the art of recording and interpreting them was practiced by an elite group of experts who had ample time to devote to the subject. In ancient Egypt, in Syria, and in Babylonia dreams were interpreted by priests and seers, and only a brave or foolhardy man ignored their warnings and judgments. Yet priests had no monopoly. Such was the universal faith in dreams that people deciphered their own dreams.

The Bible is full of tales about dreams and their consequences. When Jacob went out from Beer-sheba toward Haran and stayed there after sunset, sleeping with stones as his pillows, he dreamed of a ladder reaching to heaven, with angels ascending and descending it. He had a vision of the Lord and heard His voice: "The land whereon thou liest, to thee will I give it, and to thy seed. . . ."

41

In Genesis XVII it is told how

Joseph dreamed a dream, and he told it to his brethren, and they hated him yet the more. And he said unto them, "Hear, I pray you, this dream which I have dreamed: for, behold, we were binding sheaves in the field and, lo, my sheaf arose, and also stood upright and, behold, your sheaves stood round about, and made obeisance to my sheaf." And his brethren said unto him, "Shalt thou indeed reign over us? Or shalt thou indeed have dominion over us?" And they hated him yet the more for his dreams, and for his words.

And he dreamed yet another dream, and told it to his brethren, and said, "Behold, I have dreamed a dream more; and behold, the sun and the moon and the eleven stars made obeisance to me." And he told it to his father, and to his brethren; and his father rebuked him, and said unto him, "What is this dream that thou hast dreamed? Shall I and thy mother and thy brethren indeed come to bow down ourselves to thee to the earth?" And his brethren envied him; but his father observed the saying.

Joseph, we read, not only interpreted his own dreams, but those of others. When he was sold to the Egyptians, made a favorite in Pharaoh's court, and then consigned to jail because he had refused to be seduced by the wife of Potiphar—one of Pharaoh's officers—he interpreted the dreams of two fellow prisoners, the chief butler and the baker. The former, he predicted, would be restored to favor in three days. The baker, he predicted, would be hanged. Both prophecies came to pass.

When Pharaoh dreamed of the seven fat kine and the seven lean kine and the court magicians could not interpret the dream for him, the chief butler remembered how Joseph had correctly interpreted his own dream. Thus Joseph found himself brought from prison and taken to Pharaoh. He subsequently warned that the dream foretold a long famine, and advised the ruler to stockpile grain while there was time. As he had predicted, the famine did occur after seven plenteous years.

The Greeks believed that dreams were direct communications from the gods, and from the spirits of the departed. Aristotle, who wrote long and learnedly on the subject of dreams, did not accept the Greek view, and he also noted what modern research into dreams has confirmed: that external sensory stimuli—light or sounds or color or even some physical discomfort such as an over-full bladder—can intrude themselves into dreams and become part of the dream story. With a prescience that is little short of amazing, considering that the existence of electricity, or the basic electrical nature of all matter—animate or inanimate—was then unknown, Aristotle believed that actions could leave some trace in the air, a kind of vibration that gave them a prolonged life.

There is at least a basis for not closing one's mind to this possibility. For example, witness the unpleasant "atmosphere" that attaches itself, often permanently, to a place that has been the scene of great or violent tragedy and intense emotion, and the fact that certain people—who did not necessarily know each other, and in some instances are separated from each other by generations—have received, sometimes as phantasms or ghostly voices, similar impressions in the same place.

This theory of the permanence of emotion appealed strongly to Saint Augustine. He believed that these vestigial traces of past drama and tragedy not only pervaded the atmosphere, but in certain instances obtruded themselves into dreams. The importance of dreams is also stressed in the Jewish Talmud.

Much interesting research into the nature of dreams has been carried out, and is still being pursued, by scientists and psychologists. But the assumption that fears, conflicts, buried memories, and physical discomforts (such as the effect upon the nervous system of the body's attempt to eliminate poisons from the physical system) are factors in making us dream, and affecting the content of our dreams, does nothing to explain why foreknowledge is conveyed in some dreams, why difficult or seemingly impossible problems have been solved in dreams, why inspiration of the highest order has been transmitted in dreams before being executed in a state of consciousness, or why information that could only have emanated from one long since dead or who has just died appears to be conveyed to the sleeper.

Consider the strange case of Professor H. V. Hilprecht, as reported in the *Proceedings of the Society for Psychical Research* for August, 1900.

Professor Hilprecht was a Babylonian scholar. He had long been trying to decipher inscriptions on two small pieces of agate. Their purpose was a complete mystery to him, yet he was convinced of their importance because agate, a difficult material to work due to its extreme hardness and permanence, was very popular with the ancient Assyrians for holy, ritualistic, and other purposes.

Wearied by a long period of searching through various tomes, and speculating on what the scraps of agate might mean, the Professor went to bed and had a strange dream. He dreamed that he was in a temple in the ancient city of Nippur. A tall, thin priest led him to the temple treasure chamber. It was a low-ceilinged room, and to make access difficult, it was without windows. He saw in his dream a large wooden treasure chest. Scraps of semiprecious stones, including lapis lazuli and agate, were scattered on the floor.

The priest then spoke to him in these words:

"The two fragments which you have published separately belong together, and their history is as follows:

"King Kruigalzu [1300 B.C.] once sent to the temple of Bel, among other articles of agate and lapis lazuli, an inscribed votive cylinder of agate. Then we priests suddenly received the command to make for the statue of the god Nidib a pair of earrings of agate. We were in great dismay, since there was no agate as raw material at hand. In order for us to execute the command, there was nothing for us to do but to cut the votive cylinder into three parts, thus making three rings, each of which contained a portion of the original inscription. The first two served as earrings for the statue of the god; the two fragments which have given you so much trouble are portions of them. If you will put the two together you will have confirmation of my words."

At that time Professor Hilprecht was engaged, with Dr. John Henry Haynes, in the excavations which unveiled the secrets of Nippur, the holy city, seat of the famous shrine of En-Lil or Bel, lord of the air, god of the hurricanes, master of men's fates, and ruler of nature.

To understand the concern of the priests one must remember not only the supreme power of the ancient rulers who punish summarily and with great cruelty those who displeased them, but the enormous importance attached to the person of the ruler himself, for it was believed that the god Bel held the insignia of royalty, dispensing them to persons of his choice. In the same way that the Pope, according to Roman Catholic belief, is considered to be the

44

Vicar of Christ on earth, so was King Kruigalzu the appointed representative of Bel.

The consternation of the priests at receiving an order they could not fulfill makes entirely credible the explanation of the cutting of the votive cylinder into three rings, which, of course, made the truncated inscriptions incomplete and unintelligible.

The information imparted in the dream turned out to be correct. But before research proved it so, Mrs. Hilprecht confirmed how her husband had related the dream to her, jumping out of bed in a state of great excitement, exclaiming, "It is so! It is so!"

The Hilprecht case is one of the most baffling on record. The explanation of how information more than three thousand years old reached him in a dream raises many issues at once. Are there, then, "spirits" capable of communicating with human beings? Can inanimate things become imbued with the thoughts and emotions of others, or retain in some strange way a record of the events in which they have played a part? Did Hilprecht "pick up" from the temple surroundings some knowledge which reached him only in his dream?

How does it happen that information concerning murders is occasionally revealed in dreams? One can sympathize with police forces which are plagued by mystics and quasi-mystics offering to solve a particular crime, at a time when the police have their hands full in pursuing the usual lines of empirical investigation. From their point of view, there are too many unbalanced or illogical informants as opposed to the isolated case of a genuine intuition or revelation.

One can understand the irritation of the police in Chicago, Illinois, when a nineteen-year-old girl, a Miss Loganson, urged them to arrest a farmer named Bedford for the murder of her brother, Oscar. No such killing had been reported to them. Yet she asserted with such vehemence that she had witnessed in a dream the killing of her brother—a farmer at Marengo, fifty miles northwest of Chicago—that authorities reluctantly dispatched a telegram to Marengo.

It brought the reply "Oscar has disappeared."

In company with another brother and the police, Miss Loganson visited Bedford's farm. She led the police directly to a paved henhouse and, pointing to a certain spot, said, "My brother is buried here."

Under the paving her brother's coat was discovered, and several feet below the police came upon his body.

Miss Loganson declared that the dream had been continually repeated to her for seven days. In every dream the spirit of her brother had appeared to her and given her the information, which she had accepted as unquestioned fact.

There is a parallel between that case and the case mentioned by Cicero which was retold in Chapter One. Both raise several problems at once. Miss Loganson appeared to have received information *after her brother had died.* Is there, then, a duality of self, something approximating what is vaguely described as a spirit? Do thoughts, when projected telepathically, have a kind of permanence, so that they can be continually received? Furthermore, since it is established that not all the cells of the human body die at once, may not some cells of the brain remain active for a time, after death, and messages be transmitted by telepathic means? In other words, are we so sure that all the millions of cells that comprise the brain die at once?

The fact that the cells governing hair growth are believed by some to remain active when the heart has ceased to beat and the blood to flow is a warning that we ought to perhaps to be less dogmatic than we currently are about the actual moment of biological death.

I am not postulating as a certainty that human consciousness survives with the body for even a short period after death. But the brain, as I have said, is a complex organ with areas concerned with different aspects of cognition. When the motor areas cease their function, do we know for certain whether the memory areas are simultaneously out of action?

There is, of course, another theory: astral projection. It is maintained by some researchers whose scientific grounding gives special weight to their conclusions (for example, Dr. Robert Crookall*) that there is indeed a duality of self and that the other self can wander away from the body and can even be made to do so at will. This is obviously too large a subject to deal with in this context. We will come to it later.† But if this other self

---

*Dr. Robert Crookall, formerly Demonstrator in Botany, University of Aberdeen; late Principal Geologist, Her Majesty's Geological Survey, London; Member of the Society of Psychical Research; Member of the Churches' Fellowship for Psychical and Spiritual Studies.
†See Chapter Nine of this book.

is a fact, manifesting itself under certain conditions while a person is alive, may it not be this other self that survives a person after the death of the physical body?

Most religions postulate the existence of the soul or spirit, but it is an assertion impossible to prove. The behavior of some people, whose religions presuppose survival of personality and the exercise of divine judgment, hardly indicates that they pay more than lip service to the notion of immortality. But their belief or disbelief or pretended belief cannot affect the nature of truth. There may well be a soul. We cannot prove by scientific demonstration that there is. Nor can we prove there is not. But there are bizarre happenings, of the kind I have quoted, that would cease to be mysterious if the existence of the soul could be proved a fact.

☐ 4. Exploring the Unconscious

THE nature of dreaming has interested scientists for more than a century. All over the world brain specialists, psychologists, psychiatrists, electronic engineers, doctors, and workers in the broad field of parapsychology are trying to establish certain unquestionable and demonstrable facts concerning sleep and dreams.

The debt owed to such men as Edmund Gurney* and J. W. Dunne must always be acknowledged. But in Britain, as in many other countries, parapsychology is the Little Orphan Annie of the sciences. It is easy to raise 12 million pounds to build an airplane that proves too big to fly (e.g., the *Brabazon*), but it is virtually impossible to raise a few thousand pounds to finance any specialized branch of psychical research. Many of the biggest names in psychical research in Britain have had to finance their own research, and following it, the cost of making their findings generally available.

Only the Soviet Union gives official governmental support to the study of phenomena covered by the general term "psychical research" and which, to avoid any implied inference of mysticism, the Soviet prefer to call *paraphysical* research. However, many richly endowed faculties in the United States give substantial sup-

*Edmund Gurney (1847–1888), M.A., Fellow of Trinity College, Cambridge, a pioneer in psychical research, and one of the founders and first honorary secretary of the Society for Psychical Research.

port to projects in this field, involving many workers of a specialized kind as well as the purchase of computers for the processing and analysis of data.

Foremost among the American pioneers is Dr. Nathaniel Kleitman, of the University of Chicago, who has been studying dreams for more than thirty years. His book *Sleep and Wakefulness,* first published in 1963 by the University of Chicago Press, ranks with *Phantasms of the Living* as a trail blazer and has since been reissued in up-to-date form, embodying research, case histories, and analyses covering more than a quarter of a century.

The beds of volunteers were fitted with recording equipment, cinecameras, electroencephalographs, and similar apparatus. Not only have thousands of dreams been recorded, but also the mental activity of the sleeping persons. So have their movements in bed, establishing the fact that from twenty to sixty major movements are made by the average sleeper during the night. The sleeper tosses and turns, alters the position of an arm or a leg, mainly to ease the strain on muscles and avoid stiffening from bodily inactivity.

Claims are sometimes made by people that they have not slept for years. A Spanish farmhand, Valentin Medina, of the tiny village of La Gineta, Albacete, claimed a few years ago that he had not slept for sixty years. Personally, I doubt it. Protracted lack of sleep causes excruciating suffering, for which reason the interrogators of the Inquisition deliberately prevented their victims from sleeping, as do the Soviet secret police and their equally cruel counterparts in many non-Communist countries today.

Dr. Kleitman investigated many reports of people alleged "not to sleep a wink," but came to the conclusion that the longest period of real sleeplessness compatible with health was ten days. A volunteer who was awakened every ten minutes began, after four days of this treatment, to have hallucinations and show symptoms of paranoia.

Dr. Kleitman has also discredited the long-held belief that dreams happen in a flash, and that at the moment of drowning a man sees his whole life pass before him as if he were watching a speeded-up feature film. Electrical recording, by revealing eye movements during sleep, shows whether the sleeper is dreaming or not. Sleepers who were aroused when such eye movements were

49

noted were usually found to have been dreaming. Everyone has four or five dreams a night, each about half an hour long with regular gaps between.

A distinguished neurophysiologist, Dr. William C. Dement, of the Stanford University School of Medicine in Palo Alto, California, found that volunteers suffered derangement when they were prevented from dreaming. Dreams, he concluded, are the release of unconscious thoughts and emotions in fulfillment of the dreamer's psychological needs.

His findings were based on experiments with volunteers and on observation of patients who had suffered brain damage and who, as a result, were prevented from dreaming.

There is some comfort in the thought that distressing nightmares are often merely a mental safety valve. One could wish that the same situation held true for aggressive dreams. Dr. Calvin Hall, Director of the Institute of Dream Research in Miami, Florida, then working with Bill Domhoff, found that a high proportion of dreams were aggressive in their content. Also, aggression occurred more frequently in the dreams of children aged two to twelve, the degree of combativeness diminishing to a low level by the age of thirty. In dreams, boys were more prone to physical aggression than girls, who expressed themselves in nonphysical attacks such as rudeness and obstruction. After the age of twelve, males experienced more aggressive dreams than females.

It is interesting that adult men, in their dreams, showed little reduction in aggressive encounters. The person in their dreams whom they hated or attacked, or who was hostile to them was in 56 percent of the cases a male figure. With women, the diminution in aggressive dreams was also accompanied by the disappearance of aggressive males in their dream world, especially of unidentifiable males.

One curious fact emerging from this detailed analysis of dreams is that the epitome or symbol of hostility in the dreams of both males and females is the *male*. According to psychologists —whose dogmas are not always axiomatic—a figure seen in dreams, whether identifiable or not, is often a disguised version of oneself. When one "sees" in a dream two people involved in action, it is possible that one of them represents the dreamer. But whereas men dream of men in conflict, women, when they dream of conflict at all, more often see a female and male in conflict. If we accept the premise that the woman identifies herself with the woman in her dream, both sexes associate the male with aggression.

Another statistical result of this investigation was that, while some people seemed scarcely ever to have dreams involving aggression or hostility, others were in the midst of a fight as soon as they dozed off. Whether there is any measurable relationship between aggression in dreams and aggression in waking life remains to be seen. There may be, but if so, it might well be a relationship in reverse. The mild person, too timid to express his aversions and hatreds in open defiance and hostility, might experience the most fearfully sadistic dreams. Every psychiatrist is familiar with the mild little man whose main interests appear to be breeding hamsters and attending evangelistic meetings, but who emerges under hypnotism as a potential monster.

The dreams of John George Haigh, the Yorkshire "acid bath" murderer, were said during his trial to be as horrific as his acts. Despite an eminently respectable early background—his parents were Plymouth Brethren, he sang as a choirboy in Wakefield Cathedral—he became a petty criminal. Then, "inspired" by dreams of forests spouting blood and other vampirish imageries, he began a series of murders, luring his victims to a storeroom in Crawley, in Sussex, shooting them, and then dissolving their bodies in acid. After a sensational trial, Haigh was found guilty of the murder of Mrs. Henrietta Durand-Deacon, a retired widow, and executed at Wandsworth Prison on August 6, 1949.

Few men in the world have devoted more time to the mystery of dreams than Dr. Calvin Hall. His collection of dreams from all over the world runs into tens of thousands, filling the filing cabinets, closets, drawers and almost every inch of his home, now in Santa Cruz, California. His attitude toward a new dream incorporates the excitement and interest a coin collector experiences with reference to a coin not yet identified or inspected: Is it something unique? Does it carry knowledge a stage farther? Will it prove a missing link in an evolving theory?

It is a strange idea, a library of dreams—the Dream Research Institute's collection is unquestionably the world's largest—but it may contain the key to the mystery of human personality.

Dreams *are* a reflection of the individual, and who is to say that the mirror is a distorting one? Does the hidden stream possess less reality than the visible one? There is, furthermore, a universality about the content of dreams. However much they vary in their superficial symbolism—which reflects the cultural environment and emotional background of the dreamer—there are still the familiar fear dreams, the falling from great heights, the floating through air, the pursuit by something unpleasant, whether it is a faceless man or monster or forest fire or flooding waters. On the other hand, there are still the dream gardens, heavenly cerulean skies, deep green forests; there are orgiastic grottoes and temples in which imagination and physical desires run riot.

No wonder the ancients placed such importance upon dreams, and why it is said in the Koran that "a dream not understood is like a letter unopened."

This chapter would not be complete without a word about the Maimonides Dream Laboratory attached to the Psychiatric Department of Maimonides Hospital in Brooklyn, New York, and under the direction of Dr. Montague Ullman, assisted by Dr. Stanley Krippner and Dr. Sol Feldstein.

Many experiments have been conducted there, whose thoroughness and scientific discipline make them a worthy contribution to this important subject.*

A volunteer, having been told the purpose of the experiment and the techniques to be followed, goes to sleep in a quiet, comfortable room, with electrodes attached to his head. These give no discomfort and involve no physical danger whatever. They simply transmit the electrical impulses generated by thought.

The volunteer, in the language of parapsychology, is the subject. He will have met the agent, somebody in another room, who will be looking at a picture in an attempt to affect the dream imagery of the sleeper.

The pictures chosen by the agent are picked at random from a pile of envelopes. He does not know their contents beforehand, or the order in which they have been placed. His choice, therefore, is purely chance. In another room a researcher watches the fluctuations and graphs recorded by the electroencephalograph and the impulses of the rapid eye movements which show that the sleeper is having a dream. When a dream has taken place, he awakens the sleeper over the intercom. The sleeper or subject

*See "Experimentally-induced Telepathic Dreams: Two Studies Using EEG-REM Monitoring Techniques" by Montague Ullman, M.D., Stanley Krippner, Ph.D. and Sol Feldstein, B.E.E., *International Journal of Neuropsychiatry*, Sept.-Oct., 1966.

relays over the intercom to the agent the substance of his dream. The agent, by the way, is quite isolated, and cannot communicate by intercom or otherwise with anyone while the experiment is in progress.

Such experiments enable the researchers to follow the dream cycles of individuals, and also to measure with certainty the extent to which the content of dreams may be affected by telepathy. Not surprisingly (because for a hundred years of experiments there have been clear links between telepathy and dreams, especially with dreams at the moment of death or crisis), there were indications that the thought messages from the agent in his closed room had registered to some degree with some of the dreams.

Dreams involving telepathy, or thought transmission, or mental suggestions are far too numerous and factual, as well as being authenticated, to warrant any assumption of coincidence. Miss Catherine Crowe, in *The Night Side of Nature* (London, 1852), quotes the following remarkable case:

> I will relate a dream that occurred to two ladies, a mother and daughter, the latter of whom related it to me. They were sleeping in the same bed at Cheltenham, when the mother, Mrs. C., dreamt that her brother-in-law, then in Ireland, had sent for her, that she entered his room, and saw him in bed, apparently dying. He requested her to kiss him, but owing to his livid appearance she shrank from doing so, and awoke with horror of the scene upon her.
>
> The daughter awoke at the same moment, saying "Oh, I have had such a frightful dream!"
>
> "Oh, so have I," returned the mother. "I have been dreaming of my brother-in-law."
>
> "My dream was about him too," replied Miss C. "I thought I was sitting in the drawing room, and that he came in wearing a shroud, trimmed with black ribbons, and approaching me, said *'My dear niece, your mother has refused to kiss me, but I am sure you will not be so unkind.'* "
>
> As these ladies were not in the habit of regular correspondence with their relative, they knew that the earliest intelligence likely to reach them, if he were actually dead, would be by means of the Irish papers; and they waited anxiously for the following Wednesday, which was the day these journals were received in Cheltenham. When that morning arrived, Miss C. hastened at an early hour to the [library] reading-

room, and there she learnt what the dreams had led them to expect: their relative was dead; and they afterwards ascertained that his decease had taken place on that very night [of their dreams].

They moreover observed that neither of them had been speaking or thinking of this gentleman for some time previous to the occurrence of the dreams; nor had they any reason whatever for uneasiness with regard to him. It is a remarkable peculiarity of this case, that the dream of the daughter appears to be a continuation of that of the mother. In the one he is seen alive, in the other the shroud and black ribbons seem to indicate that he is dead, and he complains of the refusal to give him a farewell kiss.

It is, indeed, a most curious dream story, and reveals several phenomena operating at once:

1. A dying man somehow transmitted his thought to someone dear to him.

2. A woman (Mrs. C.) received a clear image of him and a message.

3. Mrs. C. transmitted her dream, let us say, by telepathy, to her daughter sleeping by her side.

4. The factual dream having reached her by two stages of telepathy, the daughter carried the dream a stage farther, as though the faculty of precognition had been "sparked off" by the deathbed scene. For at the time she had her dream, the dead man had not been prepared for burial. He was in his night attire, not in a shroud.

A curious case of double telepathy affecting a dream was reported in the *Journal of the American Society for Psychical Research,* 1967:

Two years ago my parents were away on a short vacation. Shortly after they left on their trip, my small son (Bobby) became very ill and had an extremely high temperature. Early the next morning I was surprised to see my mother and father driving in the driveway. Mother rushed in and said, "I had a terrible dream. I dreamed I kissed Bobby and he was burning with fever and when I turned around Bud (my brother) was standing there with a big hole in his head, pouring blood."

I told her that Bobby was terribly sick but that my

54

brother Bud had gone to work as usual that morning and was just fine. In less than an hour my brother, a lineman for Southern Bell Telephone Company, had been brought home by his foreman with a big hole cut above his left eye, and was bleeding profusely.

If the parent had simply dreamed of Bobby suffering a fever, the case would be a straightforward one of dream content influenced by telepathy. But her dream also contained an element of precognition—she saw an injury to her son which happened only afterward. The impression had been vivid enough to make her abandon her holiday and hurry back.

In the *Journal of the [British] Society for Psychical Research,* Vol. XLIII, No. 727, of March, 1966, Rosalind Heywood gives details of "an apparently telepathic dream" which she received from a psychologist who had, in turn, been given the details by a physicist and Fellow of the Royal Society.

His correspondent was the same William Freed whose telepathic experience was described earlier. Knowing the physicist to be interested in extrasensory perception (ESP), a subject about which Freed himself had hitherto been very dubious, he described the experience that induced him to change his attitude:

On Thursday, November 19 (1964) I was awakened just before 5 A.M. by a short nightmare—my eldest daughter, Jane (aged twenty-five, a violinist with the Queensland Symphony Orchestra), gasping for air, choking, a picture of agony. Now I hardly remember my occasional dreams, but that one struck me because of its vivid quality.

Next day I learned from press reports that on the 18th, the day before my nightmare, Jane and two fellow musicians picnicking south of Brisbane were carried out to the open sea by a strong rip tide, and that she and another person had been rescued and taken to a hospital. The rescue operations were aggravated by the huge waves and breakers, and it took about one hour before a life-saver managed to reach Jane on a line. . . .

Having received the "signal" at 5 A.M. (4 A.M. Brisbane time), I assumed that Jane "sent" it while in the hospital at that time, suffering from delayed shock, thinking of her Wellington home, father, etc. Wrong. Jane assured me in a subsequent letter that she was under heavy sedation in the hospital, but that she was thinking of me only when, in the final stage of her struggle, she gave up hope and intended to go under deliberately to shorten the agony. . . . That happened twelve to fourteen hours before my dream. Does it mean that it "reached" me at that time, but became submerged by my daily routine activities . . . to come up later while asleep?

Mr. Freed described his relationship with his daughter as "very strained prior to that episode," although usually they were much attached to each other. He had over the past year criticized and ridiculed his daughter's interest in such occult subjects as astrology and palmistry, dismissing them as senseless superstitions.

Jane Freed had a terrible struggle to breathe in the heavy breakers: "Worst of all, my hair was all over my face and if the waves didn't manage to suffocate me the hair would have!"

Mr. Freed experienced this nightmare just a few hours after his daughter's ordeal. As Jane put it in a letter to Miss Heywood, "Imagine his state. But, oddest of all, he had a nightmare only a few hours after it actually happened and long before the news had traveled. He dreamt that I was being strangled or asphyxiated —I couldn't breathe. He woke in a terrible panic, but didn't tell anyone next day in case he was laughed at! Now for Dad that must have been quite an experience!"

An amusing but no less impressive example of information being conveyed in a dream was reported by Dr. Louisa Rhine, wife of Dr. J. B. Rhine and herself a distinguished parapsychologist, in what is now known as the "crazy egg" case:

A Colorado man, recuperating from an operation and spending some time with his grandmother in the country, dreamed one night that she came in from gathering eggs and showed him one three times as large as usual, and longer in proportion. He mentioned the dream at breakfast and they laughed at the oddities of dreams. But later that morning, as he says, "She came in with that crazy egg!"

That might be foreknowledge of a singularly useless kind— but foreknowledge it was.

But such knowledge is often far from useless. That is why the famous physicist, Albert Einstein, kept a notebook by his bed to jot down the solution of any mathematical problem that might come to him in a dream, as soon as he woke up. Valuable creative ideas, even whole, integrated works of artistic creation, have emerged from dreams.

One of my favorite musical pieces (it captivated me the moment I first heard it years ago) is *The Devil's Trill,* composed by Giuseppe Tartini, who was born at Pirano in 1692 and died in Padua in 1770. He was educated for the Church, the law, and the army, in that order, and became a skillful violinist.

His life was just as adventurous and varied. He married secretly, was pursued by an outraged cardinal, and managed to reach Rome disguised as a monk. We may take it that, as was the case with all Italians at that time, when the Church was the primary source of power and education, theology colored his thinking. The fact remains that the entire sonata, which has given the world pleasure ever since, was heard by him in a dream.

He had sold his soul to the Devil, and handed the Infernal One his violin. He told his friend Lalande: "What was my astonishment when I heard him play with consummate skill a sonata of such exquisite beauty that it surpassed the most audacious dreams of my imagination. I was delighted, transported, and enchanted. I was breathless, and I woke up. Seizing my violin, I tried to reproduce the sound I had heard. But in vain. The piece I composed, *The Devil's Trill,* was the best I had written, but how remote it was from the one in my dream!"

That Tartini should dream of the Devil is not so surprising since he was aware of, even if he did not knowingly accept, the constantly repeated teaching of the Church that eternal damnation under the Devil's supervision was the reward of the guilty. He was twenty-one at the time, and leading a wild life. His conscience may have worked on his imagination while sleeping. This incident was not what William Booth had in mind when he asked, "Why should the Devil have all the best tunes?"

Samuel Taylor Coleridge composed his famous poem, *Kubla Khan,* as the result of a dream he experienced while convalescing after a severe illness in a lonely farmhouse. A soporific painkiller he had taken caused him to doze off in his chair at the moment that he was reading how Kubla Khan ordered a stately palace to be built within a huge walled garden. During his three hours' sleep the poet saw in the most vivid imagery the scenes described in his poem. Later, on awakening, he committed them to writing.

Robert Louis Stevenson often re-created as stories his fantastic but coherent dreams. *Dr. Jekyll and Mr. Hyde* was one of them.

When Professor Friedrich von Kekule was addressing a convention in Ghent in 1890 he surprised the delegates by suggesting that they learn to dream. He then described how, after trying in vain to work out the arrangement of trimethylbenzene, he saw the solution to his problem in a dream. A snake biting its own tail offered in a strange way the answer to his problem—the closed-chain or ring theory of the constitution of benzene.

Let us accept the fact that some other form of mind, which psychologists choose to call the subconscious mind, exists. We can prove it does by tapping its hidden resources under hypnotism, whose possibilities and nature I propose to discuss later. We know that the subconscious mind has an immense storehouse of memories; we know that it affects conscious behavior, usually without our being aware of it.

For example, hundreds of things which have to be learned, such as walking and balancing, become automatic. It would also seem that the subconscious mind is often uncritical. Tell a hypnotized woman that there is a mouse present, although there isn't, and she will show all the reactions appropriate to the real event. Tell her it is freezing cold, and she will shiver. Touch her with a cold iron, which you declare is a hot iron, and she will withdraw in pain—and the iron will raise a blister.

In a way the subconscious mind appears to be uncritically suggestible. But it certainly has powers and potentialities that have yet to be fully explained, codified, and applied.

Why did Spencer Perceval, Prime Minister of England in 1812, dream of his assassination (a dream he confided to his host) shortly before he was shot by a deranged man in the lobby of the House of Commons? Why did Mrs. Collins, of Muswell Hill, cancel her holiday in Scotland a few years ago after a vivid dream of standing on a bridge and watching a train crash? She saw the railroad cars standing up on end and overturned in a horrifying fashion and was so upset that she canceled her booking and went by bus. It was well she did, because she heard on the radio that night that the train on which she had intended to travel had crashed. And in the cinema she saw, on the newsreels, the re-enactment of her dream.

There is the more recent case of Mary Richards who just

before her marriage had a nightmare, repeated three times, in which her honeymoon plane developed engine trouble and circled the airport, unable to land. She and her husband boarded a Viscount of Cambrian Airways at the end of their honeymoon in Jersey to fly with thirty-six other passengers to Cardiff, where they lived, via Guernsey and Bristol. But as they approached Guernsey the starboard landing wheel jammed, and for forty minutes the pilot circled the airport before being diverted to Bournemouth.

Mrs. Richards had been so impressed by her dreams that she had tried to talk her husband out of making the flight, but he had dismissed her fears as silly.

Dreams possessing a prophetic content are sometimes associated with sleepwalking. The loss of the submarine *Thetis* on June 1, 1939, was seen in a dream by Mrs. Ada Rudkin of Algburth, Liverpool. Although she has never sleepwalked before or since, she felt impelled to go to the window, through which she saw a submarine bobbing up and down, reeling sideways, and then becoming seemingly absorbed in the soil.

Sometimes dreams have actually caused a disaster to be averted. A dramatic instance of this was reported in 1870. A Colonel Reynolds, an engineer of Cheltenham, Gloucestershire, was in charge of building a length of roadway together with the bridges that carried it. Occasionally there were floods which endangered the bridges, and his job entailed, among other things, keeping a sharp watch for damage in its early stages.

He wrote in his account as follows:

It had been my daily life for so long that no anxiety remained in my mind about it. I regarded my duties as merely routine work. I was in a fairly good state of health. One night I dreamed in a most vivid manner that I saw an exact picture of a certain small bridge. All the surroundings were complete, and left no doubt as to which bridge it was.

A voice at the same moment said to me, "Go and look at that bridge." This was said distinctly three times. In the morning the dream still persisted in my mind and so impressed me that I rode off at once about six miles to the bridge. Nothing was to be seen out of the ordinary. On walking into the water I found to my astonishment that the foundations of the bridge had been entirely undermined and washed away. It was a marvel that it was still standing.

Of course, the work necessary to preserve the bridge was done. There is little doubt that but for the dream the bridge would have fallen, as there was no reason to attract my attention specially to this bridge. Though small, the bridge was an important one, as its situation was peculiar. The picture that was dreamt was so strong that it is even now fixed in my mind as plainly almost as it was then.

It is to be regretted that a prophetic dream in one instance saved one life at the expense of millions of others. When Corporal Adolf Hitler dozed off in his trench during the Battle of the Somme in 1917 he had a vivid dream of being buried alive under an avalanche of earth and exploding shells. He left the trench for open ground, and so was the only member of the group to survive when the trench was shelled.

In a broadcast for the BBC Home Service in 1947, Lawrence Durrell, the distinguished poet and novelist, touched upon an aspect of dreaming that I have not encountered before or since. Two experiences, separated because of the intervening war by several years, and in two different places, made him ask, "Can dreams live on when dreamers die?"

However outlandish the question seems at first, there seems no logical reason why they should not. Since thought is a form of energy, we have no guarantee that, in given circumstances, it does not register in some way on places and objects. The atmosphere of many buildings and the "creepy" feel of many objects may be due to this. There is actually no proof that thought disappears. On the contrary, there is a volume of evidence to suggest that it does not—for example, the enormous number of hauntings that have been reported. But if thought energy does not vanish, why then should the thoughts that run through the mind during a state of dreaming? May not dreams register, too? These are my own speculations. Now for Mr. Durrell's story:

"In the ancient world they set great store by dreams. One ancient author divides them into five classes, of which the fifth is dreams of divination. People practiced what is known as incubation—that is to say, sleeping within the precincts of a temple—in order to have the dreams which might give them guidance in their lives or settle problems for them. When the great cult of Aesculapius arose, dreams played a great part in the technique of healing the sick; those who were sick traveled to one of the many temples where they entered a special building and spent the first night in incubation.

"There were hundreds of temples all over Greece, and today we think that those which we have unearthed at Epidaurus and Cos must have been the most famous. On arrival the suppliant made his sacrifices and performed some act of ritual whose details are not known to us today. Then he slept in the special dormitory set aside for him, and during his sleep the god appeared and either healed him outright or prescribed a course of treatment for him to follow. . . .

"I was thinking along these lines one hot August day in 1939 when some friends suggested a trip to Epidaurus in southern Greece. . . ."

The car in which Mr. Durrell and his companions were riding bumped down into a valley so beautiful that it was easy to understand why it was considered the abode of the gods. They spent the whole day wandering about the theater and the temple and inspecting the museum treasures.

Rather to Mr. Durrell's surprise, the guide, an amiable and typical Greek peasant, said that he had managed to get work in another town. But why, queried Mr. Durrell, should he want to change from such an idyllic spot?

"If I told you why," the peasant replied, "you would think me mad. It is because of the dreams. I can't bear the dreams we have in this valley."

"What dreams?" Durrell asked.

"Everybody in this valley has dreams," the guide told him. "Some people don't mind, but as for me, I'm off." He added that "the old man in the fresco" appeared in his dreams frequently and, odder still, he appeared in the dreams of his two children, who had never set foot in the temple.

Six years were to elapse before Durrell was reminded of this strange episode. He was in the island of Cos, working for the British administration that took over the Dodecanese Islands. At Cos is a temple of Aesculapius which was as famous in ancient times as the temple he had visited in 1939. Archeologists were busy at the temple, and he decided to visit this center of the

61

Aesculapian cult. Chatting by chance with two British soldiers reading in their tent, he was asked about "the blinking temple." He told them what he knew about the place and asked them if they had ever noticed anything about their dreams while camping near it.

"Well, as a matter of fact," one said, "we used to camp up there inside the blinking temple, but we didn't like it, so we came down here. Better atmosphere, ain't it, Charlie?" The fact was that when they had slept up there they had had several nightmares.

Durrell asked himself afterward:

"Was it possible, I found myself wondering again, that dreams do not disappear—that long after we are dead our dreams remain behind us? And especially in a place like this, which must have been charged with hundreds of thousands of dreams and with the fervent belief of the ancient Greek dreamers. Had Charlie—that red-faced, unimaginative British soldier—somehow made a contact with the ancient Greeks by letting their dreams invade his sleeping mind?"

☐ 5. A Vision of the World

For I dipp'd into the future, far as human eye could see,
Saw the Vision of the world, and all the wonder that
would be;
　　　　　　　　　　　　　　—Alfred, Lord Tennyson

ON March 4, 1966, Dr. Hirsch Gregory Jacubson came to see me. Although he was eighty-two years old, he was a heavy, thickset man of extraordinary physical vigor and intellectual energy. His complexion was pink and fresh and he walked with a firm and confident stride as though set on some important purpose.

I had for many years been helping him with a thesis—a long and complicated exposition that brought us often together, in the course of which I had come to know him well. He had been a prominent doctor in Latvia, then part of the Czarist Empire, before the First World War, and had been conscripted into the Red Army in order to combat an epidemic of spotted typhus that accompanied the Bolshevik holocaust.

He once nearly lost his life because, having refused a fee for saving a friend's life, he had accepted a "gift" of a gold watch so as not to offend his friend, and had insisted on paying its full value to him, keeping the watch as a memento. His delicate surgeon's hands and the expensive watch had stamped him in Bolshevik eyes as one of the hated capitalists, and the revolutionaries had converged on him with the obvious intention of killing him. Only by jumping on a table, presenting a bayonet at them, and shouting that they would all be shot when their crime was discovered, did he succeed in making them desist.

World War II brought still more terrible trials. His mother and father were murdered by the invading Germans, his brothers and sisters died in concentration camps, his wife was flung from a fourth-floor window, and his paralyzed mother-in-law was stomped to death by the Gestapo outside her home.

Yet there was about him not a trace of self-pity and he seldom spoke of his trials. He busied himself by helping and encouraging the surviving nephews and nieces of his scattered family, lived abstemiously and modestly as a lodger in the apartment of another doctor, gave almost every penny he had to charity (he received a small income from royalties earned by the sale of certain medical formulae), and kept abreast of modern life with a zest and informed shrewdness that could have put many younger people to shame. He was a happy man, free of guile and ambition and bitterness and fear.

He was also a very garrulous man who hardly ever stopped talking, as all his friends, including Sir Isaiah Berlin, knew. He simply bubbled over with observations about things around him, and if his friends found this sometimes exhausting, they also found it stimulating, and his interest in life and people admirable.

On this particular morning of our meeting he seemed subdued and thoughtful. "I see a great decadence," he said, "everybody chasing money and power, obsessed with their selfish needs, learning nothing from the past. You'll see—they will have the atom bomb, some fool will unleash it, and then. . . ."

"It's unlike you to be depressed," I said. "Of course, the world's in danger; it always has been. Come, we have done enough work. Let's go and have some lunch."

We went to an Indian restaurant nearby. We had often eaten there, and I suppose the little Pakistani waiter must have overheard scraps of our conversation while serving us. While we were eating, he approached the doctor:

"You are a doctor, sir, please?"

My friend looked up. "Yes?"

"I have a bad bump here." The waiter indicated a bump on the left side of his forehead. "I get terrible headches."

"How did you get it?" Dr. Jacubson asked him.

It seemed that one day a demented person had come into the café, attacked the waiter, and hit him over the head. The police had been called, and the man was arrested and in due course sent to a mental home.

The doctor asked him a few routine things, such as whether he had had it X-rayed, advised him to have another checkup at his hospital, and left it at that.

Thereupon the doctor fell silent. For almost a quarter of an hour he said not a single word. It was so out of character that I could only suppose that he had been thinking hard. After lunch he seemed to be his old self again. I had promised to visit a friend in a hospital, so I walked with Jacubson half of the way toward Queensway, where the doctor lived, then hailed a taxi.

At half past eight that night I had a presentiment to telephone him. My friend's associate answered. Her voice was quiet, tuned almost to a whisper, and she was greatly shocked. Dr. Jacubson was dead, she informed me. He had gone to post a letter in a box only two doors from the block of apartments where he lived. He had been molested by a mentally unbalanced woman who started quarreling with him, while passers-by were vaguely amused by what seemed to them merely two old people having an argument.

Suddenly, the woman pushed him in the chest, and he fell heavily into the gutter. Two men helped him up, and into the foyer of the apartment building nearby. Somebody rushed to find his associate, but she was with friends and it took a few minutes before she came with her bag. It was too late, however. His pulse had stopped. He was taken to a hospital, but was dead on arrival.

The tragedy set me thinking once more on the subject of precognition—those glimpses of the future that come unaccountably and prove in the fullness of time to be accurate. Had the doctor experienced a premonition? Was it not strange that he should be questioned in the morning about an attack by an unbalanced man, and find himself attacked by an unbalanced woman within a matter of hours? Coincidence—perhaps. I can only speculate about what his thoughts were when he fell silent, or why he had that feeling of depression in the morning. But I remember that he himself believed in premonition. Once, in Russia, he had had the strongest aversion to taking a train journey, although he was a man of indomitable courage. The train had crashed into some cattle that had chosen that moment to cross the line. There were many deaths and casualties, although he himself escaped comparatively unhurt.

Approximately a year later I attended a lecture given by Dr. J. C. Barker, Psychiatric Consultant to Shelton Hospital, Shrewsbury. His subject was precognition, a subject which had long interested him. He was convinced that the precognitive faculty did exist, although how and why it operated he did not know. The lecture was held under the auspices of the Society for Psychical Research at the English-Speaking Union off Berkeley Square, and to illustrate his points he used projected color transparencies. He also brought with him two correspondents who had cooperated with him in his research into premonition—Mrs. Lorna Middleton, a London teacher of pianoforte, singing, music, and tap dancing, and Mr. Alan Hencher, an Essex telephone operator.

I should, at this stage, explain that before the terrible disaster of 1966, in Aberfan, Wales, when an immense slag heap slid down the mountainside killing one hundred and forty-four people, one hundred and twenty-eight of them children in Pantglass Junior School, both Mrs. Middleton and Mr. Hencher had received a strong premonition of a disaster of just this kind. Dr. Barker, being the first doctor to reach the scene of carnage at Aberfan, had wondered afterward whether a tragedy of such appalling dimensions and involving so much emotional shock was or could have been sensed beforehand. If so, it would be a matter of significance and might even, if precognition could be established as a fact, point the way to a sort of "psychic early warning system" of such disasters, so that effective preventive action might be taken.

The most spectacular example of precognition of this particular tragedy is, certainly, that of nine-year-old Eryl Mai, who dreamed of it several weeks beforehand, and had startled her mother by saying, "Mummy, I'm not afraid to die."

"Why do you talk of dying, and you so young?" her mother asked. "Here have a lollipop."

"No, I shall be with Peter and June," the girl replied.

The day before the disaster Eryl told her mother of a dream she had had. She dreamed that she had gone to school and found it enveloped in black. The sinister sequel is that she and Peter and June *did* die when her school was buried under the mountain of slag that fell upon it from a height of six hundred feet.

66

Dr. Barker had conducted his inquiries with the help of Peter Fairlie, then Science Editor of the London *Evening Standard*. The extraordinary case of Eryl Mai was embodied, together with much other collected evidence, in Dr. Barker's book *Scared to Death,* published in 1968.

Dr. Barker encouraged many of the people who contacted him to send him forecasts, and he would wait and check their forecasts against events at the period predicted. The point is that he was convinced, as I have long been, that instances of precognition *do* occur. His scientific training was sound, and he had ample experience in assessing facts and weighing them against their source.

One day in July, 1967, at 12:50 A.M. Alan Hencher, who had told me at Dr. Barker's lecture that he frequently felt "a sense of constriction, a sort of lump in the throat" as a presage of some coming disaster, telephoned Dr. Barker at home. He had a strong premonition of the doctor's death, and urged him to take care, and to drive with caution.

Most people, even a psychiatrist well reconciled to the uncertain hazards of life and death, would not welcome being awakened at ten to one in the morning to be told that there was a likelihood of early death. But Dr. Barker, impelled as he was by intellectual curiosity and a search for truth, did not dismiss the warning as absurd. Suppose, he reasoned, the forecast came to pass? Presumably, he would be in no position to continue his researches, but others might be interested.

Accordingly, on July 21, 1967, he wrote to a few selected friends, informing them of the prediction made. "My reactions to this were naturally to be somewhat alarmed," he said. "I found it a little difficult to get off to sleep again and have, of course, decided to take extra care while driving. It would be wrong for me to say that I was not frightened by a prediction of this nature.

"I intend keeping a diary from now on and to record my reactions to this on a daily basis. I suppose anybody who plays about with precognition in this way to some extent sticks his neck out, and must accept what he gets. The important thing, though, is for this information to be recorded so that if anything does happen it should cause some interest and may stimulate others to continue in this important work.

"Having recently written a book on people, *Scared to Death,*

I am perhaps beginning to feel what this would be like. On the other hand, there is a powerful opposite reaction which involves a desire to cheat the fates and to attempt to prove that Hencher, who has been right apparently on a number of occasions, is wrong in this one."

Only two months previously Dr. Barker had been warned by Mrs. Middleton, who like Hencher had had a premonition of the Aberfan disaster, to be very careful while driving and to get the steering of his car checked. This he did, but there was nothing wrong.

Dr. Barker had asked my advice about lecturing in the United States. I gave him a few tips and the name of an agent there, adding that the work, though interesting and remunerative, could be very exhausting because of the constant travel and the great distance to be covered. But he felt extremely fit, was in his middle forties and looked forward to his tour, which he accomplished in 1968 with great success and pleasure.

In July, 1968, almost exactly a year after the nocturnal warning, Dr. Barker fell ill. Plagued by terrible headaches, he entered a hospital. After an investigation that lasted two weeks, he returned home to his wife and four children in Shrewsbury. On Sunday, August 18, he suffered a stroke, first a light one, and then slipped into deep unconsciousness from which he did not recover, dying in the hospital on August 20. The mysterious world of precognition had fascinated him. Did it also claim him as a victim?

There we must leave that mystery, being thankful at least that in the time remaining to him he tried to draw aside the veil which seemingly, but not irreparably, separates the future from the present. Every scrap of evidence on this subject is of importance and his contribution in this unusual field of research is of permanent value.

One night in December, 1968, a hundred firemen with forty pieces of apparatus fought a huge blaze at the Ponsonby Court Hotel, in Ladbroke Gardens, Notting Hill Gate, London. It was one of those hotels consisting of several houses joined together—residential houses of the Victorian period, with their heavy porticoes and rooms reached by a staircase. The building was five-storied. As is the custom with many similar hotels, it housed a large number of residential guests, many of them widows or unmarried women living on modest investments or upon their pensions. For women beyond the age of seventy, and especially for those over the age of seventy-five, finding a home if they have no families of their own, or no members of their family to live with, is never easy. The assumption is that their physical powers are bound to decline, and that they will need more attention than it is practicable to give them, or more than people are willing to provide. Conditions at the Ponsonby Court Hotel were comfortable and homely, and it is understandable that only for the most exceptional or unexpected reasons would any elderly resident wish to leave.

One of the older residents was Miss Elsie Moore, aged eighty-four, and crippled with arthritis. She had lived at the hotel for twenty-eight years.

On the day before the fire Miss Moore's sister came to visit her. She was surprised to hear her sister say that she wouldn't be there for Christmas.

"I said to her that I was certain I wouldn't spend Christmas in the hotel," Miss Moore told me, immediately after the fire. "I don't know why I was so convinced, but I was. I just felt it in my bones."

I saw Miss Moore because I had heard of her premonition through a friend, and because it is always best to get somebody's statement as soon as possible after an occurrence of this kind. She was being housed temporarily by a kindly city councilor and his family, who assured me that she was quite willing to discuss the matter with me, and had recovered sufficiently from the shock of the blaze to be able to do so. I found her, indeed, cheerful despite the habitual pain, thankful for her narrow escape from being burned alive, and grateful to the firemen who had no easy task in rescuing an old woman nearly six feet two inches tall and, as she cheerfully put it, "no lightweight either."

She had gone upstairs to her room when she realized that the whole hotel was ablaze. Glass was falling all around. Acrid smoke crept in everywhere. There were cries for help, and outside in the street she could hear the wail of the fire engines' sirens.

"I could hear the glass falling, and put a cushion on my hand," she told me. "I didn't panic. I was as calm as anything. I looked out of the window and saw the firemen."

She watched them bringing up the ladder, was told to get as

close to the wall as she could and they would get a man up to her. The ladder veered toward the window. She heard somebody call, "Every second counts." A young fireman came in through the window, against a background of smoke and flames. Like her, he was calm.

"Now I'm coming into the room with you, and you must do as I tell you. I'm going to get you on my back; you must put your arms around my neck and hold tight. Don't let go. And then I've got to swivel you round onto the ladder, so that you get your legs down the ladder."

She did as she was told, and the agonizing descent began, her crippled legs one on top of another instead of parted against the rungs for support. Huge sparks and scraps of burning material blew their way in the wind, and firemen played their hoses close to them to keep the flames away. The unaccustomed strain on her crippled limbs made her cry with pain at one point, but as they neared the ground she heard a fireman say, "You're doing fine, Gran." At last she made it.

And so she sat in the flat of Councilor Meekin, blessing the firemen and knowing now that she would not, indeed, be spending Christmas in the Ponsonby Court Hotel as she had the twenty-seven others. *How* did she know? We cannot call this a clear case of precognition, since she had no premonition of a fire or disaster. But that she should have had this conviction is, at the very least, a precognitive hunch.

What *is* precognition?

It is not prediction. The economist, the military strategist, the chess player, the punter following form, the weather forecaster, the political expert are all capable, at their best, of accurate prediction. Their knowledge is empirical. They are guided by countless precedents, they have studied cause and effect, they can survey past sequences of events, they are familiar with the natural laws underlying their respective subjects, and, limiting possibilities to a few probabilities, they decide which of these is the most probable.

Crystal gazing, card reading, divination by tarot cards, sand divining, reading tea leaves or palms, phrenology, psychometry, astrology, and the rest are not precognition but a form of sooth-saying, even though, if successful beyond the degree considered normal by ordinary processes of deduction, reasoning, and observation of character, they may imply some element of hypersensitivity or paranormal faculty.

Having a "hunch" or premonition is not precognition. Mental illness, incipient or deep-rooted, represents about 50 percent of all illness in the Western world, and one of the commonest symptoms of mental illness is depression. There are millions of people going around with a perpetual sense of foreboding, and it is scarcely surprising, taking into account the vast number and variety of their gloomy thoughts, if some of their misgivings come to pass. The fearful anticipations that prove unfounded are not heard of or at least not remembered by their associates; those that do prove accurate coincidentally inspire surprise and awe. There is no reason why they should. Scientifically and mathematically, they mean nothing.

Precognition is knowledge, in detail, of something that has not yet happened. It is as though one's consciousness had skipped ahead of the present and found itself in the future. Because precognition seems inherently unlikely, not to say philosophically impossible, there is an understandable reluctance to give much credence to it unless reliable witnesses have been informed of the vision, or prevision if you like, beforehand.

However, I recognize that this is merely my own definition, and that as is the case with so many psychic phenomena, premonitions, predictions, prophecies, and precognitions tend to merge. The same situation governs hallucinations. Here the terms ghost, poltergeist, telepathy, and telekinesis jostle with each other because the precise causation must often remain a matter of speculation.

Precognition does not necessarily involve topical matter. There are cases from the ancient world and cases reported quite recently, and in every period and every country examples are quoted in literature and archives. But since the validity of any account must depend upon the veracity and objectivity of the narrator and supporting witnesses (if any), the most valuable collection is that accumulated by the Society for Psychical Research, which, as I have mentioned earlier, was founded in 1882 for the scientific investigation of unexplained phenomena. Its founders included scientists and scholars uncommitted to any dogmatic assumptions, whether religious, philosophical, or superstitious, among them Henry Sidgwick, the brilliant if complex F. W. H. Myers, Sir William Barrett of Dublin, and others of similar caliber.

In the course of time distinguished scientists and public figures have served as President of the society. They include Professor Balfour Stewart, Earl Balfour, Professor William James, Professor Henri Bergson, and Lord Rayleigh. Nor must we forget Sir William Crookes, the English chemist and physicist, who discovered that so-called simple bodies are, in fact, compound molecules and was one of the first to take up the study of the properties of radium. He was President of the British Association in 1898, besides serving as President of the Chemical Society and the Institution of Electrical Engineers.

Sir Oliver Lodge, the physicist famous for his investigations into lightning, the voltaic cell, electromagnetic waves, and wireless telegraphy, also served as President (1901 to 1904) of the society. Fortunately, he remained impervious to the ridicule heaped upon him because of his expressed interest in the occult and his conviction that human personality survived death.

A scientist is not a demigod, and we all know that a man may be expert at some things and singularly inexpert in others. But in the field of psychical research a background such as Sir Oliver's is significant because the last accusation which can be made against a man is one of credulity or superstition.

Over the years the Society for Psychical Research has investigated every type of phenomenon with a care and depth that no other body attempts, and its reports and proceedings constitute the most valuable records of their kind in the world. Inevitably, then, I shall have occasion to quote later from them to illustrate particular points because of their imprimatur of authenticity. To do so is not to "rehash" old material because the society's proceedings normally reach a limited and specialized audience.

I should add that the society holds no corporate view and is not committed to any particular interpretation of the underlying causes of various phenomena. Its function is to encourage members to pursue research, to collaborate, and to share information so that they may be made aware of facts and theories that may impinge upon their own research efforts.

Its purpose is officially stated to be "to examine without prejudice or prepossession and in a scientific spirit those faculties of man, real or supposed, which appear to be inexplicable on any generally recognized hypothesis"—in effect, to examine in a critical and constructive spirit phenomena which are to all intents and purposes a mystery. The society formed six committees with these objects:

1. An examination of the nature and extent of any influence which may be exerted by one mind upon another, apart from any generally recognized mode of perception.

2. The study of hypnotism and the forms of so-called mesmeric trance, with its alleged insensibility to pain, clairvoyance, and other allied phenomena.

3. A critical revision of Reichenbach's researches with certain persons called "sensitive," and an inquiry whether such persons possess any power of perception beyond a highly exalted sensibility of the recognized sensory organs.

4. A careful investigation of any reports resting on strong testimony regarding apparitions at the moment of death, or otherwise, or regarding disturbances in houses reputed to be haunted.

5. An inquiry into the various physical phenomena commonly called spiritualistic; with an attempt to discover their causes and general laws.

6. The collection and collation of existing materials bearing on the history of these subjects.

Its American counterpart, the American Society for Psychical Research, was founded in 1888 with a broadly similar structure and purpose and its archives also are a treasure-house of the bizarre and unexplained.

In the ancient world every kind of precognition, divination, and prophecy was practiced. One may say that the people were riddled with superstition, although there is no reason to suppose, from the fortunes made by people who cater to superstition today, that things have changed much in this respect. Yet there seems no reason to doubt—although, after so long a lapse of time, one clearly cannot prove—the veracity of the scholars and philosophers who relate as fact stories of precognition.

Pharaoh's dream of the plagues to come was fulfilled. The Egyptian King Ptolemy owed his life to Alexander the Great, who saw in a dream the root that healed him. It is difficult to believe that the prophecies of Isaiah would have been retold for thousands of years if their fulfillment was merely apocryphal. Isaiah maintained that God's kingdom would never perish, and that the Hebrew people through all their trials would remain a great people

73

so long as they kept their faith. And despite every trial and fearsome persecutions and massacres they have retained their eugenic and cultural identity.

Assassinations are very frequently foreshadowed. Henry III foresaw his assassination by a crazed monk three days before it happened. The assassination of President Lincoln was predicted by William Douglas Home while looking into a crystal at Dieppe in 1863; it was also foreseen by Lincoln himself. John Forster, in his biography of Abraham Lincoln, mentions that the President three times had a dream presaging his death. In one he saw a great crowd of mourners in the White House, and, approaching the coffin which lay upon a catafalque, he saw his own body.

The assassination of President Kennedy was predicted not once, but several times by the Washington psychic Jeane Dixon. Before President Kennedy was elected she had told a friend, Miss Eleanor Bumgardner, that it would be "disastrous" for him to run, and several days before the final tragedy she told the same Miss Bumgardner that she saw "a dark cloud moving down on the White House." She told others, too—a Mrs. Cope, a David Greene, and a Kay Halle, whom she actually begged to persuade the President to abandon his trip.

On the very eve of the fatal journey to Dallas she exclaimed, "Dear God! In a very few days the President will be killed. . . . I hope that Kaye Halle reaches him in time to tell him not to make the Texas trip."

What had given Jeane Dixon this fixed idea? It could not be a desire for self-advertisement or a wish to attain the reputation of possessing prophetic powers, for she had told so many people of the assassination, as a predetermined fact, that had the tragedy not taken place the effect on her reputation would have been the reverse of such a hope. It is one of those things beyond explanation. As the event neared, her prevision became more specific and factual, her anxiety more acute.

Sir Oliver Lodge once recounted how an English parson dreamed of a violent storm, in the course of which a fireball crashed into the dining room and caused destruction to chimneys opposite the table. It was a fine sunny day and there was no reason to expect a storm, but the dream was so vivid that he asked his wife that they should eat their lunch earlier than usual. Within hours it happened exactly as he expected. A storm blew up, a ball of fire crashed into the room where they had eaten, and the force destroyed the nearby chimneys.

Great disasters of the past have been said to have been predicted. Four years before the Great Plague of London in 1665, George Fox, the younger, made a prophecy allegedly received by him by supernatural means: "The people are too many, the people are too many, I will thin them, an overflowing scourge shall come upon the land."

The Great Fire of 1666 in London was predicted by at least three people—by the same George Fox, by Thomas Ibbott of Huntingdonshire, and by Thomas Briggs, an itinerant preacher with a special penchant for predicting doom and damnation. The French Revolution, the American Civil War, and the First World War were also prophesied. Incidentally, the most extraordinary prediction of the latter was made by Nostradamus in 1555—three hundred and fifty-nine years before the event. The interesting thing about Nostradamus's forecast is that he foresaw war *in the air* as well as by land and sea: "A flock of ravens high in the air, and throwing fire from the sky on the cities, and on the soldiers below." He foretold the overthrow of the Ottoman Empire and the breakup of the Hapsburg Empire, both an aftermath of the First World War.

Generally, it is not so much the precognitions of great cataclysms but the more personalized stories that impress, for their detail is easier to pinpoint, and the greater the number of correct details, the greater the odds against foreknowledge. For the number of permutations of detail runs into millions.

Samuel Pepys, the diarist, was particularly interested in second sight or what we now call extrasensory perception. We owe to him the highly factual account, related to him on May 27, 1701, by the Queen's uncle, the Earl of Clarendon.

Toward the middle of 1662 the old Earl of Newborough came to dine with the Earl of Clarendon's father at Worcester House, accompanied by a Scottish friend. They were standing talking after dinner when Lord Newborough, having noticed that the Scotsman had been staring fixedly at the Earl of Clarendon's wife, Lady Cornbury, demanded of him: "What is the matter, that thou hast thine eyes fixed upon my Lady Cornbury ever since she came into the room? Is she not a fine woman? Why dost thou not speak?"

"She is a handsome lady, indeed," the man replied, "but I see her in blood."

Lord Clarendon laughed at him, for his wife was "perfectly well in health, and looked as well as ever she did in her life."

Nevertheless, in the beginning of the next month he told Pepys, "She fell ill of the smallpox. She was always very apprehensive of that disease, and used to say, if ever she had it she would die of it. Upon the ninth day after the smallpox appeared, in the morning, she bled at the nose, which quickly stopped; but in the afternoon the blood burst out again with great violence at her nose and mouth, and about eleven of the clock that night she died, almost weltering in her blood."

The Scotsman's precognition is impressive because it is highly unusual for a guest at a social gathering to stare at a woman and declare that he sees her covered in blood. His remark and his behavior in staring at her were taken in good humor, although in less friendly company they might not have been.

A still more bizarre story is on file in the Society for Psychical Research. It is an account written by Mr. Alfred Cooper, a medical specialist, and is countersigned by the Duchess of Hamilton:

A fortnight before the death of the late Earl of L., in 1882, I called upon the Duke of Hamilton, in Hill Street, to see him professionally. After I had finished seeing him, we went into the drawing-room, where the Duchess was, and the Duke said to me "Oh, Cooper; how is the Earl?"

The Duchess said, "What Earl?" and on my answering, "Lord L.," she replied, "That is very odd. I have had a most extraordinary vision. I went to bed, but after being in bed a short time, I was not exactly asleep, but thought I saw a scene as if from a play before me. The actors in it were Lord L., in a chair, as if in a fit, with a man standing over him with a red beard. He was by the side of a bath, over which a red lamp was distinctly shown."

I then said, "I am attending Lord L. at present; there is very little the matter with him; he is not going to die; he will be all right very soon."

Well, he got better for a week and was nearly well, but at the end of six or seven days after this I was called to see him suddenly. He had inflammation of both lungs.

I called in Sir William Jenner, but in six days he was a dead man. There were two male nurses attending upon him;

one had been taken ill. But when I saw the other the dream of the Duchess was exactly represented. He was standing near a bath over the Earl and, strange to say, his beard was red. There was the bath with the red lamp over it. It is rather rare to find a bath with a red lamp over it, and this brought the story to my mind.

The vision seen by the Duchess was told two weeks before the death of Lord L. It is a most remarkable thing.

The Duchess of Hamilton knew Lord L. only slightly, and was not asleep when she saw the vision. The strange picture was so disturbing that she closed her eyes to be rid of it, but it was still there when she opened them again. The whole concatenation of circumstances was so unusual that this can be considered a case of true precognition, a glimpse into the future, a moving forward in time.

The Proceedings of the Society for Psychical Research, Vol. XI, No. 517, contain another authenticated and extraordinary case:

A porter working at Escrick Station, Yorkshire, dreamed at the beginning of March, 1883, that he saw Mr. Thompson, the stationmaster, lying with his legs cut off against a small cabin at the back of the station. Nearby was a heap of coal. The porter, Thomas Carbert, saw that the accident had been caused by a freight train and, with that strange sense of time we have in dreams, felt that it was in the month of May.

He related his dream to the stationmaster, who laughed about it but, still amused, related the story to a friend, a Mr. Hartas Foxton. This terrible precognition was later enacted in reality, true to every detail. On May 18 the stationmaster was run over by a freight train which severed both his legs—in the exact place where Carbert had seen him in his dream.

A story in Lord Halifax's *Ghost Book* is a clear and corroborated case of precognition. It is a story attested by the chaplain of Exeter Prison, the Reverend John Pitkin, two warders, and the prison governor. On February 23, 1885, a murderer, John Lee, was led to his execution. On the scaffold he was stood upon a double trapdoor, whose two parts, hinged and opening downward, would insure his drop when the bolts were withdrawn. To make certain that the pressure was even, a prisoner had to stand with a foot on each door.

On the night before his execution Lee had a strange dream:

"I was led down through the reception out to the hanging place," he told the warders the next morning, "but when they placed me on the drop they could not hang me, for there was something wrong with the machinery of the drop. Then they took me off from the drop and took me (instead of the way I had come) around the A wing and back through the A ward to my cell."

The warders related the story to the prison governor. At the execution the drop refused to work, despite several attempts and the fact that it had been many times tested and found effective shortly before the attempted execution. Furthermore, when they gave up the attempt, they led the prisoner back to his cell by the route he had seen in his vision.

It may be added that the prisoner had not entertained the least hopes of his dream coming true and had given it no more thought until, after the fruitless attempts to hang him, the chaplain visited him in his cell. His sentence was commuted to penal servitude for life.

Lord Dufferin, while staying in Ireland, reported seeing one night a vision or ghost of an ugly and terrifying man, carrying a coffin. Hallucination or not, that is what *he* saw. A subjective hallucination is not less frightening or impressive because nobody else saw it.

Lord Dufferin and Ava, to give him his full title, a British diplomat of old Irish stock, was a brilliant, worldly man, a skilled negotiator and diplomat, and a wit, who was by no means given to dreaming and morbid thoughts. It is hardly surprising that the phantom made a deep impression upon his mind. He could think of absolutely no reason or explanation for its appearance to him.

Later, when he was British Ambassador in Paris, he was waiting for the hotel elevator with a gathering of people. But when the elevator descended and the doors opened and the people made way for him to enter first, he drew back in horror, and refused to enter. *He recognized the operator as the repulsive phantom he had seen.* The others crowded into the elevator, which began its ascent. The cable broke and the elevator with its screaming occupants crashed down the shaft, killing them all.

Lord Dufferin was naturally very curious to discover the identity of the operator whom he had recognized. This proved impossible. Nobody, not even the hotel manager, who had engaged him, knew anything whatever about him.

A clear case of precognition (among many others) appears in the records of the American Society for Psychical Research. It happened to a Mrs. McCahen, who wrote:

> Last year . . . (my husband and I) went to the Grand Canyon. The first evening I saw a woman walking up to one of the cabins with a man and a boy carrying the luggage. I turned to my husband and said "There is Mrs. Nash, a lady I served jury duty with a year ago. Her husband has one arm. But I will see her in the morning as she is probably tired."
>
> The next day I saw her sitting on the verandah, and I went to talk with her. Our husbands met each other and we had a pleasant chat until I mentioned I had seen her the evening before but didn't speak then. Mr. and Mrs. Nash both looked astonished and said they had just gotten here with a busload of tourists.

Mrs. McCahen was certain it was Mrs. Nash she saw, using the words "There is Mrs. Nash."

How did Mrs. McCahen see her friend before she was there? How was it that the wife of the English sportsman, Jack Marshall, watching the *Titanic* steam through the English Channel on her maiden voyage, screamed: "That ship is going to sink before it reaches America! . . . I can see hundreds of people struggling in the water!" It was, of course, on that voyage that the *Titanic* struck an iceberg off Cape Race, Newfoundland, on April 14, 1912, and sank with a loss of 1,517 lives.

The precognition which Mrs. Marshall experienced went far beyond the sort of gloomy thoughts engendered by depression or illness; there was a degree of detail and emphasis that were remarkable because the *Titanic* was considered virtually unsinkable.

Mrs. Marshall was literally frantic with fear. "Why doesn't somebody *do* something about it?" she sobbed—and we may imagine the bewilderment of her husband, wondering what the authorities would say if he demanded that the ship stop in its course, the passengers be taken off, and the proud new vessel returned to port!

Clearly, planes can't be taken out of flight, railroad schedules upset, coaches and cars immobilized, and ships prevented from setting sail because somebody foresees a disaster by some flash of precognition. The general inconvenience would far outweigh the benefits of the few tragedies which might by such drastic precautions be averted.

But disasters *have* been averted by precognitive instinct. The following account, related to me by Mrs. Katherine Satterlee of East 82nd Street in New York City, is an interesting example:

"In the 1930s, both my parents being dead, I joined forces, for financial reasons, and went to live with a cousin considerably older than I. A few years later she suffered a stroke and our life after that was like that lived in a hospital. We had a nurse. She had the mornings off, I the afternoons. For that reason, after the death of my aunt, my mother's sister, I could not give as much time as I should have liked to my uncle. He was nearly blind, arthritic, and his once fine mind had become a bit confused. One afternoon, after doing some shopping, I made up my mind to go home and get a cup of tea. But some impelling force seemed to order me to go down to Washington Square instead, where my uncle was living.

"It was then after four, and I argued with myself that it was too late for that long trip—that I would go down early the following day. But it was hopeless. I was *forced* to go to Fifth Avenue and take a bus downtown, though by that time I was beginning to have serious doubts about my own mentality.

"My uncle lived in a small hotel and had a nurse. The arrangement was that she went off in the afternoons while the chambermaid on the floor, who was very fond of him, looked in on him from time to time to see that he was all right. When I got there he was smoking his pipe and listening to the radio, as usual, and, still shaken by my own queer behavior in going there at all, I went into the nurse's room to take off my coat.

"When I went back to my uncle, it was to find that the bowl of his pipe had caught fire in some strange manner and he had not noticed it. I quickly removed it and put it out, but it did not take much imagination to know what would have happened if I had not been there. What impelled me to go there? Who sent me?"

Well, at least Mrs. Satterlee did not feel the impotence of Mrs. Marshall in the face of impending tragedy. Nor did she have the weird experience of Mr. A. S. Wiltse of Skiddy, Kansas, as related in F. W. H. Myers' *Human Personality:*

Mrs. Wiltse and myself had spent the day with her mother and stepfather, Mr. and Mrs. Todd. I had passed most of the day in the field where he was planting corn. We retired early, and Mrs. Wiltse almost immediately fell asleep.

Mr. Todd and myself being wakeful, lay and talked. There was but one room, in which there was an open fireplace containing fire . . . so nearly buried in ashes as to give about a one candle power of light.

While we were talking, I saw a picture slide on to the wall at my feet, as such a height as to rest easily in the line of my vision. I called to Mr. and Mrs. Todd and told them what I saw. The picture . . . remained before me long enough for me to describe [it] in detail to them. It was a landscape. . . . When I had given a full description, the picture disappeared with a quick movement like that with which it had appeared.

While we were talking, another picture slid on to the wall in the same manner as the first one. It was the same picture as the first, with the addition of several open fields and wooded lands along the banks. In one of the fields was a log-house. . . . The picture remained stationary until I had described it thoroughly, when it disappeared similarly to the first.

Both Todd and his wife said I had described the Cass Davis house, which was about a mile distant, across the river. At this another picture slid on to the wall. . . . The house was there, the door of which was closed, and as I announced its reappearance, I heard the muffled report of a gun on the inside of the house, and immediately afterwards the door flew open and a man rushed out seemingly in a great fright.

At this point Todd said, "See here, Doc, are you seeing these things, or just playing off a drive on us?"

I assured him that I actually saw, or seemed to see the things I described, although they did not seem possessed of solidity but were more as if one should breathe over a looking-glass, then stand at some distance from it and observe his image; it would look shadowy and dim.

In the meantime the door of the house in the picture

had been left open so that I could see into the house, where I saw a man staggering toward the door with blood running from his mouth. He reached the door, where he supported himself by leaning against the door-facing, and steadied himself off the doorstep on to the ground. In so doing he left the print of his hand in blood upon the door-facing.

At this point the picture again disappeared and was immediately replaced by another much the same . . . but in it the dead body of the man was lying on the ground some few feet from the door, while from the field advanced several people, with hoes and mattocks in their hands, who gathered around the body in apparent excitement and consternation, when the picture vanished and I saw nothing more.

I asked Todd if he was sure of the house; he assured me that it bore the exact description I had given. I asked if . . . a tragedy [had ever] occurred there. "Not that [he had] ever heard of" [he said]. I believe I said that "something of the kind has occurred there or else will. If it is past we may never know it; if it is to come, we may see."

[On the day] the corn which Todd had planted was ready for hoeing . . . we heard of Henderson Whittaker killing himself [that forenoon]. Whittaker went into the [Cass Davis] house, where Mr. Haun was sitting alone, and asked Haun to loan him his rifle. . . . Haun pointed to the corner where the rifle stood, saying, "I don't know whether it is loaded or not."

Whittaker put his mouth over the muzzle to blow into the gun, pushing back the hammer with his foot. The foot slipped off and the gun was discharged into his mouth. Haun ran out into the field for help. The hands came up and I think found the young man dead in the yard. I have also been told that the hand-print of blood was left on the door-facing . . . the main points are absolutely certain. The tragedy occurred in the house I had described, and was of substantially the nature I had described from the picture-writing on the wall.

The facts of this case were corroborated by several witnesses, including Mr. Todd and Mr. Haun.

Somehow, Mr. Wiltse's mind or perception had become displaced in time. He had seen the effect before the cause, something contrary to all logic. His experience, and others similar, raise the most complicated philosophical and scientific points. Is there, then, predetermination: is the whole of destiny laid out like a monster tesselated pavement, retreating far into the distance, every part in its place? It seems a preposterous and even a depressing prospect, as summed up in Maurice Hare's rhyme on free will and pre-destination:

> There was a young man who said, "Damn!
> It appears to me now that I am
>   Just a being that moves
>   In predestinate grooves,
> In fact, not a bus, but a tram."

For how can man be said to have free will if the future is all planned or at least its pattern determined irrevocably beforehand? And if man by his actions and decisions cannot affect the eventual outcome, what of moral responsibility for a man's actions? What is the point of prayer if the outcome is a foregone conclusion?

From Mrs. Harold H. Darnstein of Fort Wayne, Indiana, I have the following curious and sad story of her prevision of an accident:

"I was very ill just before our son was born, very weak afterward, but by the evening of the second day I felt better. About 5 P.M. or 6 P.M. I knew there would be, at 11 P.M., a three-car accident and that three ambulances would be used—a very rare thing in our town—and that one of the victims would have a broken leg and would be in the room across from mine.

"Lights were out at 10 P.M. for the rooms, but I waited for the 11 P.M. accident. Shortly after that hour there came the three ambulances, and one victim did have a broken leg and was placed in the room across from mine.

"On another occasion I saw a policeman walking up to our door and I knew that my father-in-law was dead. When he asked if we were the Darnsteins, I said, 'Yes, come in. My father-in-law is dead, isn't he?' He was so stunned he was speechless, as it had happened about seventy miles away, and his sister was in shock and could not have telephoned me. . . ."

A *premonition,* which makes you take a particular course and avert disaster (but a disaster of which you have no clear fore-knowledge), is one thing; it is like the decision not to catch a scheduled plane or train; or the impulse to visit somebody, for no known reason, with results important to them or to you; or the strong feeling that somebody is in danger, or has died.

Precognition, in the sense that I am considering it, consists of detailed foreknowledge. Broadly speaking, precognition can be accepted as a fact when the arguments and odds in favor of chance coincidence are so farfetched as to constitute the fantastic.

Mrs. Janice Lissauer, of Broadway, Boulder, Colorado, is a well-educated housewife-secretary with her feet well on the ground. Her hobbies are far from mystical—reading, cooking, gardening, real estate management, interior decorating, and fishing.

In June, 1966, a small girl in Denver disappeared one evening while playing with some local children. A search was organized, but for a time it was totally unsuccessful; there was not a single clue, and it was commonly assumed that she must have been kidnapped.

Mrs. Lissauer within two days had strong feelings and "persistent images." Their insistence prompted her to note them down, but if she did not approach the authorities about her inner conviction, one can scarcely blame her. Police work along established empirical lines, and have a distrust, if not contempt, for any metaphysical approach. Mrs. Lissauer noted down these comments:

> I see a door, a very ordinary door, and beyond it is dark, and it goes down, and there is a turn after a few steps. I feel the real solution is not at this location. The important thing is that the child is right at hand—right close—and why searchers have missed her I do not know. But she is not far away.
> I feel she is no longer living, I suppose because so much time has passed. She is close, and I do not mean nearby states, but very close here in Colorado, and I feel strongly that she is not too far from her home, and never has been. I feel very strongly that somebody close to the situation is not telling the truth, and is in a position to stick by it. . . . I feel the significant part is a very ordinary door opening into a dark place, down, and I believe this is the last place police would spend much time, that it is the most important place to search.

This little girl had been killed in a moment of panic by a

somewhat older neighbor, a boy, who had concealed her body in a dugout storage space beneath an outbuilding in his backyard. Until she was found he denied all knowledge of her disappearance and helped in the community search for her.

But if premonitions are not as detailed as flashes of precognition, they are still examples of the well-known saying: "Coming events cast their shadows before."

☐ 6. *Their Shadows Before*

JUST as Jeane Dixon foresaw the assassination of President Kennedy, so Jackie Kennedy (now Mrs. Aristotle Onassis) had a premonition of her brother-in-law's assassination.

She lunched frequently with Gian-Carlo Menotti, the American-Italian composer who is a close friend of the family. When Menotti asked if she was happy about Senator Robert Kennedy's running for the Presidency, she replied: "I can't be very happy because I know he's going to be shot like my husband. They're going to shoot him."

According to the Washington *Daily News,* Jeane Dixon also forecast the killing of Robert Kennedy months before the event. She had confided her misgivings to Alex Bilanow of the *News* and to Frank Boykin, former Alabama Congressman. She also forecast the assassination of Dr. Martin Luther King, Jr.

"My wife, Jeane, and I," said Boykin, "were having lunch on the Washington Hotel roof. Jeane told me that King would be killed and that he'd never come to Washington. She also said that Bobby would be next."

A British spiritualist, Minnie Bridges of Ebbw Vale, South Wales, recorded for a friend a forecast that there would be a further tragedy in the Kennedy family "very soon."

It could be argued that prominent people are liable to assassination, either as part of the jockeying for power or the fact that the unbalanced seem to prefer prominent people as the objects of their spite and hate.

"I knew that he would kill himself on this one, and I think he knew it, too," was the comment of Donald Campbell's wife, Tonia Bern, the Belgian-born singer, after her husband's death on Coniston Water in the course of the world speed record attempt in 1967. She had the clearest conviction that it would end in disaster.

This was the only record bid in the course of their eight-year-old marriage when Tonia was not with Donald Campbell. When she had to visit London, she asked him to await her return before making his next attempt, but he did not do so.

She told a reporter: "It is strange, but we both had a premonition about today's run. He said to me last night, 'Take care of yourself' on the telephone, as though he was saying goodbye. . . . I really did have a feeling about this attempt; I begged him not to go on with this particular series until the weather was better."

It is strange that Campbell, a deeply superstitious man, should have ignored both his own feelings and his wife's misgivings. But he knew also that record-breaking attempts always involve an element of risk; it is not easy to draw a line between caution and fear. They tend to merge at a certain point, and a proud and brave man prefers the hazard. He kissed a Polynesian charm every day for luck, carried a teddy bear mascot. A few weeks before his death he had delayed a bid in perfect weather because he realized that he had left his mascot ashore. He avoided important activity on the thirteenth, and avoided a third match on a cigarette like the plague.

Yet on the night before the fatal accident Campbell told a *Daily Express* reporter: "I have the most awful premonition that I'm going to get the chop; I've had the feeling for days."

To ease his mind they played cards, in the course of which Campbell turned up the ace and queen of spades—the same combination Mary Queen of Scots had turned up, convincing her that she was going to be beheaded. Then, with a look at the sky, he said, "Well, I reckon it will be over tomorrow, one way or the other."

Prophetically, Donald Campbell's record-breaking father, Malcolm, once said of his son: "I hope to God Donald doesn't go in for this business. . . . If he does, he will kill himself."

A remarkable story was recounted in *Weekend* magazine by R. Brownbridge, a miner from Middlesbrough, Yorks, whose life was once saved by a voice. Every day he would leave the coal face to find some spot to eat his sandwiches. But one day he had no sooner sat down than he felt uneasy and heard a voice say, "Move! Move!"

Impelled by this strange feeling, he moved a hundred yards away. Later he saw a crowd of workmates around the spot where he had been sitting; he had no sooner moved than a huge rock fell on the spot he had vacated. Indeed, the mates he saw thought he was under it and were trying to rescue him.

Miss Joan Bourne of Crewe, Cheshire, received her premonition in a very strange way a few years ago. She was working in her office when she felt something heavy fall on her head. It actually caused her pain, yet there was simply no object to account for it. It was simply an impression, though real enough in the physical sense. In fact, she had to abandon work for about fifteen minutes to recover from the shock. At the exact time she had this experience, a roof had collapsed on her father's head.

Similarly, Mrs. G. Owens of Bristol had a strong premonition of disaster in 1959. Indeed, it was so compelling that she begged her husband not to go to work. He merely laughed, and insisted on going to work as usual. So convinced was she that she was dressed ready to go out and was standing by the door when a policeman approached.

"You are looking for me?" she asked him. She then inquired how badly her husband's head was injured and named the place where it had happened. The policeman was astonished. He had come to tell her that as a result of an accident on his motorcycle her husband was suffering from a concussion.

The terrible Ronan Point disaster, in which an East London block of flats collapsed like a pack of cards, was vividly foreseen by a fifteen-year-old schoolgirl, Jacqueline Challis, who lived opposite. A fortnight beforehand, she saw in a nightmare the block collapsing, heard people screaming, and saw them running around in a frenzy. She told her mother and friends about it.

A kind of second sight saved the life of Leslie Hockenhull. Giving evidence at the official inquiry into the Hixon train disaster in January, 1968—a grade-crossing crash in which eleven people were killed and many injured—Hockenhull, who was second man on the footplate of the London-Manchester express, said that for no accountable reason he broke his normal habits on that occasion.

He had completed his duty when the train reached Stoke-on-Trent. His usual habit was to stay in his cabin. Instead, he decided to travel as a passenger and went to the seventh coach. The three railroad men in the cabin were killed.

Many passengers who were on the train that crashed at Thirsk in August, 1967, owe their lives to a premonition, it was revealed at the official inquiry into that accident. The driver's "inner voice" prevented what could have been a far worse disaster (as it was, seven people were killed and forty-three were injured). The British Rail driver, John Evans, brought his speed down from nearly eighty miles an hour to about forty miles an hour before he could see any danger.

He told the inquiry: "At this stage there was nothing to show that anything was wrong. To break even, though, I should have been *increasing* speed."

Something made him slow down, and slow down considerably. Later he saw a cloud of dust and knew that something was wrong, and he took his foot off the "dead man's handle" to increase the braking before crashing into the derailed wagons of a cement train. Had he been traveling at his normal speed there would have been a major catastrophe.

In 1967 Gina Beauchamp, who was due to fly from Manston to Perpignan, saved her life by acting on a premonition, despite angry and puzzled remonstrances from her mother, with whom she was to have made the journey. When she arrived at Victoria Coach Station to catch a bus to Manston, she point-blank refused to continue, ordered the driver to remove her luggage, and instead traveled home to Tranmere in Cheshire. The plane crashed with a loss of eighty-eight lives, and her mother was among those killed.

Sir Alec Guinness, the famous actor, had a clear and powerful premonition about James Dean, the Hollywood film actor whose memory has become a world cult. Dean was showing Guinness a new car he had bought, which was still in its transparent wrappings.

"How fast can it travel?" Sir Alec asked.

Dean beamed with pride. "One hundred forty miles an hour."

In a flash Guinness had a strong premonition of doom. *"Please,"* he begged, "don't drive that car. I have a feeling that if you do, you will be dead within a week."

Within a week James Dean was killed in the car.

A moving and a strange story comes from Queensland, Australia.

Eric Franks, an estate agent, was dismayed and alarmed when his nineteen-year-old son came home one day drunk. But it wasn't simply the usual and understandable anger of a parent wanting to keep his family along the right lines. He had a strong premonition that the boy's drunken habits would cause his death. For the youth loved driving fast. I suppose one could say that the assumption of an accident in the future was a matter of common sense—an accurate but almost inevitable assessment of probability. But was it? Mr. Frank's reactions to this incident, by no means unique in families nowadays, proved the conviction of his premonition.

He tried talking to Rex, telling him that he was convinced he would meet with a fatal accident if he continued hard drinking and hard driving. Rex simply laughed it off. Next, Mr. Franks inserted in a Southport, Queensland, newspaper, a bold-spaced advertisement warning that he would sue anybody supplying his children with liquor and would claim forty thousand pounds in damages.

As a sequel to that, he wrote an article for the newspaper describing the horror of a father finding his son dead in a car crash after he had been drunk.

Shortly afterward Rex Franks was killed when his car crashed while traveling at high speed. The trunk was full of beer bottles, and the state analyst found that there was alcohol in Rex's blood at the time of the crash.

In 1958 a thirty-six-year-old tennis star known professionally as Gem Gilbert had to visit a dentist for an extraction. Her mother had died while having a similar extraction, and it is understandable that the trauma could have affected her own attitude to her forthcoming dental appointment. She was convinced she would die, so much so that she wrote a farewell letter to her husband, Major George Kerswell, then serving in Jordan. The next day she died just as the dentist was about to begin his work.

What "instinct" (if it is instinct) gives a person certain foreknowledge of his own death? We know that people with crippling, painful, and highly dangerous afflictions can live on for decades after medical experts have given them up as hopeless. Many faith healers have a record of cures comparing favorably with those of qualified men who have spent a third of their lives in studying orthodox medicine. If a medical man cannot say with certainty when a person is likely to die (except in the case of grievous physical injury, or damage to the brain, and certain fairly obvious cases), how can the person himself know?

But know he often does.

Children seem to have extrasensory perception, and fore-knowledge, to a very marked degree. It is interesting that this should be so. It tends to confirm that these mysterious faculties may have an atavistic source, that they may be perceptions inherited over millions of years of development and born of the dangers and fears that have beset people ever since they began the long, perilous, upward journey to what we call civilization.

Some years ago Edwina Taylor, aged four, was playing happily in her parents' bedroom in East London when she stopped suddenly and said to her father: "Daddy, I'm going to die today."

Of course, her father laughed it off as a childish fantasy. Infants habitually mix reality and unreality, living their dreams in wakefulness as well as in sleep.

"Don't be silly, darling," he told her.

A few hours later Edwina was dead. Her murdered body was discovered days later in a disused cellar four hundred yards from the home in which she had had her premonition.

What had happened? Had she received a glimpse of the future, her tragic future?

Once the *British Medical Journal* carried accounts submitted by various doctors of instances where patients had known with certainty, and often with a certainty of timing, of their coming ends. Dr. A. Cameron, of Southborough, Kent, wrote of a case which had interested him when he was working in a large Arab refugee camp in Jordan:

> Amongst my patients was a youth of sixteen, whom I knew well, suffering from pulmonary tuberculosis.
>
> We were able to confirm radiologically that the condition was not far advanced and clinically his condition did not give cause for undue anxiety, though facilities for treatment were unfortunately limited.
>
> There were two noteworthy features about this boy—firstly, he was simple-minded and was regarded, in fact, as something of a joke by his friends and relations; secondly, he was a very devout Moslem.

His father, a sheikh, had formerly been a man of some wealth, but the son had always eschewed material possessions and all he had earned he had given away to the poor.

Some weeks later, when he seemed physically no worse, rising very early in the morning, he walked from end to end of the huge camp (in which dwelt some seventeen thousand people), bidding farewell and blessing them.

He then walked about five miles (eight kilometers) to Jericho, where he had relatives, and repeated his action.

Returning to his tent at the camp, where his father sat cross-legged upon the ground, he kissed him and invoked the blessing of Allah upon him; he then laid down his head in his father's lap and died instantly.

The doctor added, "I hope the Gradgrinds* will not try to rationalize about these things. Let us recognize that there are still imponderables behind both the jargon and the stupendous achievements of present-day medicine."

Dr. Madeline Allen, of Gravesend, Kent, told of a bronchitis sufferer who summoned her family around her because she was convinced that she would die that night. The doctor did her best to dispel her conviction, but the patient, who was "perfectly lucid" said: "I shall die soon after midnight tonight." She died at 12:40 A.M.

A Glasgow doctor gave the following facts about the passing of a cancer patient:

On paying my usual routine visit one Tuesday afternoon, the patient took hold of my hands, thanked me for all my attention, and then proceeded to tell me that I would not need to call and see him after Thursday, as he was going to die at 2:30 that afternoon. Needless to say, I comforted him the best way I could, told him to exclude such thoughts from his mind, and promised to look in again.

On late Thursday afternoon I received a message from a member of his family that their father had passed away peacefully.

A few days later two daughters of the deceased came to consult me, and in the course of our conversation told me

*"What I want is facts," says Mr. Gradgrind, in Dickens' *Hard Times;* hence the term has come to be applied to a man who can trade in nothing but facts, and refuses to use his imagination.

that the day before their father had died he had summoned all the members of the family together and repeated to them what he had told me—namely, that he would die the following day at 2:30.

On the predicted day, all the members of his family were with him except his wife.

As 2:30 was approaching, he urgently called for his wife to come in, saying, "Hurry, hurry, before it is too late."

She came running into the room, and on the stroke of 2:30, according to his two daughters, "He sighed, raised both hands behind his head, smiled, and passed away."

Dr. J. C. Jones, of Worthing, Sussex, told how a mother came to see him because she was worried about her four-year-old daughter, who had told her mother that she was going to leave her, but that she was not to worry because she was going to "a very beautiful place."

"The mother," the doctor told the *British Medical Journal,* greatly scolded her and said, "How unhappy I would be if you left me. How unhappy we would both be." To which the little girl replied, "I shall be able to see you, but you will not be able to see me." This was repeated over a number of days.

The girl was healthy and full of bounce, both physically and mentally, and psychologically normal.

"After a short period," the doctor said, "the child suddenly developed acute meningitis and died in a few days. This was before the advent of antibiotics."

Dr. J. B. Collinson of Broxburn, West Lothian, described an incident in a ward for tubercular patients in a Glasgow hospital. Naturally enough, because of their proximity and common suffering, such patients develop intense relationships with each other:

> The patient concerned had, however, been partially separated from his fellows, mainly since he was clearly dying and subject to rather frequent and distressing hemoptyses. Day and night about, each turn of duty by the nursing staff carried with it the expectation of this man's death and each return to duty brought renewed surprise at his continuing existence.
>
> His bed, I remember, lay in a corner at the end of the ward farthest from the door, and on the night of his death,

and on that night only, that man called from behind his screen, in turn, correctly, bed by bed around the ward, the name of each of his fellows, most of whom he had not seen for months. To each he wished good night, and one who was already asleep drew the comment, "Aye, Lachlan, ye old bugger, ye're sleeping."

If this farewell was coincidental, it was certainly surprising. Most of the men in this ward came to a lingering end, and a large proportion of them had full insight extending over long periods of time. Close association with such a community is not lightly forgotten.

Many rock-and-roll, jazz, and pop singers have had clear premonitions of their deaths. It might be supposed that the strident blare of amplifiers, the constant traveling and hastily eaten meals, the packing of heavy equipment on and off their trucks and all the hustle contingent on that sort of world would scarcely be conducive to contemplation, or encourage metaphysical lines of thought. But this is not so. A considerable number of these musicians are given to mystical and metaphysical speculation, although in some cases the hypersensitivity may be induced or activated by drugs.

Eden Kane forecast his own death. So did Buddy Holly. In 1961, Eddie Cochran, at the age of twenty-two, was making a successful tour of Britain, and the general outlook for him was good. He should have been in the best of spirits. Contrary to popular conception, a pop musician's life is not an easy one. It is exacting, tiring, often frustrating, and not infrequently years of struggle produce no worthwhile benefits. But Cochran's records were selling well.

Even so, Cochran was deeply oppressed in spirits, and kept saying that he wanted to return to America. In Manchester he woke up in the early hours of the morning, and raced to the hotel manager's room. Sobbing and distraught, he banged on the manager's door crying, "I'm going to die. I know I'm going to die."

It was not a publicity stunt. On the contrary, the incident was hushed up at the time because of the adverse effects it could have had on public opinion. The obvious inference would have been that he was drunk, under the influence of drugs, or mentally unbalanced.

On April 27 Eddie Cochran was on his way to London Airport when he was killed in an automobile accident.

94

A similar thing happened with Johnny Horton, another American singer, who achieved almost overnight fame in his field with a hit record, "No. 1 New Orleans," in 1959. He was better known and appreciated in the United States than in Britain.

In 1960, Horton experienced so firm a premonition of his death that he told his wife he was going to die. Horton was frightened of death, and the effect of his conviction was to make him do everything he could think of to avoid it. As things turned out, his excessive caution proved more dangerous than the customary acceptance of normal exigencies. On one engagement he had a long distance to travel. To fulfill this engagement he would ordinarily have traveled by plane, but he decided to make the long journey by automobile. His car crashed, and Horton died in it.

Both men, incidentally, had posthumous hits in the record world—Johnny Horton's was "North to Alaska" and Eddie Cochran's "Three Steps to Heaven."

My old friend and colleague, Robert Jackson, a distinguished author and journalist with many books to his credit, in his book *Thirty Seconds in Quetta,* says that a few hours before it happened a woman dreamed about an earthquake in which thirty thousand people were killed, while a voice told her that her husband would be saved. She was Mrs. Hawes, wife of a colonel at the Indian Army Staff College at Quetta in India.

On the evening of May 30, 1935, Bernard Law Montgomery, later to become famous for his leadership in World War II, then an officer at the Quetta Staff College, had guests to dinner in his home. Suddenly his wife, Betty, who had been doing some embroidery, drew her husband's attention to something odd which was happening to a skein of silk she held in her hand. Every strand had separated and become as stiff as wire. Monty could not explain it. Colonel Hawes, a dinner guest of the Montgomerys, said: "It is the electricity in the air."

That night at Farnborough in Kent, thousands of miles away, Colonel Hawes' wife had a vivid dream. She was standing on a rock overlooking a plain, exactly as the Staff College overlooks Quetta. The sky was gray. Suddenly, cracks appeared in the plain, and in the cracks were white and black faces. A voice said, "He's going to be all right."

Mrs. Hawes woke up shivering.

In the early hours of the next morning the town of Quetta

was totally destroyed by an earthquake. The ground surged four feet into the air, with a thunderous roar like that of a monstrous underground train echoing in a monstrous tunnel. It is obviously impossible to check accurately on a disaster that caused such total havoc and destruction; a conservative estimate is that thirty thousand people were killed in those fatal thirty seconds. As Mrs. Hawes had dreamed, her husband was one of those who escaped.

The earthquake was followed by an eerie silence. The answer is that the victims were swallowed up by the earth, which accounts for the strange fact that although Montgomery, Colonel Hawes, and their fellow officers at the Staff College knew that there had been an earthquake that night, they had no idea until the next morning of the incredible havoc wrought within a mile or so of their headquarters.

The strangest and most dramatic case of premonition must, it seems, forever remain a mystery:

It was on a winter morning that the citizens of Owensville, Indiana, found this strange message painted in huge letters on the pavement in front of the primary school: REMEMBER PEARL HARBOR. That was the morning of December 7, 1939. Nobody knew what it meant. Remember Pearl Harbor? Remember what? Why Pearl Harbor?

On that same day, two years later, the Japanese launched their attack on Pearl Harbor.

Sometimes precognition is manifested by some act which proves to be related to a dramatic occurrence. It is, as I say, difficult to define where mere premonition (a sense of foreboding) ends and precognition (a glimpse of the future) begins.

For Mr. S. Rajaratnam of Alexandra Road, Colombo, Ceylon, what might seem to us mere coincidence is for him a tragic example of precognition. The documentation he has sent to me is explicit and considerable and there is absolutely no question about the facts.

Space forbids the recitation of all the details, which relate to the death of his eldest son on January 21, 1961. His name was R. Sri Skanda Rajah. He was an inspector of explosives, attached to the Police Administration Division of the Ministry of Defense and External Affairs in Colombo.

Mr. Skanda Rajah's program of inspections began on January

17, 1961, on the range, and should have ended by Saturday, January 21. Indeed, on completion of his inspection at Deniyaya, he was due to return to his station the same day and a lunch awaited him at the Y.M.C.A. hostel at Galle where he was living.

That day, January 21, his father, on the way to his ablutions between 6 A.M. and 6:30 A.M., noticed in the bare, uncemented land opposite the bathroom a cluster of seven bandicoot burrows. (Bandicoots are large rats some twelve inches long, which are very common in India and Ceylon.) He admits to being superstitious, and took this to be an ill omen. He resolved also to destroy the bandicoots.

Mr. Rajaratnam was at that time employed as a draftsman in the Surveyor General's Office, Fort, Colombo, and had to begin work at 9 A.M. each day.

At 9:10 A.M. he felt impelled to write to his son to ask him to bring some fuse with him on his next visit; he planned to use it to smoke out the bandicoots, which were doing considerable damage, from their burrows.

Five minutes later he began to write: "My dear son: When you come home, please do not fail. . . ." But a real fear forced him to stop writing. The fuse might catch fire, he thought, in the car. The feeling of fear, and of concern for his son, was so strong that he put the letter back into his desk uncompleted. The time was by now 9:20 A.M.

At that precise moment his son was killed by a gunpowder explosion at Deniyaya, one hundred miles away. The wristlet watch he was wearing stopped at 9:20 A.M.

Mr. Rajaratnam had his overwhelming sense of fear a few minutes before the gunpowder explosion which killed his son. He feels it was precognition and he knows better than anyone else how strong his feelings were at that time. On the other hand, the superstitious omen of the bandicoot burrows, and a naturally protective attitude toward his eldest son, could account for his stopping midway in his letter.

Precognition comes by way of dreams, of hypnagogic dreams, or visions, hallucinations, or daytime "inner" visions (sometimes called daydreams). Some speak of an "inner voice," such as Mr. K. K. Bhattacharya of Fairlie House, Fairlie Place, Calcutta, India:

It was in the year 1959, nearly four months before the actual

97

event, that I felt a strong inner voice communicating over the telephone with my managing director, Mr. Alexander Robertson at Kilmarnock (Ayrshire, Scotland) reporting to him of the death of Mr. James Burns, manager for India (Glenfield and Kennedy Ltd., Indian Branch) in an air crash. This powerful voice appeared some weeks later.

In actual fact Mr. Burns, a young Scotsman of thirty-one, died in Calcutta in a tragic motor accident on May 15, 1959. The accident took place near the Calcutta race course on the evening of May 12. I happened to be away then in Central India (Bhopal)—a distance of nine hundred miles—and was informed of the accident over the telephone. I came back on the evening of May 15 and put a call through to Mr. Robertson telling him what happened. I was next in command to Mr. Burns.

There is confirmation of his story. It does seem that he had a genuine precognitive glimpse of a tragic happening, and especially of a telephone call that would be made in connection with it.

Mr. Frank Menefee, formerly of Company "A," Forty-seventh Infantry, United States Army, now of South Highland Avenue, Akron, Ohio, remembers that in World War II he "knew" exactly where in the body he would be injured (he was wounded in the leg and lumbar region). He did not mention this to anyone, of course—it would have sounded odd if he had done so, for in the conditions then prevailing (a heavy artillery barrage was going on) it might have been attributed to mere apprehension. His honorable discharge certificate, a copy of which I have, shows, of course, that this was not so.

A more spectacular case of precognition is related to me by Richard Lannoy, a writer and artist, of Nairobi, Kenya. Mr. Lannoy spent many years in India, in whose culture, he says, "we have a vast apparatus, a veritable Jodrell Bank of a receiving device for registering the paranormal."

Remember the famous catastrophe at the Allahabad-Prayag in 1954 when seven hundred people were trampled to death? Now there was a certain guru at the Kumbh—which was a festival beside the Ganges-Jumma confluence held every twelve years, but this one happened to have a planetary conjunction which occurs only every, I think, one hundred and forty-four years—well, this guru, the very famous Sri Anandamayi, was residing at a riverside camp about a mile from the bathing point where the disaster occurred.

On the afternoon in question she was in her camp, not bathing (she never "participates" in rites) but resting on a charpoy, alone with her attendant. All the rest of her disciples were somewhere in the *two million* crowd.

Suddenly she arose from her cot and said, "I see hundreds of bodies being crushed. Our own people are not involved." She was quite unmoved and serene. The time was exactly the moment when a caldron of boiling *ghee* [fat used in cooking] had been overturned in the melee and the stampede began. . . .

A question arises: If coming events cast their shadows before, is it wise or useful to seek the shadows before they encompass us? Would the millions of people who, during my lifetime, have ended their lives in circumstances of horror, bloodshed, mental anguish, and sickness have been able to go on existing had each foreseen his end in all its detail?

The question occurs to me after reading an account submitted to me by a doctor who had read an appeal of mine in the *Medical News* (London) for accounts from medical men who had had experience of the paranormal.

I have recently done a locum in Norwich. One of the patients with whom I had dealings, and who was a clairvoyant, read the palm of a retired gynecologist and ex-mayor. He told the gynecologist that he would rather not say more.

On being pressed, he predicted that the gynecologist would become seriously ill and that during the course of his illness the treatment would be altered, and on being further pressed the clairvoyant said that the illness would be fatal.

Soon after that interview the subject of it was X-rayed. A carcinoma of the lung was present. Arrangements were made for a pneumonoectomy to be done at the Brompton Hospital. After admission to hospital the idea of surgery was abandoned and deep X-ray therapy carried out. . . . About last Christmas the patient died.

An extraordinary case of precognition occurred in October,

1969, when nineteen-year-old Eddie Prior, a laborer, of Harans Cross, Swanage, Dorset, was seeing six holidaymakers off on their vacation. After his friends had driven off he broke down and cried, and youth club leader Harry Parson saw him weeping distractedly.

"Whatever is the matter?" he asked.

"They're going to have an accident," said Prior. "I can't see them coming back."

Three days later the truck crashed on the M6 motorway and three of Eddie Prior's friends—Terry Villis, Reginald Lye, and Chris Wellman, aged twenty-two, nineteen, and twenty-one respectively—were killed. Yet Eddie Prior was known in the youth club —and still is—as a balanced, level-headed, and certainly not an overemotional type. His clear conviction that tragedy lay ahead is certainly puzzling.

Research into precognition and premonition, which I have been conducting for nearly two years, is uphill work. There is something elusive about it, as there is with all psychic studies. What I have been trying to discover is this: Is precognition a fact —something that happens often enough to be worth investigating? (I have, at least, the answer to that—Yes. There are plenty of corroborated cases and they *are* worth investigating.)

If precognition is a fact, can any common factor be discerned in the conditions in which it is manifested? (The only common factor I have been able to find so far is that the hypnagogic state, between sleep and wakefulness, seems conducive to precognitive imagery.)

Is any particular type of person more predisposed to, or responsive to, such a happening? Could the faculty of precognition be exercised at will? If the faculty could be so exercised, to what purposes, useful or otherwise, could it be applied? And, thorniest of all questions—does precognition presuppose predestination?

My first attempt was to see whether people could, at will, foretell what would happen on a specified date. I was, of course, thinking of those who believed that they possessed precognitive abilities, or had some previous success in foreseeing the future.

In January, 1969, the Denver *Post* gave considerable prominence to my experiment, and, after outlining what I meant by precognition (a glimpse of the future which could not be attributed to an interpretation of past sequences of events, mere guesswork, or a correct assessment of current political, economic, and social trends and their future consequences), invited readers to contact me with their forecasts.

In all, something like three hundred correspondents wrote to me, some at length, some briefly, some seriously, others facetiously. Letters were first reproduced in the newspaper and then the originals were forwarded to me.

The response was gratifying, if a little alarming. Each correspondent received a personal reply and a questionnaire which would give me some background; it is necessary, in any case, to confirm that the signatory really did write, and was not somebody playing a practical joke at his expense. Such initial letters are seldom factual enough to be satisfying as they stand, and one must inquire as to the degree of corroboration available.

It does not follow that a correspondent is not genuine because there is nobody to confirm his account. But it is scientifically more satisfying if witnesses are available. If, for example, somebody predicting an assassination accurately mentions the probability before the event to other people, writes to others informing them of his prevision, or records it at the time in his diary, one can more readily establish the validity of his prophecy.

Another general conclusion to be easily drawn was that 90 percent of these correspondents were doom-minded. Hardly anybody expects anything good to happen in the world. Of the Colorado experiment (which I extended in due course to other areas and other countries) twenty-one participants foresaw earthquakes, four predicted violent riots, and six others predicted floods. Other events prophesied included three tornadoes, five explosions, six bad storms, two atomic events, four assassinations, and two attempted assassinations. Sixteen predicted the end of the war in Vietnam, two foresaw its increased continuance, while seven forecast wars of various kinds in other parts of the world.

One odd forecast was that the Pope "would resign." An earthquake predicted for the west coast of the United States, from approximately south of Long Beach northward to San Francisco, included the added detail that scattered distances up to twenty-five miles inland would "slip forever into the sea." There had long been forecasts in circulation of earthquakes in California, so that these forecasts were not so much precognition as pure prediction.

Disasters which fortunately did not come to pass were the blowing up of a U.S. Navy ship off South Carolina or Georgia

101

killing about forty men, a tragedy over Belgrade involving one hundred and sixty-nine lives, and "a tragedy involving snow." Off-beat predictions were that the Leaning Tower of Pisa would be straightened, Kosygin would resign, a biologist would defect from a Communist country, and "a famous U.S. songstress will lose her bird."

Perhaps it was wishful thinking that made one correspondent forecast "an epidemic of bubonic plague in hippie colonies." The forecast that the U.S. would land men on the moon, although inaccurate as to the date of June 12, 1969, did at least anticipate what happened weeks later—but this was scarcely precognition, in view of the flood of publicity attending the project. For one correspondent the gift of precognition was not really necessary so far as June 12 was concerned because "On that date, at about 9 A.M. in the office of the Selective Service System, New Customs House, Denver 1, I WILL LOSE MY 2S STUDENT DRAFT DEFERMENT [capitals his]."

In due course I extended the "What will happen on June 12?" experiment to about forty other countries, including India, Pakistan, Scandinavia, and elsewhere. Whatever else might be adduced against my mail, there was never a dull moment. One Spanish correspondent predicted my death on that day, another my suicide. A member of the staff of *The Times of India,* who does not know me and had never previously heard of me, wrote in consternation to say he had a feeling I was in some danger—from burglars, footpads, junkies, mad motorists, falling scaffolding, gas explosions, jamming elevators, air pollution, wind-borne diseases, and food poisoning.

Mr. T. K. Banerjee of R.D.S.O. Camp, Tamilnadu, India, saw in his "yogi trance" a tall tower breaking and falling down; another correspondent saw Princess Grace of Monaco falling from her horse, and (strangely, since the Dutch royal family is popular and the prediction was not an obvious one) a threat to the Dutch royal family. Such a threat was subsequently made, though not on June 12. Mr. Sumil Kumar of 8 Rajah Copendra Street, Calcutta, India, foresaw that a great man would arrive to establish peace and "world peace will prevail from that date." Later news indicates that his wish, which we all share, has not yet been achieved.

An evangelist from the Persian Gulf asked me for some free Bibles; another foresaw "a diabolical attempt on some small country by big powers" (a safe enough prediction); an editor of an obscure journal invited contributions from me without specifying a fee; the deaths of Nasser, Nixon, De Gaulle, and Mao Tse-tung were forecast.

The whole thing had become a sort of psychic Russian roulette. The mail was immense and answering it all became an arduous task. It was expensive in time and money, for each correspondent was required to fill in a questionnaire so that I had some background to go upon, not to mention some handwriting, which can be very revealing as an index to character in itself. My object was to see what proportion of respondents could achieve a prediction that could fairly be said to go beyond the laws of chance —where the explanation that it was due to precognition.

One correspondent in Singapore certainly set me thinking. I was bombarded, to my initial irritation, with a series of long letters written in Chinese characters, very artistically drawn. My irritation was due to overwork and not ingratitude. After all, getting letters translated from Chinese can be expensive, and there could be no guarantee that, the money having been spent, the contents of the letters would justify it. However, here at last was one bull's-eye, even though not accurately angled to June 12. For my Chinese friend predicted, accurately, that the American astronauts in Apollo 11 would bring with them "volcanic rocks" and that the moon was subject to seismic shocks. Within hours of the astronauts' leaving, a seismic shock was recorded on the instrument they left behind.

Having isolated one or two people who appear to have precognitive gifts, my next step is to subject them to a series of tests over a prolonged period. Such work cannot be hurried, and I will attempt no general conclusion now. In such a dredging operation one is as likely to bring up mud and old boots as objects of value. To isolate precognitive people will take patience and time.

One correspondent who has been sending me predictions regularly is Mrs. Lorna Middleton, who had, as mentioned earlier, predicted the Aberfan disaster. Mrs. Middleton forecast that the Queen Mother would look worried, and that this meant some mishap in the royal family. The day after she wrote this to me Prince Philip's sister died, and shortly afterward so did his mother, who lived at Buckingham Palace.

Research of this sort is often discouraging because it does not always produce swift results. This seems to be especially character-istic of psychic research. Only telepathy appears to lend itself to laboratory experiment and permit repeatable results—as with Zener cards.

That spontaneous phenomena cannot be explained, however, does not mean that they do not exist.

Precognition has happened on innumerable occasions, some of which have been specified. That it cannot be done to order does not mean that the spontaneous phenomena did not occur. Pre-cognition, if we could ever understand and apply it, would have the most revolutionary impact on our whole conception of time and space and upon our entire way of life. Truth may not always be the beauty that Shelley thought it, but by general consent it is worth pursuing.

☐ 7. The World of Ghosts

AT 2:30 A.M. on November 20, 1965, a truck carrying a pop group then called "The Cheynes" was on its way through the Surrey village of Cobham, a picturesque hamlet on the Esher-Guildford road often visited by Charles Dickens.

The group was returning from an all-night engagement at the Bird Cage Club in Portsmouth. The truck was loaded with the electric organ, guitars, amplifiers, and the usual trappings of a pop group, so that the four youths were crammed together in the front seat.

Suddenly Mac Fleetwood, then seventeen years old and the drummer in the group, let out a blood-curdling scream. About a hundred yards ahead of him, coming toward them on the sidewalk, he had seen a ghost. At first he thought that it was an unusually tall man. I will describe his experience in his own words, just as he related it to me:

"Suddenly—we were going along normally, we weren't talking about anything that suggested this, you know, in any way—and just suddenly I looked up and saw a very tall man. The figure could have been, oh, about six feet nine or nearly seven feet. It had what I would assume to be a very long coat which was nearly down to the ground; and it was light gray, slightly fluorescent and it seemed to have a light of its own against everything. I screamed, really screamed; I was absolutely petrified, really petrified."

What, I asked him, was the expression on the "man's" face?

"It was so vacant looking—that was what was so terrifying.

105

It was just a face and it was quite an old face . . . could have been about sixty. It was walking straight ahead on the right-hand side toward us on the pavement and it was going straight along. It was walking very stiffly—could have been a military sort of thing and . . . *its face!* I really saw its face. I think that's why I was really shaken; it was quite a long face and it was expressionless, forlorn, quite drawn. . . ."

The whole figure, from top to toe, according to Fleetwood, had a sort of fluorescent grayish-yellow glow. The road was fairly dark despite a few widely spaced electric lights. "It" (note Fleetwood's use of the impersonal) wore a long, ankle-length coat—"the sort of coat my father [a World War II squadron-leader in the Royal Air Force] used to wear."

Fleetwood had never witnessed anything like it before, and, as he put it emphatically: "I don't want to see it again. I made a bit of a fool of myself in front of the rest. I was actually in tears. I was absolutely petrified."

It is only necessary to listen to the tape recording of our talk to realize that for Michael Fleetwood this was a nerve-shattering experience that few of any age would care to encounter.

My son, Peter Bardens, the leader of the group, was driving at the time. He was then living with my wife and me at home in London, and did not volunteer the information of his experience; I had noticed that he looked tired and shaken and asked what was the matter, and the story came tumbling out. I exacted a promise from him not to mention the matter to the group's publicity officer, who would certainly have given it to the newspapers, since musical groups thrive on publicity. In this instance the publicity would have led to misunderstanding which could have been a nuisance to me professionally.

By an odd coincidence, a book I had been preparing for several years, *Ghosts and Hauntings,* which embodied my research into the subject of many different kinds of hauntings and psychical phenomena, was to be published on November 29—the very next day after our chat.

"If this gets into the papers," I explained, "it will look like a publicity stunt intended to promote my book, which I have tried to make a serious and factual study. If that impression were to get around, it would be a terrible nuisance. So please say nothing about it."

106

Not until a year later, when Dr. A. R. G. Owen, a Fellow of Trinity College, Cambridge, and a member of the Society for Psychical Research, was collaborating with me on a series of articles for the *Sunday Mirror,* did I feel it possible to disclose the facts in my possession.

After recording Peter's impressions of the affair, I made separate recordings of the other three members of the group—Mac Fleetwood, the drummer; Peter Green, the guitarist; and David Ambrose, the bass guitarist. I interviewed them separately, out of each other's hearing, for it is only by this means that, in investigating a collective experience of this kind, one can establish the common factors in their respective statements and insure that one witness is not repeating—consciously or subconsciously—the statements of the rest; that they are not, in effect, influencing each other in their versions of what transpired.

Their statements show a remarkably unanimity on essential points. They all saw the figure and are agreed on the height of the figure, its curious quasi-military gait, its gliding motion—it seemed to be gliding, rather than walking—and its strong luminous quality. To quote Peter Bardens:

"All four of us realized that it wasn't an ordinary bloke, that it was something horrible. I shuddered, and gripped hold of the steering wheel, you know, temporarily lost my mind. . . . Mick screamed and was sort of semihysterical, and the other two were a bit shocked. Mick started shouting for me to drive on faster and to get away from the thing, while Peter, the guitarist, shouted at me to turn around so that he could get another look at it. But my instinct was to get the hell out."

I have investigated a good many alleged cases of ghosts and hauntings and, as I have made clear in my previous works, I have never accepted that all such things can be written off as hallucinations, freak lighting effects, telepathically induced mental imagery, mental ill health (whether incipient or permanent, embryonic or advanced), or the result of prolonged anxiety, starvation, alcoholism, or drugs. All such things can be and often are at the root of certain hallucinatory experiences, but there remains an enormous residue of carefully corroborated and authenticated cases that defy explanation.

In this particular instance, I am satisfied that the youths were telling the truth. Had telepathy played a part? Was this an hallucination of Michael Fleetwood's, which by some strange means was conveyed to the other three youths? Such a hypothesis is far-fetched, as extraordinary as the assumption that the ghost of a man was walking through the streets of Cobham.

One thought occurred to me. All had stressed the military look of the man. The truck had just passed a churchyard wherein are buried the remains of Jean Louis Ligonier (Field-Marshal Lord Ligonier), who retired to live at Cobham Place and was buried in Cobham in 1770. A Huguenot who escaped to England to avoid persecution, he was the only Frenchman to become Commander-in-Chief of the British Army, a distinction he seems to have well deserved. In battle he was fearless and feckless, and at the Battle of Malplaquet he had twenty-two bullet holes in his clothes.

The English climate had little modifying effect on his Gallic passion, for he supported—and sustained—four mistresses.

I thought it worthwhile to look in at Westminster Abbey and study the face of Ligonier which appears in profile on his memorial. All had stressed the long features of the ghost they saw. Ligonier's face could be called long and horselike. A full-scale portrait of him on horseback, silhouetted against the smoking ruins of a town under attack, his long, silk-lined, brocaded coat flapping in the wind and his tricorn hat miraculously in place, emphasizes the long-drawn features.

But whether the group saw a phantasm of Ligonier must remain conjecture. What is certain is that they *did* glimpse something and are agreed on the broad details of what they saw, and that what they saw could by no stretch of the imagination be called a human being. People don't glide, and they're not fluorescent and luminous. In the course of getting around, one meets some strange-looking people and not a few ugly or sinister individuals, but one doesn't scream at the sight of them.

Dr. Owen, who saw the boys, questioned them, and had access to my own transcript of their statements, concluded that they were "completely objective witnesses; level-headed; down-to-earth. Each seemed keen to describe just what he saw and no more, and each was anxious not to exaggerate and to be accurate."

In brief, the youths saw a ghost. There was a certain irony that it should have happened to my son, who, observing my preoccupation with the subject, had declared his own complete disbelief in such things. But of course I did not make any play on this, for his experience had been an upsetting and disagreeable one. Not all ghosts are frightening, but this one was.

What are "ghosts"? They are constantly reported, and by a variety of people from all walks of life, every degree of literacy and intelligence, and every country in the world. This has been the case throughout the ages. If ghosts are a mental aberration, then the aberration is one that is common to an enormous number of people. But such a theory is itself more fantastic than the acceptance of the idea that ghosts exist. Why should particular places acquire a reputation for being haunted? Why should different people, who have had no previous contact with each other and have not been told that a place or house is supposed to be haunted—in other words, who have not been exposed to suggestion in the first place and subsequent autosuggestion—have the same experience of the uncanny?

Many people, at different periods of time and having no previous knowledge that could have influenced them, have experienced terrifying phantasms in the Tower of London and Windsor Castle, to name only two places. Several people, at intervals of several years, reported a sinister presence in an upstairs room at Renishaw Hall, country seat of the Sitwell family. Several people, whom I have interviewed personally and at length quite recently, have seen a ghost at Littlecote Manor in Berkshire, home of the Wills family—and such reports, in the case of this house, cover many centuries.

Built between 1490 and 1520 and standing on the site of an earlier house built in 1200, Littlecote Manor is a magnificent Tudor mansion set in superb parkland and gardens, which is now the property of David Seton Wills. Once the home of Sir John Popham, Lord Chief Justice of England under Queen Elizabeth— he presided at the trials of Sir Walter Raleigh and Guy Fawkes— it remained the home of the Pophams for four hundred years. It was a Cromwellian headquarters during the Civil War and houses the finest set of Cromwellian arms in the world, as well as having the only existing complete Cromwellian chapel.

The story attached to the haunted landing at Littlecote is well authenticated and there are even magisterial depositions to support it. Briefly, a former tenant, Will Darrell, caused a local midwife to be kidnapped and brought to the house at dead of night; there he ordered her to deliver a masked woman of a child, and then threw the child into a blazing fire. Since then there have been persistent reports of a ghost's being seen.

Jamie Albutt, David Wills's cousin and a lecturer at Sussex University, saw the ghost of a lady one light, summer morning in 1961. Ron Bishop, who lives in the area, tells me that recently he saw "an old boy coming down the path to the house," who went into the front doorway. "I got down and went along to have a word with him (I was up a ladder cleaning windows when I saw him) and there was simply nobody there. And that was ten o'clock on a bright summer morning."

Since Mr. Bishop used to serve with the Corps of Military Police, he is a man more used to realities than to fanciful flights of the imagination.

Longleat, the palatial home of the sixth Marquis of Bath (although he himself lives now in a mill house and has deeded the home over to his only son and heir, Viscount Weymouth), is another place where reports of hauntings have been persistent. Longleat has two ghosts—one, of Bishop Ken, the man who came to dinner and stayed, as a religious refugee, for twenty years, which he spent in the tremendous rambling apartment now known as the Bishop Ken Library—the other of Sir John Thynne, who built the house in 1580 and sometimes stands in spectral contemplation in the magnificent Red Library.

When Guy Montag, a German reporter from United Press International, was on a visit to England, he asked me if I could suggest a haunted house where he could spend the night.

"Why not spend a night at Longleat?" I suggested. "Of course ghosts don't keep appointments—they merely make them."

In due course Mr. Montag *did* spend the night there, in the Red Library. And he got the surprise of his not unadventurous life. He phoned me in a state of high excitement to say that the ghost of Sir John Thynne not only appeared during the night, but stayed for several minutes before fading away.

I may add that, although a house open to tourists and sightseers gains in interest by being haunted, Longleat has enough attractions of itself, with its parks, its architecture and history, its incredible art treasures, and its lions and baboons, to draw visitors without the aid of legend. And the ghosts were seen by many people long before, in 1946, the Marquis of Bath decided to open his estate for the first time to sightseers.

Ghosts and hauntings, or poltergeist disturbances, are not

110

found exclusively in historic houses and buildings, or at the scenes of bygone tragedies. Nobody knows by what criterion a place can become haunted. Nor do we know what makes one place more likely to be haunted than another, or whether the ghosts that are seen are entities with an independent existence, or whether they are subjective experiences of the percipient. Their appearances and their manifestations may be due to factors of which we are either imperfectly informed or merely ignorant.

The abandonment of long-held beliefs in the disciplines of science, physics, and chemistry, due to the discovery of laws of nature hitherto not even suspected, and the fantastic breakthrough in such fields as space travel (anyone predicting some years ago the amazing achievements man has made in the past couple of decades would have been branded a lunatic) are a warning that we should adopt an attitude of humility when we are confronted with happenings we do not understand.

To say that one doesn't believe in ghosts is as egotistical and nonsensical as to say he doesn't believe in quasars—whose existence on the outer periphery of known space had hitherto not even been suspected—because he cannot observe them and does not know precisely what they are.

The late Professor Margaret Murray, a great authority on witchcraft, comparative religions, and anthropology, once reminded me that ghosts are frequently seen, or appear to manifest themselves, during the course of demolitions. This was true years ago and is still true. The number of strange happenings on or near the sites of old buildings that have had to be dismantled is quite extraordinary. There are repeated cases where the workmen have been so scared that in some instances they haven't even come back for their wages.

In May, 1969, there was the strange case of the elevator that worked on its own, despite the fact that it was an electric elevator and the supply of electricity had been cut off.

Demolition men, generally speaking, are a fairly tough breed. Their work is hard and exacting and involves an inescapable element of physical danger. This fairly describes Joe Smith and his demolition crew, an eleven-man team assigned to knock down the abandoned Palace Hotel at Birkdale in Southport, Lancashire.

The hotel was built one hundred and twelve years ago, and there is tragedy associated with it. It was built back to front, and

111

the architect who designed it committed suicide by jumping from the top landing. He is said to have landed on the spot where the elevator later stood. A woman was once found dead in one of the rooms—on the floor to which the elevator moved of its own accord when the electricity had been disconnected and the workmen were engaged in demolishing the premises.

At first the workmen stayed in some of the hotel rooms during the night, though most of them reported hearing sepulchral voices and other unaccountable noises. However, it was the elevator going up and down by itself, against all the laws of gravity, mechanics, and common sense that most alarmed them. And there is absolutely no question that this did happen, because independent witnesses confirm it. A local housewife, Mrs. Kathleen Templeman, and a newspaper reporter saw the elevator move seven feet from the second floor upward. To remove any possibility of a hoax, even the winding handle had been removed. No mechanical explanation was ever discovered.

In 1966 still another hotel produced its unexpected quota of unlikely happenings. In this case it was the Crown Hotel in Poole, Dorset. An old building which was standing in the yard was being converted into a youth club. One of its members, twenty-four-year-old Malcolm Squire, was talking to his friend, Eric Dayman, and Paul Eeles who lives at the hotel, when all of them heard a single note being struck on a piano in the upstairs stable.

They mounted the flight of stairs and found the room empty except for the piano and no explanation whatever of how the note came to be struck. Then, to their horror, a number of objects on top of the piano projected themselves onto the floor and the front of the piano collapsed. They were petrified with fear and raced down the stairs. But their scare was by no means at an end. As they fled into the courtyard, a sort of "fluorescent mist" flowed down the stairs after them. They were immobolized with fear as the weird thing drifted across the yard and through the arch.

The disturbances started coincidentally with the demolition work. But the landlord, Mr. Stan Brown, had noted other curious happenings. Sounds like a body being dragged along the floor were heard from the top floor, and in the stables a handle was seen to move and a door opened by itself. One guest tried the exacting test of bolting the door of the stable room and going back into the courtyard. Standing there, he watched the door open.

112

A similar type of disturbance was reported from the Rose and Crown Inn at Basingstoke—footsteps and knocks being heard from the public bar when the place was closed. In the Sir Ralph Abercrombie Club, Bootle Street, Manchester, a thick glass shelf cracked unaccountably after the removal of the portrait of Sir Ralph, who is reputed to haunt the pub.

Workmen carrying out alterations to a house at Bosham in 1967 claimed to have been addressed by an elderly lady who told them they had done enough. Her description tallied with that of Lady Allen, the former owner, who had died two years before.

Buchanan Castle, where Rudolph Hess was imprisoned during the war, and which is now derelict, has been reported by numerous observers as resounding to the noise of heavy breathing. One visitor was puzzled, as well as a little frightened, when a powerful flashlight which he was carrying went out of its own accord. Inspection of the flashlight showed nothing amiss, and when the man returned downstairs again it flashed on again, unaided.

Having had a similar experience myself, I do not find this story at all improbable. I have related in a previous book how, sensing a sinister presence in a room in Highgate—and the friend who was with me sensed it, too, and was very frightened—I went over to the wall switch and turned the light on. The bulb lit with unusual brilliance and then went out, and nothing would make it light again. Yet in the morning the light switched on without the least trouble. The most detailed examination of the switch, circuit, socket and bulb revealed that nothing whatever had been changed or was amiss.

During the demolition of the Royal Ascot Hotel five years ago workers reported hearing horses neighing and seeing the apparition of a white horse. Following the hearing of unexplained footsteps in Mowbreck Hall Country Club, near Manchester, a false wall was broken down in the hope of discovering a legendary secret chapel said to have been used by a priest who was executed during the Reformation. The chapel could not be found, although priests' hideouts are a common feature of English country houses.

Mr. Norman Hutchinson was involved in an unpleasant happening when he was driving to work past Castle Dykes, North Stainley, in February, 1968, near a section where a new highway was being built. A white but faceless form appeared outside his car, moving at the same speed as his for a distance of several hundred yards. It is not unusual for ghosts to be seen on the public highway, but extremely unusual for one to be capable of maintaining this rate of speed.

It would be easy to add to the volume of such reports surrounding alterations and demolitions, both from those available in Britain and in other countries as well. Puzzling as such reports are, and fantastic as are the hypotheses by which one attempts to explain them, the easiest explanation of all—that the informants are mistaken—is simply not good enough. The broad spectrum of witnesses covers every type of person and degree of literacy and common sense, and the assumption that they are mistaken, or lying, or neurotic simply will not suffice. It is particularly interesting that so many of these hauntings occur when old premises are disturbed. *What* is released, and why?

There are two schools of thought among the considerable body of people who do not dismiss reports of ghosts and hauntings as nonsense, and are prepared to examine the facts. Explanations come easiest, of course, to those who accept the premise that the body has a soul or spirit, and that the soul or spirit is a distinct entity, self-motivated and possessing some kind of active intelligence.

I do not wish to digress into the field of theological dispute. Human survival after death has not been proved to the satisfaction of those who demand controlled scientific conditions; but as the factors underlying it are a mystery anyway, it is difficult to see what types of controlled laboratory experiments could be attempted.

Here it seems to me the scientists and physicists are unreasonable, because their rejection of the possibility of a nonhuman form or "spirit" is based upon what is known. But what is known is not, necessarily, all that exists, or all that could be or may be known one day. If the existence of the soul or spirit cannot be proved scientifically, neither has it been disproved. Therefore, it must remain an open question.

That sounds are heard and things seen, when alterations are made or buildings pulled down—sounds and sights relevant to the place's past history—suggests that "inanimate" things can become imbued with something of the personality of people long since dead, and that sounds and sights can in some strange way be retained. It would not surprise me if this proved to be the case, because experiments have revealed that the human presence can affect the be-

114

havior of electrons, which are a fundamental component of matter. Electrons being part of the atomic architecture of all substances, it may be that their behavior in certain conditions may be repeated long after the person who affected them has died.

Wood, for instance, the main material of furniture, is composed largely of carbon atoms. Each atom has its little universe of electrons. Do the doors, window frames, and paneling of rooms retain, so to speak, a sort of emotional photographic image?

Even if this vague theory proved to be true, it would not explain how an elevator goes hurtling up a shaft unaided, or a door opens of its own accord. One can only remember that thought, human activity of any kind, sound, and light are all forms of energy. We *assume* that they are all transient; but we have no proof of this.

Besides, what kind of explanation can we advance for the circumstance of the workmen being told by the phantasm of a dead person that they had done enough work? Their story, if accepted, implies that the ghost had a consciousness, was capable of conveying its thoughts or intentions, and able to observe what the men were doing. The "imprintation theory"—if I may call it that—would not account for such an experience, nor would it account for a piano note's being struck. It would leave us just as much in the dark in cases of poltergeist disturbances, when objects are moved or thrown about by invisible forces. Poltergeist reports are extremely numerous all over the world and cannot all be attributed to fraud or illusion.

One reason why stories of ghosts and hauntings are either accepted uncritically or rejected without sufficient weighing of the available facts is that investigating even the simplest case requires the expenditure of considerable time and money. Firstly, the people concerned must be traced and contacted. Meetings must be set up, fares paid, and possibly arrangements made for hotel accommodations. Since unilateral evidence is of limited value (though not necessarily valueless) the testimony of anyone able to corroborate the story will be needed. The site or building must be visited and inspected, plans drawn, notes taken, the history of the place established—as distinct from legend—through the testimony of old inhabitants and study of the archives and books of the local library or town hall or parish register. Geological maps may have to be consulted because pockets of underground gas, subsidences, or either an excessive flow or a drying up of a subterranean water course may account for certain movements and noises which, if not otherwise explained, may well seem mysterious or sinister.

The testimony of witnesses must be transcribed, and the main points of their statements compared to reveal common factors and points on which they are at variance. Photographs may be necessary. Even the environmental and health background of the principal witnesses assumes importance. Have they been subjected to undue environmental strain, so that their judgment is warped? Is there a record of mental stress, nervous breakdown, or mental imbalance?

When watch is kept under scientific conditions in an allegedly haunted house all sorts of physical and mechanical requirements must be considered. Is there a lighting source? If not, flashlights or butane lamps will be needed. Walkie-talkies may be necessary for members of the team to keep in touch with each other and report immediately anything unusual seen or heard.

Cinecameras, using either color or black and white film, infrared cameras for operating in the dark, electrical circuits that will release a flashgun and take a photograph when broken, talcum powder for window sills and floors, thin black thread for affixing to windows or doorways to reveal whether they have been opened, whistles for giving signals in a dark house that silence is to be observed by all for a given period (necessary when listening for strange sounds), and tape recorders—these are just a few of the physical aids that may be necessary.

Some time ago, with other members of The Ghost Club, I sat up all night in a council house on Bilborough Estate, Nottingham. We had gone there to see if we could isolate any cause or facts following repeated stories of a haunting. I referred to the case briefly in Chapter One; the detailed facts are as follows:

A few months previously, Charles Hill, an employee of Nottingham's transport administration, his seventeen-year-old daughter Sandra, and his two other children—Margaret, aged fifteen and John, aged twelve—moved into the house. Hill told me that early one morning he was sleeping in the upstairs bedroom when he awoke suddenly, and saw what seemed to be "a young French Foreign Legion chap" cross the room and disappear into the wardrobe. The man might have been about twenty years old, and Hill

116

mentioned the Foreign Legion because the man had a sort of kerchief about his neck. He saw the figure again on another occasion and was in no doubt that it was a ghost. He was also considerably frightened. Nothing like it had ever happened to him before and he had never believed in ghosts.

Later, Sandra was alone in the house when she encountered a similar figure on the stairs. She was so terrified that she fled the house and refused point-blank to go back again. The advice of their doctor, who could see the state of shock they were in, was that the family should not return to the house.

They were, in fact, too scared to contemplate returning. Accordingly, they left their furniture and fittings in their new home—to which they had moved from vastly inferior accommodations after many years of waiting—and went to stay with neighbors.

The house was quite comfortable, as such houses go, and might have been any council house anywhere in England. It had a small front garden, a larger garden at the back, a comfortable parlor and kitchen on the ground floor and three upstairs bedrooms. It was in the largest bedroom, overlooking the back garden, where Mr. Hill twice saw the ghost.

One point Mr. Hill made to me was that he had several times heard a young man singing. This fact is interesting because for many years the house was the home of a widow and her young son, who was a window cleaner. One day he fell from the cradle which supported him while he worked, and on account of the fall was paralyzed from the waist down. Becoming depressed by inactivity, he eventually shot himself in the upstairs bedroom where the phantasm had been seen. Another interesting point is that the young man was in the habit of wearing a kerchief about his neck instead of the usual tie. And he indulged the habit of singing to himself.

Fortunately for us, neither the electricity nor the gas had been shut off, the house still being the official home of Mr. Hill and his family, although they had been forced to abandon it. There were thirteen in our party, and Mr. Hill and Sandra agreed to spend the night with us. It was a bitterly cold night, but luckily a fire was lit in the downstairs parlor. It seemed to me that the upstairs bedroom (in which the phantasm had appeared) was inordinately cold, even allowing for the frigid weather.

The rules were explained to all taking part in the watch. Any rooms not being used would be sealed and the seals checked at the end of each observation period. If footsteps were heard, observers were asked to try to judge the direction, note the duration, and observe the type of step—whether heavy, soft, pattering, or shuffling. If an apparition or form was seen, nobody was to approach it. It should be observed carefully, the watcher being careful not to move, and meanwhile drawing the attention of the nearest person, without speaking, to the direction of the form.

Should knocks or raps be heard during this period of observation, the procedure was to try to ascertain the exact location and intensity (whether soft or percussive) of the sound. Observers were invited to initiate knocks or raps and see if they were repeated.

Certain objects were ringed with chalk so that their movement could be noted, if they did move. One was a bell which could be rung.

Our party included Peter Underwood, Chairman of The Ghost Club, Colonel Ralph Morris, a retired Indian Army officer, David Cutler, a "saw doctor," or specialist in refurbishing saws, whose hobby is parachute jumping, and Richard Howard, a sound recording engineer employed at Pinewood Studios. We were later joined by Leslie Parker, a friend of Mr. Hill, who was giving the Hill family temporary refuge from their "haunted" home.

In the late evening we all entered the haunted room upstairs, closed the door, extinguished the lights, and sat absolutely silent in a ring. There followed an eerie silence, followed by knocks and measured footfalls from above us. The gas fire flickered as if it were about to go out (even with it fully on the temperature of the room was arctic).

Then the silence of the house was shattered by a piercing scream nearby, followed by hysterical sobbing. Immediately we switched the lights on and raced to the scene of the cries—the small back bedroom in which Sandra and a friend, Mrs. Preece, were keeping watch. This room had a small hand basin, whose two taps on an earlier occasion had been turned on as though of their own accord, although they are extremely stiff and difficult to turn. The house had been flooded as a result.

We found Sandra shaking with fear, hysterical and distraught. She said she had seen *the legs* of a man step over something on

118

the floor and walk into the wardrobe, straight through its closed door. Mrs. Preece had witnessed nothing unusual. I noted that the wardrobe was of varnished wood, which could have reflected the faint light entering the room through the uncurtained windows.

Sandra was emphatic. "It wasn't a reflection," she assured me. *"It moved."*

We assembled in the downstairs parlor beneath the haunted room. At a given signal, everyone was absolutely quiet and motionless. At last the silence was broken. From the empty room above came the sound of measured footsteps, lasting for about a minute.

An element of experiment was tried. I myself have little faith in glass tipping or the ouija board, but some people claim success with them. There being nothing to lose, we tried glass tipping first.

The technique is simple. On a single glass, upturned on a polished table, a number of people place their index fingers. Arranged about it are the letters of the alphabet. Eventually the glass begins to move. It seems to every sitter that he himself is doing nothing to move it, but I have never made up my own mind how anyone can be sure who is leading and who is following. At any rate, it slipped crazily over from one letter to another in a sequence that made no sense to us.

At one point Peter Underwood asked a question: "Did you commit suicide?"—as a result of which the glass went immediately over to YES.

We tried the ouija board, where a pointer moves to various letters of the alphabet, although touched by several fingers at the same time. The same reservations that apply to glass tipping apply also, in my view, to the ouija board, although if spirits exist and have means of exerting physical force in any way, there would seem no reason why they might not assert themselves by the means presented to them. Whatever the merits of that thought, the pointer did spell out the names of all of Charles Hill's children and those of his friend, Leslie Parker, including an unusual name, DENICE. Then, in sporadic bursts of lettering, it spelled out the message: SANDRA I LIKE.

None of the bells we had placed strategically were rung. None of the ringed objects were disturbed. No ghostly footprints appeared on the sprinkled talcum. But something happened when

119

we held another session in the haunted bedroom. In the pitch dark, relieved only by the faint glow of the flickering gas fire, we fell silent and waited.

It could have been an optical illusion, but it seemed to me that there was a faint smoky haze in the wardrobe recess. I had no sooner noticed it than there was a sharp, agonized cry of panic from one of our circle: "The light! For God's sake put on the light!"

We rushed to the light. David Cutler, whom twenty-four parachute jumps had failed to frighten, was shaking with fear.

"I had a terrible feeling," he explained, "a tightness about the chest. I heard heavy breathing just by me. My head is spinning. I never want to experience anything like that again!"

We watched different parts of the house and compared notes. Les Parker heard a "slight scuffle" in the bathroom followed by two thumps from above. Others heard footsteps from the haunted bedroom. Peter Underwood, on watch in the hall, heard a noise like moving furniture.

As I left in the early dawn, and took a backward look at the house, I found myself reflecting how ordinary and normal it looked —so much like hundreds of thousands of similar dwellings. Yet for the Hill family it was a place of terror. What was the answer?

"Some people say that we're trying to get a better house from the City Council," Sandra told me. "But why should we? The place is a palace compared with our old home. But we wouldn't live in it again."

□ 8. Ghosts Galore

THE Nottingham council house is only one of many ordinary dwellings where bizarre happenings are reported.

Ghosts drove a truck driver, Robert McGhee, and his family out of an old terraced house in Spenser Grove, Stoke Newington, London, in 1969. The disturbances got so bad that the family began sleeping away from the premises, just as Mr. Hill and his family had done. There were loud bumps in the night, "a beautiful woman" came out of a wardrobe, and a hunchback cobbler, said to have lived in the house ninety years before, appeared from nowhere.

For Mr. McGhee, who first moved into the house in 1963, the tenancy became a nightmare of occult and legal complications. Apart from the appearance of apparitions and the frightening noises at night, no less than four fires started unaccountably, the last of which made the house uninhabitable.

As a result, the rent officer assessed the rent at five shillings a week. The landlord appealed to the rent assessment committee, and that group ruled that the fire, which completely gutted the house when the McGhee family was not in residence, must have been caused by Mr. McGhee's negligence in leaving the place at night with the gas and electricity connected, and that ghosts had nothing to do with it.

The suggestion that a tenant fleeing from ghosts ought to shut off the gas and electricity though still officially in residence in the house and liable for rent (Mr. McGhee would have lost his right to be rehoused somewhere more suitable had he merely abandoned the house) is a strange one, because thousands of people have left their houses without disconnecting the utilities.

The case was argued out in the Queen's Bench divisional court, Lord Parker sitting with Mr. Justice Melford Stevenson and Mr. Justice Willis. The court decided that the committee was wrong and that Mr. McGhee was in no way to blame.

The fires starting unaccountably are a typical poltergeist disturbance. The word *poltergeist* means "mischievous spirit" in German, and through the ages there have been innumerable reports of poltergeist activities. It is usually found that the disturbances involve a boy or girl approaching or going through some phase of puberty. It has been postulated by many experts that such drastic bodily changes may cause a person to emit some kind of telekinetic energy (e.g., causing the movement of objects without actually touching or applying any direct physical force to them).

Mr. McGhee and his wife, together with his daughter, son-in-law, and granddaughter had moved into the house seven years before. Then three-year-old Elaine Strachan said she saw strange white forms at night. Naturally, her parents thought she was having nightmares. But one evening her mother, Mrs. Sally Strachan, saw the forms, too, and ran in terror from the house. After that the whole family made a practice of leaving at night to sleep with relatives.

A strange feature of the haunting was that on several occasions, as the family was leaving for the night, they saw smoke and flames coming from the windows. Mr. McGhee stated that, on going back to investigate, he saw a great ball of fire moving around the room, setting fire to everything it touched.

A couple who moved into a brand-new house in Howden, Livingston New Town, in December, 1968, complained of bumps and thumps, a gas stove moving a couple of inches, ghostly impressions of a hand on the insides of windows, and an apparition —a sad-faced man sitting in a chair in the living room.

The local priest, Father John Byrne, was contacted four times by the distracted couple, both of whom were rapidly losing weight because of their anxiety. Mrs. Cassells, aged twenty-three, refused to stay in the house alone, with the result that her husband, Hugh, had to stop his work on a building site. The house was blessed by the priest four times but, although no more handprints appeared, there was a continuation of the strange noises.

Councils are getting used to complaints from tenants that

122

a house is uninhabitable because it is haunted. Any sensible official, and certainly any doctor, would take the reasonable view that if living in a particular house imbues the tenant with fear and terror, the house is not being occupied in any proper sense of the word, and alternative accommodation should be found. It must, of course be established that the complaint is not merely a device to stampede the council into offering better housing facilities, and that the complainants are neither neurotic nor unbalanced.

In any event, there are plenty of occasions when totally inexplicable happenings puzzle the most sober and methodical officials. A very unusual case occurred in Wales fairly recently (May, 1969) when the Rev. Emlyn Stephens was called to a council house at Rogerstone, near Newport, Glamorganshire, to exorcise a poltergeist creating havoc there.

When Maurice Walters, housing inspector for Magor and St. Mellons Rural Council, called to inspect the disorder he was so astonished by what he saw that he hurried home to fetch his camera. The furniture was in utter confusion, with piece piled upon piece. It would, as Mr. Walters realized, have been impossible for seventy-two-year-old Mrs. Edmunds, the tenant, to have done it.

The family had been living in the house for only three weeks when knocking noises started. According to Mrs. Edmunds, her daughter, and her granddaughter, they all saw a table lifted up, and a tray float away, spilling eggs, coffee, and cups over the floor. Later on, the furniture was turned topsy-turvy.

Yet another council house—one built over an unofficial burial ground—at Waddon New Road, West Croydon, Surrey, was alleged to be haunted; the complainant was a new tenant, Mrs. Mary Wild, who moved into it with her two children, a ten-year-old girl and a two-year-old boy.

During their first night there, Janet heard footsteps, was frightened, and came into bed with her mother. Then, Mrs. Wild told a reporter, "Something pulled the sheets off us—and Janet was thrown out of bed."

They tried pushing a heavy chest of drawers in front of the door, but it was shoved aside. The terrified family moved into the garden and waited there until dawn. Mrs. Wild's experiences fully justified her decision to move out a month later. She complained of footsteps, and the noise of someone dragging a sack. There was the sound of a "barking dog," screams, and vases were turned upside down. Another puzzle was the loud ticking of a clock, although they did not have such a clock.

On one occasion Mrs. Wild said that her daughter had seen the figure of "an old woman in a long black dress" at the top of the stairs.

Here we have a not unusual situation of the council house (actually an eighty-year-old two-bedroom cottage bought by the local council in May, 1968, as part of a future road-widening scheme) being associated with a burying ground. Waddon New Road was built over Waddon Marshes, which were used as an unofficial burying ground during the Great Plague three hundred years ago. Such was the panic prevailing at the time, and so low was the general standard of medical knowledge, that according to historians many of the "corpses" flung into the marshes were probably still alive.

When it comes to physical disturbances of the kind outlined, the theory that inanimate objects retain some sort of charge as a result of past emotional upheaval or display by previous generations is clearly inadequate. Unless, of course, one entertains the hypothesis that the "buildup" of emotional force is so great that, as with psychokinesis, it can have an actual physical effect. But how do objects come to be "thrown"? If a vase is turned upside down by an unseen hand, that is not a repetition of a past action; the vase didn't exist as part of the environment when the Great Plague ravaged London.

In cold print these accounts must seem bizarre, incredible, and exaggerated; but when one realizes that one tenant had waited six long years for a decent home, it is inconceivable that he would subject himself to the inconvenience of sharing living or sleeping quarters with neighbors, and incidentally find himself legally committed to paying rent for a house he does not use, without having very good reasons. One must accept in such instances the validity of a person's feelings. Spontaneous and mysterious phenomena cannot be dismissed as nonsense merely because the happenings seem to be improbable.

While more than a hundred castles in Britain and an even greater number of historic houses are reputed to be haunted, an immense variety of places have been the scene of strange phenomena. Haunted places include a sewage farm, a deserted air base, a small tobacco store, a garage, a blast furnace, and London's newest underground extension—the Victoria Line—which is being bothered by a ghost.

And there is an ample variety of ghosts, too. They have their quirks and personalities—mostly, I am sorry to report, malevolent and terrifying. Recent reports include a ghost that has a penchant for stealing teaspoons; a ghost who draws his own beer; an animal-loving ghost who frees pets; a phantom motorcyclist; a phantasm of an old woman who likes to watch television; and, as a welcome but rare touch of light relief, the ghost of a young girl bared to the waist.

Alan Whittacker told a strange tale of a haunted R.A.F. camp in the *News of the World* recently. For years the old R.A.F. air base at North Weald in Essex lay deserted. It was from here that the Spitfires darted into action over England's skies during the Battle of Britain. Being obsolete as an R.A.F. base, it was used instead by the Army.

Before long many soldiers—hardened men who had served in Cyprus, Aden, and North Africa—were saying that the place was haunted. There was talk of "the ghost of block 101," part of which was bombed during the war, and comprised the old airmen's sleeping quarters, sealed by barred doors.

In a room next to the closed doors, Corporal Roderick Broomhead would find that the window of his room had opened despite the fact that he had been sleeping and his door had been locked. He decided to change rooms after finding, one morning, that the light in his room was switched on, although the previous night he had locked both the door and the window, and switched off the light.

Lance-Corporal Steve Lovatt, with whom Broomhead exchanged his room, suffered a surprise, too. For when he opened the door one night, a heavy blanket that had been neatly folded under a heavy case suddenly spread out like a parachute and fell on him! The window was closed at the time. Not even the strongest draught could have caused such a phenomenon.

The ghostly rider of the A38, a main highway, was seen by an eighteen-year-old motorcyclist. David Pyke, a construction worker of Priory, Wellington, was riding home from work in the nearby town of Taunton late one January night in 1969. When he approached the crossroads leading to Poole, the phantom rider on a motorcycle came speeding toward him from the other direction, on the other side of the road, followed by a Triumph. He was outlined in light that resembled a halo embracing the entire area of his body.

As the phantom motorcyclist neared Pyke, it tilted toward him as though it were going into a skid and rushed right across his path. Frantically Pyke, who was going at about 45 m.p.h., jammed on his brakes. Just as the phantom was about to collide with him, the whole thing vanished.

"I cannot understand why I didn't hit him," Pyke said. "If there had been anything there, I know I would have done so."

Pyke, of course, stopped to examine the area. There was nothing to see—no track marks, no motorcyclist disappearing into the distance. The rider and his machine, which had seemed so real, had simply vanished. The driver of the oncoming Triumph looked out of his car in surprise. He had neither heard nor seen any other motorcycle.

Two years previously a Wellington motorist, Dudley N. Sanders, of Bovet Street, had also seen a "ghost" on the A38. The police of Poole, Dorset, being responsible for keeping the neighborhood roads clear would, not unnaturally, treat stories of the A38 ghost with some impatience. But the fact remains that several people have had a similar experience near the same spot. Is this due to telepathy? Had the imprint of what once happened been picked up by living people? A motorcycle is a material, tangible thing, a machine needing fuel; any such thought sounds wildly improbable. Yet a human body is also a kind of machine needing fuel, and the appearance of a seemingly human form that vanishes is no less remarkable. Even so, the very idea of a ghostly machine seems utterly impossible. How can anything so real and solid in appearance vanish?

I believe that the youths saw what they said they saw. I believe that it may have been a trick of time; somehow or other, although existing in what we call the present, they got a glimpse of the past. This is called "retrocognition," of which I will adduce examples later. But it is retrocognition with a difference, since the present and past appear to be mixed. This happens frequently in dreams, when past, present, and future commingle in the strangest way. The mind being untrammeled by the restrictions of consciousness wanders at will.

126

To the experienced driver most of his actions are built-in reflexes. Even his responses to emergency situations—and the road always produces plenty of those—are automatic reflexes. A particularly unusual situation may involve conscious thought because there is no precedent to act upon, no empirical criterion. Even then most of the responses to the situation, as quickly assessed by the mind, will be automatic reflexes.

All of us have vestigial faculties which for most of the time are inactive. In the slow upward development of mankind over millions of years, many instincts necessary to survival must have been developed, which were the product of early but continuous environments of which we have limited knowledge.

The numerous distractions of conscious life—and they are infinitely more numerous than when the pattern of human life was basically simpler—allow vestigial instincts no play. But once a person is doing something *automatically* or is in a hypnagogic state (half-asleep, half-awake), these subliminal instincts have freer play. We must remember that the human body still retains several vestigial and seemingly useless physical characters—the appendix and the coccyx to name only two. If we are born with physical parts and retain them long after they ceased to serve their original purpose in the evolution of man, it is equally probable that we have vestigial instincts whose nature and methods of operation are unknown to us.

The House of Bewley, a tobacco store in Eastgate Street, Chester, was the scene of strange events from 1968 onward. The unnerving incidents were said to include a picture crashing to the floor, bolts popping out of an oak door, and unaccountable wailing and stamping sounds. It reached the point where staff members were too terrified to go anywhere in the building by themselves. On one occasion the staff people turned to serve a customer who had entered the shop, and found no one there. The interesting thing is that the manageress, Mrs. Lilian Jones, and her staff all experienced the same reaction, at exactly the same moment. The feeling of a presence was very distinct.

The day after this occurrence a picture crashed to the ground. Later, it was discovered that the screw was cut in half. Then a huge stud from an old-fashioned door fell out. The picture was replaced, hung upon a substantial screw firmly fixed into the wall. The stud was put back in the door. Two weeks later the picture fell again. The screw had been cut in half. The same stud fell out of the door. A strange "wailing noise" came from the center of the shop, and was heard by customers as well as by the staff.

Poltergeist activities seldom make any sense at all. The acts seem purposeless, often trivial. Yet they can be unnerving.

There is nothing especially alarming about a wisp of smoke, but it depends on circumstances. Both Geoffrey Bernerd, land-lord of The Grenadier pub in Wilton Place, Knightsbridge, London, his chief barman, Tom Westwood, and an ex-Superintendent of Scotland Yard all saw, in the downstairs bar, a wisp of smoke that had no apparent origin. The pub had been closed for the afternoon. Tom Westwood provided me with this account:

"Mrs. Sheffle, who was here at the time, called me and said, 'There's a fire over there.' So I came across there. There was no fire there whatsoever. It had all been swept up and cleared. The smoke was just drifting away."

Geoffrey Bernerd, who sometimes stays at The Grenadier with his wife, has often answered to loud, distinct raps on the door upstairs. But this has happened when the pub is locked and nobody could get upstairs; in any event he has found nobody there when he has opened the door. And, as he explained to me, they are not the mere creakings of expanding or contracting timbers, common enough in old buildings. They are the sharp, rhythmic, deliberate knocks of a sort one would expect from a caller.

What are described as "wisps of smoke" are a phenomenon often mentioned in connection with haunted premises. The smoke mentioned to me by Tom Westwood was also seen by Mrs. Bernerd and ex-Superintendent Hallett of Scotland Yard. The smoke was, says Mr. Bernerd, "like cigarette smoke being pulled from a nonexistent cigarette. These puffs went on for three or four minutes."

The Grenadier, sold by the Duke of Westminster to the original Mr. Watney, the brewer, in 1818, was once the haunt of the Duke of Wellington and his officers. It is believed that an officer, found cheating at cards, was flogged to death in the small downstairs bar.

When one speaks to people who live or work in haunted places one accepts, at least, the reality of their experiences. The sincerity and directness of witnesses is obvious, while the notes of fear, uncertainty, and puzzlement that sometimes creep into their accounts could hardly be simulated except by an experienced actor.

Another pub, The Chequers, at Weldon, Bedfordshire, is said to have a thirsty poltergeist who draws his own beer—four pints of it at a time! The hostess, Mrs. Madge Walker, a forty-five-year-old widow, was awakened early one morning by "something indescribable." It wasn't a sound—just a feeling that something was going on in the centuries-old inn, and that she ought to investigate. She went downstairs quietly, conscious of a "creepy" feeling. There on the table stood four glass tankards of beer!

She checked with other members of the staff who sleep in the hotel, but everyone was mystified. It happened on two other occasions. Might some member of the staff have been playing a joke? Mrs. Walker is satisfied that that cannot be the explanation. The taps are turned off in the cellar, and the cellar door locked, before she retires. It is possible to drain off about a pint once the taps have been turned off, but never four pints. There the mystery must be left.

Is there a sort of time limit between a tragic happening and the appearance of a specter having some relationship to it? I have mentioned the abandoned air base and the happenings there. Another ghost from the period of World War II is said to have entered a small paper, confectionery, and tobacco store run by Mr. Roy Thomsett near Barnwood Court in East London's dockland.

One morning he turned to serve a customer who, somewhat strangely, seemed to be wearing a helmet and carrying a bucket. He was about to ask him what he wanted when the man simply vanished. Hardly able to believe his senses, Mr. Thomsett rushed outside. There was absolutely nobody in the vicinity.

During the war, a land mine was dropped by the Germans near the site of the store. It caused heavy casualties, including deaths and injuries to many staff people of the Air Raid Precautions organization. What Mr. Thomsett had seen sounds to me like the phantasm of an air raid warden.

A very strange poltergeist phenomenon is the actual disappearance of physical objects, as well as their being merely moved. Mrs. Joyce Henshaw, of The White Cottage, Claverley, has often awakened with a feeling of foreboding, to observe a phantom gliding silently around the room and vanishing through a door. The most irritating feature of this haunting is that things disappear;

an engagement ring left on her dressing table at night vanished, never to return. Vases have been upset and flowers strewn about the room. Four out of a set of six new spoons disappeared without explanation. Usually the phantom takes the form of "a plump, motherly woman with a shawl around her shoulders," but sometimes she is leading a boy who appears to be about nine years old.

From the thirsty ghost and the spoon-stealing ghost we come to the animal-loving ghost, which was alleged to be upsetting the private menagerie of Mr. Stanley Hughes, owner of a small bar in Flintshire, Wales. He complained that the cases in which he kept his pets were mysteriously opened at night. He has lost six squirrels, two desert rats, and a bat. Although most of us would be quite thankful to lose them all, Mr. Hughes was quite annoyed about it.

Each morning when he found the cage doors open, there were no footprints visible on the sanded floor.

In this case the pub (the Blue Lion, at Cwm, near Rhyl) has a very long tradition of being haunted. The building is nearly a thousand years old. There is a legend that John Henry, a farm laborer, was murdered inside the building, which was then a farmhouse, in 1646. Mrs. Eccles, a partner in Mr. Hughes' business, says that her three-year-old boy has told her he has spoken to a strange person upstairs. Both Mrs. Eccles and Mr. Hughes get the occasional feeling, so common to people in haunted places, that they are not alone.

One doesn't often hear of a ghost watching television, but since ghosts seem to appear anywhere and television is now everywhere, I suppose it was bound to happen sometime. Mrs. C. E. L. Roberts recently advertised an antique chess table for sale in the columns of the *Surrey Advertiser*. The table was one hundred years old and had been given to her by her grandmother, who had died nearly seventy years earlier. The table was bought by a Mrs. Bunnett of Morningside Road, Worcester Park. It was proudly installed in her living room, and Mrs. Bunnett sat watching the Dave Allen show while her husband went to the kitchen to clean his shoes.

Suddenly Mrs. Bunnett felt her attention diverted, and noticed the figure of a short, plump, motherly woman looking at the television set as if she were surprised. The figure was wearing glasses, and had light brown hair streaked with gray. Mrs. Bunnett felt icy cold, although the temperature of the room was over seventy degrees, and noticed that the downy hairs on her arm were standing on end. She telephoned Mrs. Roberts, the original owner of the table, and described what she had seen. The description fitted Mrs. Robert's grandmother exactly.

This is by no means the only instance of a ghost being seen when the percipient was watching television.

Early in 1966, Canon J. B. Phillips, D.D., of Swanage, Dorset, was sitting in the living room of his home. He does not keep a regular diary, but tells me that the time was about 6:15 P.M. While his wife was preparing supper in the next room, he was watching a news program on television, the set being about twelve feet away from where he was sitting.

He had just become absorbed when he was astonished to see the figure of his old friend C. S. Lewis (author of *The Screwtape Letters* and other notable, popular theological books), sitting in an armchair three feet away. He was looking "as large as life and wearing his favorite tweeds."

Their gazes met. C. S. Lewis—who had died three years earlier—smiled and said, "It's easier than you think." Then, after a stay of about two minutes, he vanished.

I should explain that Canon Phillips does not consider himself psychic and is not a spiritualist, though he does not deny genuine psychic phenomena nor disapprove of proper researches by people of integrity. But he took C. S. Lewis's words to be a personal message, a reassurance that death is not the end of existence, and that the transition from mortal life to another form of life is not something that need be feared.

The Canon tells me that he was not shocked, as some might expect, but merely surprised. I am grateful to him for troubling to answer nearly thirty questions which I put to him on this particular experience, whose implications are of immense importance. Whether people believe or disbelieve, fear or welcome, what is termed an afterlife, the fact remains that if anything survives of human personality after death, and particularly if what survives has active intelligence and will, it looms as a fact of tremendous importance. The Canon very patiently met all my factual queries:

> DB: How long had you known Professor Lewis?
> CANON: We first corresponded in 1943, and we had a

desultory correspondence over the years amounting in all to less than a dozen letters.

DB: Did you see much of him in the closing years of his life?

CANON: No, I did not see him at all.

DB: How frequently did you see him?

CANON: I only met him once, after he had given an address in Southwark Cathedral on Ascension Day during the war years.

DB: Did you ever discuss with him the question of survival?

CANON: Only indirectly, since we both believed the orthodox views of Christianity. I was at the time inclined to suggest that death should be looked upon as more of a beginning than an end. Unhappily I have lost his letter in reply, but I do remember that he said that physical death was "ambivalent" and could be both disaster and triumph in one.

DB: Did he express the view to you that human personality and active intelligence survived physical death?

CANON: No, we did not discuss it. I found myself very much in agreement with what he had written in his books. He, as I, was not so much interested in "survival" as in the unknown realms beyond the limitations of time and space. But he would not be dogmatic, and neither would I, since the New Testament is extremely reticent about life and death and, indeed, it is possible that there are no human words to describe it which we could understand at present.

DB: Did you ever have any agreement with him by which he would attempt to prove survival by appearing to you? I have no reason, in posing this question, to suppose that he did. I merely ask because such compacts have been made in the past—e.g., the Rev. Theodore Alois Buckley and his close friend MacKenzie and their pact at Oxford in 1850.

CANON: No.

DB: What was the date of the appearance?

CANON: Early June, 1966.

DB: In which room of your home did this happen?

CANON: The living room.

DB: At what hour?

CANON: About 6:15 P.M.

DB: What was the lighting like in the room at the time?

CANON: It was bright outside, a curtain was drawn

behind the TV which I was watching, but there are four other windows so the room was pretty light. (He went on to say that he was watching television on a set twelve feet away.)

DB: I gather that the figure looked solid, not transparent?

CANON: Yes, there was nothing "ghostly" about his appearance. He looked as natural as any human friend who had looked in to see me.

DB: Did you attempt to speak to him?

CANON: No.

DB: Was the appearance colored or monochrome?

CANON: Colored. Not only was his countenance rubicund, as in normal life, but he "glowed with health" as the old-fashioned saying had it. He was wearing old tweeds.

DB: Had C. S. Lewis been in your thoughts lately?

CANON: Not particularly. He died in 1963, and I have probably been influenced quite a bit in my own thinking by reading and rereading his books.

DB: You had been unwell lately. Was this a serious illness, the course of which troubled you, or something unpleasant but more transient, such as influenza?

CANON: No, I was not seriously ill, but suffering from a long period of overwork. This resulted in headaches, but I was not at this particular time suffering in that way.

DB: Have you ever had any sort of "psychic" experience before?

CANON: No. I have always had a vivid imagination and I normally dream in color, but this "appearance" was certainly not imaginary and had no dreamlike quality about it.

DB: Was his appearance accompanied by any sort of noise?

CANON: No.

DB: Did his voice sound like a normal speaking voice, or did you hear it "mentally"—that is, in your head?

CANON: Yes. At the time he seemed to be speaking to me in his ordinary voice which, naturally, I did not know well. But on reflection I would be prepared to accept the thought that I heard his voice "mentally."

DB: Was his appearance accompanied by any other phenomena of any kind, such as a drop in temperature?

CANON: No.

133

DB: Was anyone with you at the time, and did they see him, too?

Canon: No, I was alone.

DB: To whom did you first relate your experience?

Canon: To my wife.

DB: How soon was this after the event?

Canon: Immediately, as my wife was in the next room preparing supper.

DB: Has C. S. Lewis appeared since, and would you wish him to?

Canon: The experience was repeated almost exactly a week later. This time I was in bed reading and, as in the first instance, my attention was drawn, not by any noise, but by seeing out of the corner of my eye this very solid figure smiling happily and repeating the same sentence, which was, "It's not so hard as you think, you know." This could plainly bear a variety of meanings, but on these two occasions the general sense was one of encouragement. I have an open mind on whether I should wish to see him again. I certainly should not make any attempt to communicate with him. But if he did appear I should regard it as a bonus and I do not see why I should be any more frightened than I was before.

It will be seen that Canon Phillips submitted patiently to questioning, and it is of obvious value to a researcher when people who have these experiences are willing to do so. The point of most of my questions is obvious, others perhaps less so. Descriptions of phantoms vary considerably and it is always best to establish whether they appeared to be solid, transparent or wraith-like, or certain of form; or in color or black and white; luminous or reflecting light. Health is also a factor. In certain physical or mental conditions, hallucinations are a usual symptom, but none of the predisposing conditions were present in this instance.

Psychic News in November, 1968, sent a reporter to interview workmen engaged in construction of the new Victoria Line for London's subway system. John Daley, an Irishman, took him deep down into the newly dug tunnel where he and his workmates had seen a ghost.

Daley said that he watched it for fifteen minutes. Another man rushed out of the tunnel after seeing a figure. He collected his pay and never returned. Considering the high pay that some of the workmen collected—many as much as eighty pounds a week (close to two hundred dollars) it is obvious that he must have been very frightened indeed. Yet another man saw a figure walk into a cross-passage—a *cul-de-sac*—that was still being cut. He followed to ask for a light—and found the uncompleted passage empty.

One doesn't often hear of naked ghosts or even near-naked ghosts. On the face of it this is odd, for people shed their clothes completely with fair regularity. Although it is only comparatively recently that people have been willing to expose themselves to public view wearing little or nothing, one would expect to hear more reports of unclothed ghosts than one does.

Rattlesdon Rectory, near Ipswich, was said half a century ago to be haunted by a naked ghost—an extremely unpleasant specter that is alleged to have appeared to a Stowmarket carpenter while he was engaged in making alterations there. He was doing some work on the ancient paneling when he became conscious of a musty smell. The next thing he knew was when his white dust sheet came through the pantry with a head seemingly on it. He accused his assistant of playing jokes and told him to stop his nonsense. Immediately the figure dropped the sheet, revealing a naked apparition with blotchy skin the color of "old parchment."

Supposedly it is the ghost of a parson who once lived there and, for some reason or other, was buried under the house instead of in an ordinary grave. I have been unable to establish that it has made any appearance in the last half century.

One ghost hunter, however, James F. A. Mann, a chartered accountant practicing in Moray, Scotland, claims to have seen a half-naked ghost (by no means as disagreeable-looking as the corpselike apparition of Rattlesdon) in the large stone house that is his family home near Aberdeen. The time was 1935, and when he arrived at the house he found it full of relatives home from India. The only accommodation that could be found for him that night was a small room on the ground floor that was seldom used and had not even been wired for electricity.

Mr. Mann sensed an unpleasant atmosphere about the room. However, having no choice in the matter, he read by the light of his oil lamp. Soon he experienced a strange but distinct tension— a conviction that he was not alone. It developed into real fear.

Then, through the wall, the ghost of a young girl in her twenties appeared. She wore only a petticoat and was otherwise naked to the waist. She was almost transparent. Gliding to the end of the bed, she seemed to say, "What are you doing here?" Then she smiled and disappeared.

Comparing notes with a relative later, Mr. Mann discovered that the girl had been seen before, and their versions of her appearance tallied exactly. The interest of this lies in the fact that nobody had told Mr. Mann about the existence of a ghost. He is satisfied that he really saw her, and that it was not an hallucination.

In my book *Ghosts and Hauntings* I gave the testimony of a colonel who once played billiards with a ghost. However outlandish the story sounds, the man in question is an ordinary, balanced sort of person who does a responsible job in a government office. He does not strike me as a man given to fantasy or outlandish declarations. He had happened across the ghostly billiards player while stationed in an old country house during World War II. (Obviously, he didn't immediately recognize the presence as a ghost; he observed a shy young man in blue uniform, who played a few shots, and then went into a bathroom that had no other exit, and did not emerge again. When he inquired about the apparition's identity, he discovered it was the ghost of the son of the owner, who had shot himself in that bathroom.)

However, the Lads' Club at Hyde, Manchester, was said in 1968 to have a ghostly billiards player. Mr. André Davis and his wife, who live on the premises, heard the clicking of billiard balls at night, followed by a loud crash. When Mr. Davis hurried to investigate the noise, he found nothing. His dog refused to enter the room. Similar noises have been heard by boys staying overnight. On one occasion Mr. Davis, on going to investigate, saw an old man playing billiards, who simply looked up, smiled, and continued playing. When he went to lock up, there was no sign of the old man, and the billiards table was covered.

Every week in Britain, without exception, several cases of alleged appearances of ghosts, or manifestations of poltergeists, or stories of unexplainable noises, removal of objects, movement of objects, and so on, are reported. Over a third of these are of ghosts recognizably human. About a tenth are of indeterminate shape; a fifth of the reports include the hearing of ghostly footsteps; there are sounds of some sort in nearly a third of the cases; and in a few instances there are reports of people having the physical sensation of being touched by an unseen presence. In at least one instance— at the Exchange Hotel in Thornbury, Gloucestershire—the poltergeist was said to have pinched a barmaid's bottom. I have no confirmation of this, but if true it would imply that there is a human side, even to ghosts.

What is the explanation of all these reports of ghosts and hauntings? They cannot all, in my view, be dismissed as illusions, self-delusions, or fakes. Not only are many of the stories related by people of substance and unquestioned veracity, but the percipients themselves include too many people who have nothing to gain, and sometimes even something to lose, by revealing their experiences.

There are certain common factors discernible from an analysis of the reports over the years. In a large proportion of cases there is a drop in temperature before the appearance of the phantom; heavy breathing, footsteps, and a "dragging" noise are very common; a gliding motion is often remarked upon; quite often the poltergeists—or whatever influences are making themselves felt—play havoc with electrical installations and circuits. So often lights go on when they shouldn't, or refuse to turn on when they should. In nearly a third of the cases reported—a high percentage—objects are moved.

We have been speaking of apparitions which in most instances are recognizable as those of somebody dead. Where they are not so recognizable, and are not seemingly in period clothes, it would be unjustifiable to assume that they are not phantasms *of living* persons. On the few occasions when experts have had time, patience, and money enough to devote to a census of some kind, it has invariably transpired that there are more "ghosts" of living people than of the dead. Or to put it more precisely, more cases reported (we cannot assume that all spontaneous phenomena are reported) are of *living* people.

Here, of course, telepathy may play some part. I have listed in my references to telepathy many instances of this. In *Telepathic Hallucinations: A New View of Ghosts,* published toward the end of the last century by Frank Podmore, an analysis of visual hallucinations—as he called them—showed that there were three times as many "realistic human apparitions of living persons" as there were of dead people.

The appearance of apparitions coincidental with death proved far more numerous than the laws of chance would permit. The committee that examined cases reported to the Society for Psychical Research over the years found thirty ghostly appearances coincidental with death in an examination of thirteen hundred cases.

The prevalence of this type of phenomenon was, in the committee's opinion, far beyond the laws of mere chance. There is a positive relationship between somebody dying, and somebody attached or related to the person in some emotional sense seeing the dying individual's apparition.

The ghost of Noel Gay, popular composer of "All the King's Horses" and other songs, appeared to his brother, the late Rev. Cyril Armitage, Rector of Saint Bride's Church in Fleet Street, London, at the moment of his death in a hospital. Mr. Armitage was sitting in his study in a very old and rambling rectory a few streets away from the church itself. Suddenly he saw his brother standing by him, smiling happily. The figure stayed for several minutes, then faded away. He told me about it immediately afterward, knowing my interest in the subject, but I have not revealed the fact until now. He was very attached to his brother, and my view was that for a few years the incident should be forgotten.

A strange, and rather sad, story of unusual phenomena coinciding with death was related to me by a professional photographer, Mr. David Ingham, of Isis Street, Wimbledon. In 1967 his young brother Dennis, then aged fourteen, was living at home with his mother in Octavia House, Ladbroke Grove, London. One night he and his mother tried glass tipping—putting their fingers on the glass, asking questions, and watching the glass move, apparently of its own accord, toward the encircled letters of the alphabet.

The glass moved over to certain letters, and Dennis felt frightened, and stopped the session.

Shortly afterward, Dennis died from a heart attack in the playground of his school in Warnington Road, Kensington.

On the night of Dennis's death David Ingham and his wife, while lying in bed in their home in Wimbledon, were both terrified by strange noises in the passage outside their bedroom. Mr. Ingham described it to me as "a walking outside in the passage" and admitted frankly that he was too scared to go and investigate. It is not altogether clear to me why they should have been frightened, since they were not the only tenants in the house. Indeed, there was an elderly man in a room opposite them, on the same floor. In any event, Mrs. Ingham remembers that they were both frightened, but finds it difficult to say why the sounds should have been assumed to be other than natural. It would seem that there must have been some feeling, or atmosphere, conducing to their joint frame of mind other than the mere noise. There must have been some strange quality about the sounds, as David Ingham who was twenty-eight years old, did not seem to be a nervous type; yet he was too frightened to want to go and investigate.

David's brother, Derek, a sheet-metal worker then living in Shepherd's Bush, and his wife, were both disturbed at the same time by inexplicable sounds of the same character, and were also both frightened.

At the same time, the mother, Mrs. Ingham, Senior, with whom the dead boy had been living, heard sounds of bangings and knockings coming from the lad's room a few hours after his death.

It is probable that all concerned were suffering from some degree of shock after this sad loss, but it is unusual that three branches of the family should all have reported unexplained noises a few hours after the lad's death.

Can furniture become haunted? If a place, which is composed of materials such as stone and wood, brick and slate, steel and rubble, can retain something of past events and the imprint of personalities long since dead, why should not objects as well? Perhaps, in view of the prevalence of reports involving houses with paneled walls, the old animistic idea that trees could be the abode of spirits was based upon more substance than we think. I say "we think" because although most religions, and the Christian religion in particular, acknowledge survival (the Church of England, for example, has a service of exorcism, and you can hardly exorcise a place of ghosts and spirits unless you believe that they exist), I do not myself consider it proved beyond dispute.

An American professor, with whose theories I will deal later, claims to be able to prove immortality and the existence of the human soul as a fact. The material he has sent me in support of his contention is most impressive. However, until scientific tests under controlled conditions can produce uniform and unvarying results (observable, recordable results), the matter must remain one of theory. Spiritualists, of course, regard the case for survival as unarguable.

Which brings me to the strange case of a haunted bed. The story really starts, so far as I am concerned, when the telephone

139

rang on the desk of my friend Bernard Kelly, of the Denver *Post* in Denver, Colorado. The caller was a young, intelligent woman posing a simple question: "Do you know anybody who wants a haunted bed?"

Offhand, Kelly didn't. Most people go to bed for rest or stimulating companionship. Only a minority of dead-keen fanatics would go to bed primarily to be haunted.

Shorn of its frills, the story is as follows:

A few years ago, Mr. and Mrs. Grant A. Richmond of Arvada bought a bedroom set of mahogany and cherry wood from a very elderly woman in Alameda, California. The set consisted of two dressers and a "sleigh bed," having curved or rolled head-and foot-boards which made it resemble a sleigh in appearance.

The dressers were fine and very beautiful, but the bed proved such a headache in the home that Mr. Richmond insisted that it should be sold. Questioned further, Mrs. Richmond said that when two people were occupying the bed an unseen hand grasped the ankle or wrist of one of them in an iron grip. Or a "judo-like" blow struck the bed between them.

In due course Mrs. Richmond sold the bed to an antique dealer, through whom it was bought by Dr. Robert A. Bradley, of South University Boulevard, Englewood, Colorado. I asked Dr. and Mrs. Bradley if they had had any unusual experiences attributable to this allegedly haunted antique. It seems that they have not, although their own home is haunted, and rings to the tread of ghostly footsteps and the noise of self-slamming doors.

From Mr. Grant A. Richmond and his wife, Melba F. Richmond, of Xenophon Street, Arvada, who owned the bed previously and got rid of it because of its alarming features, I have an interesting account of their experiences with it:

> The bed . . . was a mahogany sleigh bed which we understood came from the New England coast by boat around the Horn at the turn of the century. We do not know the origin of the bed . . . we do not care to divulge the name of the family from whom we procured the bed since there are living relatives who might take offense. . . .
>
> We do not know anything of the bed's history, except that it belonged to an elderly lady who was widowed quite early, never remarried, and lived alone with her widowed mother. The bed was one of her treasured possessions. The

reason for her attachment [to the bed] is also unknown to us. She herself was found suffocated on a daybed in the same large, private bedroom where the bed was located.

Early in our occupancy of the old house we experienced uneasiness and sleeplessness which we attributed to the old house itself, its high ceilings, and its size. We did not associate this with any particular item of furniture at the outset, although our children, who were small then, would not sleep in the old bed in the original bedroom. [The Richmonds purchased the house fully furnished. It had been built about the turn of the century; the furniture included the sleigh bed, and "the original bedroom" refers to that in which the previous owner was found suffocated, and in which the sleigh bed had been kept.]

Visitors who used the room while visiting us said they did not sleep well, and awoke suddenly without reason during the night. We frequently thought we heard footsteps upstairs in the bedroom where the old bed was, although we were sure we were the only occupants in the old house.

In 1948 we sold the old house and moved to Salt Lake City, where we took up residence, taking with us, among other things, the old bed. We set it up in the children's bedroom. The children would awaken and report that someone moved the bed. Beads rolled without apparent cause across the bedroom floor. We heard footsteps in the room and the sound of doors opening and closing even though no member of the family was in the area of the house where the bed was located. We smelled the fragrance of perfume in the room, unlike any of our own perfumes—and later the actual fragrance of our own perfumes, even though members of the family had not used the perfume.

Frequently, while alone in the house, I myself or other members of the family would come upstairs from our basement area to see who had arrived home, after hearing footsteps, or the door of the bedroom open or close. It soon became apparent that we were never alone and none of the family felt comfortable alone in the house.

We took the bed down, but we placed the ancient springs and mattress on a bed for our oldest daughter, who soon reported that someone placed their hands beneath the covers during the night and pinched her mischievously.

In 1957 we sold our home and bought a new home in another part of the town, taking the old bed with us. This time we set the bed up in our own bedroom because none of the children would consider having it in their room. Some unusual things began occurring. The bed would move during the night. We would leave the house, returning to find the bed and dressers in the room moved away from the walls.

I was in a traveling position and was away from home quite frequently. Upon returning from my trips, my wife would report that she was awakened suddenly during the night by someone pulling the covers from her or touching her. Sometimes she reported that the bed moved violently. The smell of perfumes continued, without explanation.

In 1958 we were transferred to Denver, Colorado, moving into an apartment, where we again set up the bed in our own room. The same occurrence continued. The bed or dressers would be moved away from the wall, our dog would bark at unseen persons in the bedroom. Unseen hands continued to touch us during our sleep. We found ourselves answering persons whom we were certain were standing near the bed. Marbles or balls would roll mysteriously across the floor. When we took the bed down and stored it in the basement, we continued to hear the sound of footsteps.

When we moved from the apartment to our new home in 1961, we tried setting up the bed again, but no one would sleep in the bed or the bedroom, while it was there, a second time. After moving a second time into a new home, we sold the bed because, despite the fact that we tried storing it, we had constant visitations during the nights; doors opened and closed without explanation, footsteps continued in and out of our bedroom, dresser drawers were opened mysteriously, chairs were moved from under the tables, all very mysteriously.

Only somebody with an inordinate appetite for nocturnal disturbance would bother to keep such a bed, and I am not surprised that the Richmonds parted company with it, although it took them a long time to decide that the bed would never mend its ways.

☐ 9. Lonely As a Cloud . . .

I wandered lonely as a cloud
That floats on high o'er vales and hills. . . .
                    —William Wordsworth

EITHER hundreds of people in Britain and elsewhere are suffering from some mad delusion, or the air is filled with unseen presences, floating and swirling in defiance of the ordinary laws of gravity and speed, having inherent in them the faculties of hearing and sight and emotion, tied in some strange analogous way with a living body of identical propensities. It's not a spirit. Not a soul. Nothing, really, definable in everyday terms, yet alleged by many serious and sensible people to have a reality—the other self.

In the days when the supposedly separate entities of body and soul were accepted as axiomatic and enjoined by religious dogma, such an idea would not have seemed outlandish. But today how can such ideas conform to what is known of science and physiology?

Psychology has taught us—not that we really needed any proof—that Dr. Jekyll and Mr. Hyde lurk in almost everybody, in the conflicting personalities of their conscious and subconscious minds. One has only to hypnotize somebody to discover that the thoughts and motives and memory of the conscious mind are but the visible tip of an iceberg. There is far more submerged than revealed.

"I can't be in two places at the same time," you answer irritably, when priorities conflict. But according to quite a few

143

authorities, including medical men, you *can* be in two places at once. The phenomenon has many names—bilocation, astral projection, "out-of-the-body" experiences. In the technical nomenclature of psychic researchers it is known as an ecsomatic experience.

There are many examples in history of people being in more than one place at the same time. Historically speaking, the case of the monk Alphonse de Liguori is fairly recent, having taken place a mere two centuries ago. On September 21, 1774, in the monastery of Arienzo, Liguori was dressing for Mass, when he felt lethargic, groped his way to a chair, and fell into a comatose state or trance condition. Like many religious zealots of the period, he had been fasting for several days, a condition in which varieties of religious or mystical experience have been undergone.

Much concerned, and wondering whether Liguori was alive or dead, the elders gathered around him. Although cataleptic, white as a sheet, and his features as immobile and expressionless as a death mask, the monk began to describe happenings in Rome, four days' travel away. The Pope was dying. He described the deathbed scene, the personalities in attendance.

Emerging at last from his trance or cataleptic state, Liguori was surprised to find everyone at the monastery gathered around him.

"What's the matter? Why are you all here, around me?" the monk asked.

"We were concerned for you. We thought that you might die."

"It is not me you need be concerned with," Liguori replied, sadly, "but His Holiness the Pope. I have just come from his bedside in Rome. He is dead now."

This was later proved to be true, both as to time, the circumstances of the Pope's passing, the bedside scenes as Liguori had described them, and the personalities who had been there. This story does not belong to the realm of folklore but to the archives of historical fact. There is ample documentation in support of it. And the evidence is astounding, even when reviewed after this great lapse of time. For Liguori was seen at the Pope's bedside as he lay dying. In fact, Liguori led the prayers in the presence of the superiors of the Dominican, Observatine, and Augustinian orders. They had not only seen him, and heard him pray, but had spoken to him. The facts were fully attested, and examined in detail, with the help of witnesses, by the Roman Congregation of Rites which assembled to discuss the details of Liguori's life as a preliminary to canonization.

It is also related how the sixteenth-century traveler Duarte da Gama was sailing from Japan to India when his vessel was becalmed in the China Sea. Rather than drift with the tide and wander off course, he ordered several members of the crew to lower a longboat, tie it by hawser to the sailing vessel, and then row with all their strength.

While they were doing this—and it was, of course, a long and difficult job—a tremendous storm arose, filling the ship's sails and blowing it forward with such speed and strength that it bore down on the rowing boat, smashing it and spilling the crew into the raging waters.

Da Gama made no attempt to save the struggling men. Instead, he ordered the crew to sail before the wind. Father Xavier, a famous missionary who was a passenger on the vessel, implored the captain to go back and save the men. Da Gama told him bluntly that they could all count themselves fortunate if they survived the hurricane, which had reached a peak of intensity and threatened the sailing ship, its crew, and everyone else, and that there was not the faintest likelihood that the men in the longboat could survive. It was not worth going back and he did not propose to do so.

Father Xavier told the crew not to despair of their mates, but to keep a close lookout for them, never relaxing their vigilance; he personally guaranteed that they would return. Da Gama greeted this forecast with brusque derision, but the priest's intensity impressed the crew, who did as he bade them, while he himself retired to his cabin and prayed.

Two hours later, after endless buffeting, when it seemed the vessel must succumb to the fierce onslaught of the waves, the sea turned calm again. Suddenly the lookouts espied the longboat, with men still in it.

When the sailors were pulled aboard, one of them said, "Don't forget Father Xavier; he's still in the boat."

Their rescuers assumed that the abandoned sailors had become delirious. "Father Xavier has never left the ship; he's on board with us!" they insisted. The rescued men were equally adamant, insisting that the missionary had been with them in the boat throughout their trials, sustaining their hope and courage, insisting that they would be rescued.

Did Father Xavier know the technique of astral projection—a technique that modern authorities on this strange psychic propensity insist can be applied at will? The eyewitness accounts of this extraordinary episode suggest that he must have known.

Astral projection, or out-of-the-body experiences, often occur in moments of great crisis or emotional intensity and not infrequently at the moment of death. Thus, many "phantasms" of the living, seen at vast distances from their bodies, may be a projection of this other self and the explanation of many of the phenomena dismissed as being ghosts.

In *Phantasms of the Living* there is a fascinating quotation from *The Life and Times of Lord Brougham,* written by himself and published posthumously in 1871, which contains these notes from the journals he kept in December, 1799, while traveling in Sweden with friends:

> We set out for Gothenburg [apparently on December 18] determining to make for Norway. About one in the morning, arriving at a decent inn, we decided to stop for the night. Tired with the cold of yesterday, I was glad to take advantage of a hot bath before I turned in, and here a most remarkable thing happened to me—so remarkable that I must tell the story from the beginning.
>
> After I left the High School, I went with G., my most intimate friend, to attend the classes in the University. There was no divinity class, but we frequently in our walks discussed and speculated upon grave subjects—among others, on the immortality of the soul, and on a future state. This question, and the possibility, I will not say of ghosts walking, but of the dead appearing to the living, were subjects of much speculation. . . . We actually committed the folly of drawing up an agreement, written with our blood, to the effect that whichever of us should die first should appear to the other, and thus solve any doubts we had entertained of "life after death."
>
> After we had finished our classes at the College, G. went to India, having got an appointment there in the Civil Service. He seldom wrote to me, and after a lapse of a few years I had almost forgotten him; moreover, the family having little connection with Edinburgh, I seldom saw or heard anything

of them, so that all his schoolboy intimacy had died out, and I had nearly forgotten his existence.

I had taken, as I have said, a warm bath, and while lying in it and enjoying the comfort of the heat, after the late freezing I had undergone, I turned my head round, looking toward the chair on which I had deposited my clothes, as I was about to get out of the bath. On the chair sat G., looking calmly at me. How I got out of the bath I know not, but on recovering my senses I found myself sprawling on the floor. The apparition, or whatever it was, that had taken the likeness of G., had disappeared.

The vision produced such a shock that I had no inclination to talk about it or to speak about it even to Stuart; but the impression it made upon me was too vivid to be easily forgotten; and so strongly was I affected by it that I have written down the whole history, with the date, 19th December, and all the particulars, as they are now fresh before me.

After Lord Brougham's return to Edinburgh, a letter arrived from India, stating that his friend G. had died there on December 19.

Lord Brougham seems to have assumed that his friend was dead when he saw the vision. But G. may have projected himself while still alive, although near death. Furthermore, we do not know whether death, as accepted then by medical men, was as complete as they supposed. Recent developments in medicine, including the ethically difficult question of heart transplants, show that the "moment of death" is not so easily definable as the world had supposed.

But what I would call "crisis apparitions" may sometimes be due to telepathy or astral projection. *Phantasms of the Living* lists as a telepathic hallucination the case of an informant who, to quote the woman herself:

had made the time-worn arrangement that whichever died first would endeavour to return to visit the other. Some years after, I asked this man's sister to remember me to him and say, did he remember his promise, and having received for answer "perfectly, and I hope I shall appear to ———, and not she to me," the whole matter passed out of my mind.

My friend was in New Zealand, his sister, I don't know where. One night I awoke with the feeling someone was in the room. I must tell you that I always have a bright light burning on a table, not far from my bed. I looked about, and presently saw something behind the little table; felt myself grow perfectly cold; was not in the least frightened, rubbed my eyes to be sure I was not asleep, and looked at it steadfastly.

Gradually a man's head and shoulders were perfectly formed, but in a sort of misty material, if I may use such a word. The head and features were distinct, but the whole appearance was not substantial and plain; in fact it was like a cloud, formed as a man's head and shoulders. At first I gazed and thought, who is it? . . . Then the formation of the head and forehead (which are most marked in my friend) made me exclaim to myself "Captain W———!" The appearance faded away.

I got up and put the date down; and waited until news from New Zealand was possible. I made enquiries about my friend, never doubting but that he was dead. The answer always came: "No news." At last this also, "We are so anxious; it is so long since we have heard. We shall again wait another mail, and write to so-and-so." And then came the news, a mere scrap, "Have had a severe fall off the coach; can't write; head all wrong still." In due time we heard more. He had fallen off the coach, and was insensible for some time, and then, as he had said, his head was not clear for a while. *I have never had the slightest doubt but that, while insensible, his spirit came here.* The appearance was coincident with the time of his insensibility. . . .

The italics are mine. *What* was it that came to her? A mental impression, telepathically conveyed? Or something having an inherent motivation of its own, an astral projection of the man, believing himself to be dead and redeeming his promise to his friend?

There is a detail of this particular case worth noting. The phantasm or vision which appeared to her had *gray* hair, whereas when she had last seen her friend his hair had been black. It was because of this feature of the emergent specter that she had taken some time to recognize him. His once-black hair had turned gray.

The evidential value, or the implication, of a paranormal happening does not lose its importance because of a lapse of time, and I make no apology for going backward and forward to illustrate particular points. I shall adduce presently the evidence of a man who tried deliberately to master the technique of astral

148

projection, or the projection of the self to another place, away from one's recumbent body. In his case, too, he appeared to those to whom he was trying to project his image, or project himself, not as they usually saw him (for he always wears glasses) but as he lay in the darkness on his bed, *without his glasses*. In that particular instance I interviewed not only the man himself, but his son and daughter—the two people to whom he appeared.

Before saying more on the subject of astral projection, I should make it clear that I do *not* advocate experiment in this field at all. This is also the advice of Dr. Robert Crookall, whose factual and methodical surveys of this little-understood phenomenon will rank with *Phantasms of the Living* as classics on which psychic researchers will draw for many generations for case histories and a reasoned assessment of the scientific and philosophical implications. Astral projection cannot be prevented when it happens spontaneously; but to attempt it is not only frightening, but dangerous.

There are cases where it is impossible to say whether telepathy or astral projection is at work. I asked Dr. Crookall for a "classic" example of astral projection. He thought that the case of S. R. Wilmot (recorded in detail in the *Proceedings of the Society for Psychical Research*, Vol. VII, p. 41) was one of the most spectacular and unarguable instances.

The facts, briefly put, are these. In 1863 Mr. Wilmot and a friend, Mr. Tait, were returning to the United States by boat, in a two-berth cabin. Wilmot was in the lower berth and Tait in the upper.

The weather at that time was not good. In fact, Mrs. Wilmot, more than a thousand miles away, was seriously worried about her husband's safety, for one vessel had already been reported shipwrecked. She had tossed and turned in bed until four o'clock and then, as she subsequently revealed, found herself released from her body, floating through the air at great speed, impelled toward the vessel by unerring instinct. A dream? It was far from being a dream. . . .

That night Mr. Wilmot was lying asleep (or thought himself to be asleep) in his bunk when he had the vivid impression of seeing his wife. Clad in her nightgown, she had come to the stateroom, opened the door, hesitated when she saw that he was not the only occupant and then, overcoming her diffidence, reached his side, stooped over him, regarded him with love and concern, caressed him gently, and left as silently as she came. No word was spoken.

The next day Tait asked Wilmot jokingly who the woman was who had visited him the previous night. By means of questions, he elicited from Tait that he too had *seen* Mrs. Wilmot. Wilmot had not put the idea into Tait's head by first describing his strange experience.

Returned safely, Wilmot was sitting at home with his wife when she asked him, quietly, if he had received a visit from her. He tried to look surprised.

"*A visit?*" he asked, with simulated incredulity. "We were more than a thousand miles at sea."

"I know it," said Mrs. Wilmot, "but it seemed to me that I visited you."

She then described how she had had the sensation of floating away from herself, speeding across the raging seas, climbing the ship's side, and visiting his cabin. It hadn't happened to her spontaneously. In her anxiety for his safety, she had willed and wished it. The sensation of astral travel had come to her immediately afterward, at four o'clock in the morning. She described the ship's appearance, the look and situation of the cabin, and the scene inside, with absolute fidelity, even to Wilmot sleeping in the lower bunk and Tait in the upper.

This well-attested case cannot be written off as dreams induced by the mutual concern two loving people felt naturally for each other. How would Tait have described her visit with such fidelity? How could Mrs. Wilmot know what the stateroom looked like? Furthermore, her appearance in the cabin was coincidental with her own sensation.

You have probably at some time had in a dream the sensation of floating. Is it just a dream, or is it that—as the ancients called it—the soul goes wandering? The idea may sound fanciful, but Dr. E. E. Bernard, a psychologist at North Carolina State University in Raleigh, North Carolina, puts the number of people who have experienced astral projection as high as one in one hundred. Dr. Bernard is, in fact, convinced "that people can leave their bodies and drift away, uninhibited by physical barriers or distance."

Many prominent people have had experiences of astral projection. William Gerhardi, the famous novelist, has practiced it for years. He has described how on one occasion, when he was

150

asleep in bed, he awakened to find himself in midair. The room was pitch dark, and he seemed enveloped in a sort of milky light, able to look down upon his sleeping figure in bed. He noticed the flushed cheeks, the open mouth, the even breathing.

Hughie Green, the television star, found himself floating above his damaged car, seeing his body trapped in the wreckage, after an automobile accident. He saw the ambulance men arrive and pull him gently from the wreckage.

The Oxford Institute of Psychophysical Research has collected more than one thousand cases of alleged astral projection, and Celia Green has summarized these in a report, *Out-of-the-body Experiences*, which was published by the Institute in 1968. That report indicates that in more than 60 percent of the cases the people concerned had had only one such experience. The number having two to five experiences fell off rapidly, but jumped when the number of experiences reached six or more—actually about a fifth of the cases reported had undergone an experience six or more times. A third of the cases occurred when the subject was anesthetized or unconscious for some reason.

Mrs. Ellis Pitt, of Grange Estate, Crookham, Hampshire, told *Psychic News* a few years ago that when she thought she was going about the house normally she was puzzled by the fact that she tried all the lights in her bedroom without success and failed to put on the lights on the landing, and so went downstairs and put a shilling in the gas meter.

"Much annoyed at the continued darkness," she reported at the time, "I went back upstairs and happening to glance at the bed, saw my physical body lying there sleeping peacefully."

What is an "out-of-the-body" experience like? Let me quote in his own words the experience of Mr. John Eyre, a well-known writer who has long been interested in a wide variety of mystical experiences. He had been particularly intrigued by the revelations concerning telepathy recorded by Dr. Andrija Puharich in his well-known book *Beyond Telepathy*, in which, among other things, he deals with astral projection.

"In the spring of 1967, for one reason or another, I started practicing Yoga. I was following a technique described by a well-known writer, Ramacharaka—which has been published in England—and I was concentrating on the two aspects related to breathing; a breathing technique designed to slow down the heart, to reduce the amount of oxygen in the brain, and therefore to create a certain state of one's organism. I learned later (and in fact this book *Beyond Telepathy* describes the effect upon the sympathetic and parasympathetic nervous system and the endocrine glands) that in fact I was producing what is known as a "cholinergic" state. I was trying to bring about two effects under the suggestion of the books written by Ramacharaka. One: the sense of my own self as a thing that had always existed—in other words, a sense of my own eternity—and secondly, I was trying to bring about a sense of this thing that I was as a part of all the phenomena of existence. In other words, a sense of universality.

"The process involved also, of course, turning off one's thinking mind; it's the thinking mind, or sense of the ego, which creates a knowledge of time and place. Switch off the thinking, intellectual, self-aware brain and try and exist in a moment of time almost without thinking, and then you can bring about certain phenomena.

"Anyway, after I had been trying to bring about the sense of myself as having always existed, it suddenly happened. Lying on my bed in a hotel where I was living at the time, I could recognize no sounds that were reaching my ears. I could hear no sound that I recognized at all. In fact, it later transpired that what was going on in the street outside was the emptying of garbage cans, cars passing, and so on, but at that moment I could recognize none of those sounds. Secondly, I felt my head with my hand and found it too small; and also the hair was too short and coarse.

"Now this experience triggered off a whole week of very strange phenomena. The main thing that happened, arising out of this alienation, doing the breathing technique, etc.—I was on holiday from my work at the time, so I had all the day and all the night if necessary to carry forward what I was doing—was that I began to experience falling into trances. I was amazed at what was happening. I had at that time no belief in extrasensory perception; up to this point I had been a total materialist. Suddenly I would be overcome by what I can only call compulsive breathing. It was a kind of breathing that one has under anesthetic; short, forceful breaths, like this. [He demonstrated to me the rhythmic, forceful breathing; the deliberate intake and forceful exhalation.] I was suddenly overcome by this, and learned very soon to lie down on the bed quickly.

"Trance pictures appeared in my eyes and in my mind, as

soon as this happened, if I allowed them to come; and I learned how to let them come. This trance-breathing effect would come upon me at many moments in the day without warning.

"Through all these experiences I kept a diary, which in the course of the year amounted to eighty thousand words, factually describing as a journalist the experiences that came and also what I had been doing.

"I had the experience, therefore, of these trance effects and I was determined to try and record the trance experiences, breaking the trance. I tried having a tape recorder by my bed, but the effort of switching on and off I found too difficult. I tried note-taking on a bit of paper but that, too, proved too difficult. I eventually hit upon the idea of sitting at a desk if a trance effect came, with my arm resting where I could try and write what I was experiencing, even as I was experiencing it. And I had, about two or three days after the first attempted alienation, a fantastic experience of what I can only describe as an automatic writing effect coming.

"At three o'clock one morning I was going into a trance effect. I had learned not to disturb myself too much and so break the effect. I tried a tape-recording technique first, and it failed. I moved to this desk, with the light on, still in the mood of this compulsive breathing. I laid my head on a pillow on the desk with my hand resting, and I felt a most fantastic, painful, exquisite sensation coming up from the roots of my body, flowing up into my arm; a sensation of an energy trying to move the pencil I was holding; an energy—I was completely relaxed—of exquisite pain as the movement or electrical force was breaking through my tissues; but a sense of exquisite pleasure, as though something which had been inarticulate for years and generations could speak at last.

"The angle, though, that my arm was resting on the desk caused too much friction, I think, so that the arm and hand never went into movement except for just a few words that were written on a piece of paper. This had been very emotionally moving, as there had been no volition in my own brain or in my own nervous system, so far as I was concerned.

"Now during this time—a period of about a week to ten days —I was in the moment of doing this breathing, trying to create that sense of the electron and neutron force of my body being a part of all things. Universality.

"In this process I had the sense of radiating out from myself an enormous energy, and in the energy of emotional feeling, concern, peace—call it what you like—the thing to bear in mind, so far as the body is concerned, is the question of which comes first: the tear in the eye that creates an emotion of sadness, or the emotion of sadness, which creates the tear in the eye. I was bringing about certain changes in the chemical flow within my bloodstream, by altering the adrenalin content of my blood, and various other processes that this book, *Beyond Telepathy*, so well describes.

"I was altering the negative-positive forces of the body, the sympathetic, the parasympathetic system of the body; I was affecting the hypothalamus center in the brain; all these things were bringing about, perhaps, the tear in the eye which creates the emotional state. Who knows? But the emotional state of universality led me to send out from me a mood, an emotion of love and affection, to people I knew, people I knew were sick, and particularly to my two children, from whom I was separated at the time. I didn't linger upon thoughts of them; I just sent out a radiation, telepathically, as I felt concern for them; and I sent it out to other people.

"And here's an interesting thing. My own son, who at the time was about seventeen, had a number of experiences of seeing me just before he was going to sleep, the interesting thing being that he didn't know I was doing this, and he saw me without glasses. Ordinarily, I wear glasses, and he had hardly ever seen me without them; but of course, while lying on my bed in the darkness I did not have my glasses on; it is possible that he saw an image of a face as it actually was. I was sending out to him this telepathic force, or let us say this telepathic force of my presence. And he will confirm that he had these experiences.

"My daughter also, aged at that time about nineteen or twenty, had a number of experiences of being intensely aware of my presence.

"I want to describe also an attempt I made which one can describe as a mobile center of consciousness. That is, shifting the consciousness out of one's body. Now, I've tried to do this, and—why did I try? That is a secondary consideration. I tried to do this, but I found it extremely difficult. The procedure was for me to lie on my bed in the darkness. I tried to get my consciousness out of my body, with myself lying there on the bed, to shift the consciousness. Curiously enought, I found a trick of psychological reinforcement which I will describe.

"I had a strange dream. From one aspect it could be a dream of reincarnation of some previous existence—who knows? I dreamed that I was a white European, and I was dying under Red Indian torture; a very strange dream; and the Red Indian, in the moment of torture and my own death, suddenly was moved to great pity and great regret, to great concern; and I had a sense of a pledge from this Red Indian that he would serve me for all time, out of affection and regret. It was a dream. So when I came to try and shift my own consciousness from my own body, then came this dream.

"A few nights later I had the idea of using the psychological reinforcement of the presence of the Red Indian that I had dreamed of. I lay on my bed in the darkness and tried to summon up the sense of this Red Indian person, assisting me to leave my body.

"Then it suddenly happened. My consciousness was up in a corner by the ceiling. I was looking down on my body lying there. And in a flash my consciousness went out into the corridor (I was in a hotel room, remember), and I was looking back through the wall at my body lying on the bed there. So I made the effort to get out, assisted psychologically by the illusion or autosuggestion of this Red Indian figure, the sudden breakthrough and switch like lightning of the consciousness up into the top corner of the bedroom and like a flash! the consciousness had gone into the corridor looking back through the wall—and would have gone, like a flash, God knows where except . . . *I grew frightened*, alarmed, and of course I was then back inside myself on my bed.

"I tried this again about nine months later, consciously and deliberately. The attempt I have just tried to describe was under strong emotion. Under less emotion, I tried it again. And this time two things happened. An enormous sense of nausea, a tremendous sense of sickness in the whole of my body as I slowly tried to shift the consciousness out; and this time my consciousness shifted only about a foot away from my body, and as it moved I had this great, overwhelming sense of physical nausea and, secondly, fear—real fear and terror."

John Evre's experience tends to underline the warning made

by Dr. Crookall in all his books on astral projection, and to me personally in a long discussion we had on this subject. Furthermore, the unpleasant aspects of Eyre's attempts at astral projection went farther than this. In the ensuing days he became conscious of an increased awareness, a heightened perception; he seemed to be drawing impressions out of the room itself, as though the place was imbued with the presences and happenings of bygone times, a sort of retrocognition (a going back in time).

"In this sensitive state," he told me, "I began to pick up what I can only conclude were vibrations out of the room itself, impressions of the previous people who had inhabited this hotel room. Visions, picture stories came into my consciousness in these moments of trance. After I had achieved that original alienation (of consciousness), rappings started up in the room. It was very strange, and they generally started up when I began to go to sleep, to the point where they disturbed me.

"I would be just falling asleep, when suddenly the knocks would start [here John Eyre demonstrated the quick, staccato knocks] and I got fed up. All right—I had released some force or other, and so these knockings were coming, and I began to speak to the knockings—'Oh, go away for heaven's sake'— that sort of stuff. And on about the second or third night, as I was just drifting into sleep, again the knockings came. I said, 'Go! Go! Go!' and instantaneously, as I was thinking and uttering this in my mind, the picture came into my mind of a girl, aged twelve, sitting in a rocking chair, rocking herself in a drawing room. Behind her were two large bow windows, which were open, and a flight of stairs lying at those window points, leading to a garden below. And as I was saying 'Go, go, go!' she was rocking the chair, and rocked backward, rolled right down the steps, and presumably was killed. This was the sense. And I awoke with a tremendous shock, feeling that my driving her out like this had, in fact, killed her. It was all in color. I judged by the style of her dress—a little white muslin dress —that it was about 1910. As I relate it now, I see it so vividly I could draw a sketch, in fact.

"Anyway, I wondered whether something like this hadn't happened way back in the history of this old hotel, and whether she, as a small girl, had had an accident and had been carried to this room where I was, and whether I might be picking up some vibrations. The next morning I thought I would investigate the ground-

156

floor rooms of the hotel. Only one of them was open to the public; the others were locked.

"I asked the proprietress if I could look at the other rooms that were locked, explaining that I was interested because I knew that there was a garden lying at the back of the hotel. She unlocked one of the rooms, and there, sure enough, was exactly the setup that I had visualized but had never seen—the bow window, the stone steps leading down onto what I think had been an old greenhouse or patio or something there."

The experience occurred in a hotel in Princes Square, Kensington, London. This last experience would seem to be an example of retrogression, of which there are many examples, and which I will deal with later.

To return to astral projection, it is easy enough for somebody to say that they have dreamed they drifted out of their bodies. Weird dreams are more common than ordinary ones. But in cases of astral projection two factors take them out of the rut of mere mental imagery or imagination—corroboration by dependable witnesses, and detail that could not be secured from the subconscious mind or conscious memory.

I spoke to John Eyre's daughter, Trudy, a twenty-one-year-old modern languages student. I found her a self-possessed, logical person who spoke factually and without reservation of how her father's experiments in astral projection had affected her.

She told me that at the time of her father's experiments she did not see him visually, but had "a great sense of his presence" and also "smelled him." The comment may sound amusing or unusual, but it does so happen that every human being has an entirely distinctive smell—hence the ability of a dog to follow its master unerringly through thoroughfares frequented by thousands of other people. "I smelled his presence," Trudy said, "and he was all around me. I felt him touching me."

"A caress?" I asked.

"Yes."

"Did this happen once, or several times?"

"About twice or three times." This happened when Miss Eyre was in bed at home, in Neville Terrace, Montacute Road, Tunbridge Wells, Kent. "It was quite fantastic, really."

"Where were you in the house?"

"In a basement bedroom."

"And this happened when you were just going off to sleep, when you had this tactile sensation?"

"Yes."

I asked if she was in any especially emotional state at the time. Her father's marriage had recently broken up, and it would be reasonable to suppose that the children might find the change upsetting.

Trudy assured me that she had recovered from the breakup at the time. She was grown up, and retained happy relations with both parents. "Peter and I had been calling our parents by their first names for nearly two years before this, which gives you an idea of our attitude toward our parents. We regard our parents first and foremost as individuals and as very good friends rather than as merely father and mother."

"Were you frightened when you first sensed your father's presence, knowing him to be faraway somewhere else?"

"I was, in the beginning. The first time it happened I was scared because I'd never experienced anything like it before. I had a great sense of John calling me, showing concern for me. I found myself replying, in fact. And I was crying, from the nervous shock of it all, because it was an experience I had never remotely dreamed of before. Yes, he was asking me how I was, and I called out that I was fine, that he needn't worry about me."

"What happened the second time?"

"The second time was much easier for me. I realized that I was in full control of myself, when I was just dropping off to sleep. It was a fantastic sensation—I felt a sense of communion with John, though rather tentative on my side."

"And the rapport, or exchange if you like, followed the same lines?"

"Yes."

"Sort of 'How are you?' and 'I'm fine'?"

"Yes, but it was on a sort of higher plane this time as there was no fear on my part, or at least rather less fear."

"Have you tried the same experiment yourself—of transmitting?"

"Yes, I have."

"With him, or with somebody else?"

"With John. I can give you the most recent example, which occurred ten days ago. My friend Lee and I decided on the spur

158

of the moment to come up to London, and I later phoned John to ask if I could stay the night with him. Which we did. When we returned to East Grinstead, there was a card from John saying, 'Come up one evening.' We had made a sudden decision to go up to London, and at that precise time he sent us a card inviting us."

Trudy has tried experiments with her brother, but these have been telepathic and not an attempt at astral projection.

I spoke later to Peter Eyre, aged eighteen, a technical assistant in an electronics firm, who also lives in Montacute Road, Tunbridge Wells. He is a healthy, upstanding, balanced sort of youth whose recreational activities are football, chess, and bridge, but he shares the family interest in psychical research. His father, John, it will be remembered, had appeared to him while trying his experiments at deliberate projection. Naturally, I wanted to know what it was like to be on the receiving end.

"Your father says that he appeared to you—that you saw him?"

"Yes, just his head. It got to such a point that I noted down the date, place, and time that I saw him, and when we next met I checked with him. It was at the time he was trying to contact me."

"When did you see him?"

"When I was dozing off to sleep."

"What time would that be?"

"Between ten and eleven."

"How did you see him?"

"When you think about something you have a picture. He appeared in the top left-hand corner of my vision—just the face, enshrouded in darkness. The face stood out. The surroundings were dark."

"Was it in color or monochrome?"

"In color."

"Quite distinct?"

"Yes."

"And the expression?"

"Concern. And other times happiness. There was a time about a year ago when I had a bad accident on my motor scooter. My sister told my father that same night. And I saw his head, just his head, in my vision. His expression was one of grave concern. The accident occurred about five miles from Tunbridge Wells. I went to the hospital and came back home, and saw him just as I was dozing off. I saw him a bit then, but three days later when my sister saw my father, I saw his face as clear as a bell, with a grave expression of concern written all over it. It really stood there for about five minutes."

"Did you exchange any speech?"

"I told him mentally, 'I'm all right, John. Don't worry.' "

"Were you badly hurt in the accident?"

"I was bruised and shocked and had to have stitches. My eyes were closed when I saw him. The face kept the same position."

"This sort of communication with your father had become quite regular, I gather. How often do you see him in this fashion?"

"About every four days."

I asked Peter if he had had any psychic experience of his own. He told me that in 1954, when he was three years old, he saw behind some partly drawn curtains in his room the figure of a man. He screamed with fear, and when his mother came rushing in he described in detail the figure of the man. The description was of his mother's brother, who during World War II had been serving with an anti-Japanese force in Malaya; discovered by the Japanese with arms secreted under his bed, he had been led away, tortured, and eventually shot.

"The interesting thing in this case," Peter told me, "was that he appeared at the same time to my grandmother, to whom he had once said, 'Mother, if I die, I will always come back in time of trouble.' "

As it happened, there was trouble in the family at that time, when Peter's grandmother was living in Holland.

A few months ago he and a friend had visited his grandmother's bedroom, where she had collapsed and died some time before. Suddenly he felt all the strength drained away from him and sensed he was going to collapse. He was standing on the spot where she had died. Later he saw the phantasm of his grandmother in his own room. It was clear and detailed, but although Peter knew what she looked like from photographs, her dress was different in every detail. However, he described correctly an outfit in which others had seen her while she was alive, but which he himself had never seen.

"When you saw her, did you experience fear?"

"Oh, yes. I shouted 'Get out! Get out!' One is always afraid of the unknown."

160

Later, in the course of further experimentation, John Eyre experienced another "out-of-the-body" adventure. An interesting feature of this case is that he found himself linked to his other self by "a silver cord." This "cord" is said by those who believe in astral projection to be a sort of umbilical cord which elongates itself as the astral self speeds on its way. It is a most curious fact in view of the mystical phrase in Ecclesiastes (12:6):

Or ever the silver cord be loosed
Or the golden bowl be broken
Or the pitcher be broken at the fountain
Or the wheel broken at the cistern
Then shall the dust return to the dust as it was:
And the spirit shall return unto God who gave it.

Although there is manifest symbolism in this passage, such as "the golden bowl be broken," the idea of loosing a silver cord as being symbolic of the departure of the spirit is of the deepest interest; references to such a silver cord have come from hundreds of people who have submitted their accounts independently of each other and who, before they went through their strange experiences, had read nothing on the subject.

I have quoted in John Eyre's own words his weird experience in "visiting" his children while his body lay recumbent somewhere else. He continued his experimentation throughout 1968 and 1969, and in particular had been learning and practicing yoga techniques, including "the raising of Kundalini, or Serpent Fire." At the risk of oversimplifying, this may be described as a technique for releasing great waves of energy and bringing the entire nervous system under the control of the will. Eyre was trying to transfer the center of consciousness to other parts of his body, and then, he told me, "I suddenly found another body was floating above me. The queer thing was that this other body was linked by the semblance of an umbilical cord, from the head-shoulder part to mine. When I visualized my consciousness in, let us say, the hips, it was this other body above me that adjusted itself, floating in the air, adjusting itself over my real head, so that my real head was in the other body's hips now; so that my consciousness, so to speak, was in that other body's hips.

"Similarly, if I tried to move my consciousness into, let us

161

say, the legs and ankles, this body floating above me, linked by some kind of a cord, would shift and float to a position so that my real head was coinciding with the feet of this thing. When I visualized my consciousness as being in my heart, this shadowy body floating above me, linked to me with this cord, shifted so that the heart of this thing was over my head. . . ."

When he shifted his consciousness into the thyroid gland, the floating self above nearly coincided with his own body. Then came the realization that he could send this floating "body" anywhere he willed; Mr. Eyre No. 1 could decide where Mr. Eyre No. 2 should go. He thought of somebody he "wanted to send this thing to." Then he saw this floating body, its cord trailing behind it, "shooting away like a bolt into the distance and shadows. . . ."

A strange story. A ghostly figure, sent hurtling through space with the compliments of its more physical counterpart, is the sort of present most of us could do without. And not many of us would have the knowledge, courage, or patience to attempt so bizarre and dangerous an adventure. Dangerous? Yes. In my view it is dangerous to strive to achieve the alienation of personality or soul or spirit. In pursuit of truth, which has its own validity but which does not always offer consolation or comfort, the experiments may perhaps seem worthwhile to those with exceptional nervous, physical and mental stamina, but the advice of Dr. Robert Crookall remains: *Don't do it; don't try it.*

Robert Crookall, B.Sc. (Psychology), Ph.D., is a cheerful, energetic, tidy-minded man who brings to psychic research the discipline and orderliness that its importance justifies. A scientist who has worked all his life within the confines of scientific methods, he is not the sort of individual who selects only such facts as fit his preconceived ideas, or draws concrete conclusions from abstract propositions.

It is this strong practical sense, coupled with that awe and reverence for human life and for nature which Albert Schweitzer maintained was the very stuff of true religion, that gives Dr. Crookall's works their singular importance.

Dr. Crookall says that astral projection is a genuine occurrence and not an unusual one either. He has collected several hundred instances where people have left their bodies and, although his fascinating and scholarly works are eagerly read by interested people throughout the world, they are all labors of love.

Crookall lives in the beautiful city of Bath, in Somerset, famous as a spa nearly two thousand years ago and still rich in Roman remains. Although he is eighty years old, he certainly looks ten to fifteen years younger. His manner is alert and interested and he smiles readily. To keep fit he cycles daily around Bath and the surrounding countryside. He lives in a simple apartment into which he moved when his wife died recently. He cleans and cooks for himself, and works assiduously at his research into astral projection and allied phenomena, which brings him correspondence from all over the world.

How did such a man come to be interested in such a superficially weird subject as astral wanderings?

Robert Crookall was born in Lancaster in 1890. His father was a joiner who later became clerk of works in a linoleum factory. Robert received a sound education at a time when places in universities were few and precious, and were kept only by those students who applied themselves to their studies with energy and self-discipline.

He recently explained to me how he became interested in what has now become his life work.

"When I took my degree at Bristol University, I studied psychology as well as chemistry and botany. It always seemed to me that I saw odd things which the professors of psychology had overlooked, such as astral projection. So, although I didn't get a post in teaching psychology, becoming a botanist to start with, I was itching to retire and write up these ideas on psychology to try to establish them.

"I first of all lectured in botany at Aberdeen University, and specialized in fossil plants, especially the plants that made coal, which grew two hundred and fifty million years. Fossil plants are very important because they indicate the origins of many modern species and genera; and the fossil plants which made coal are important because they have a practical bearing on the discovery of new areas in which we can expect to find coal.

"And so I was asked to join the Geological Survey as a paleobotanist in 1926. I was there for twenty-six years, retiring three years before I needed to, in order to make these psychological studies. But it took years to get my ideas into proper form and it was nine years before I got a book published. This was *The Supreme Adventure* [published for the Churches' Fellowship for Psychical Study by James Clarke & Company Ltd., London, 1961].

"In the same year was published *The Study and Practice of Astral Projection* [Aquarian Press, London, and University Books, New York]. Originally I started writing one book, but it grew beyond all proportions and had to be separated. The great problem, of course, is to find some 'sieve' or screen or method of analysis for the data claimed, showing that they have some relation to reality."

Impetus to Dr. Crookall's work and encouragement to its recognition outside the Doctor's own immediate circle was given by the late Hornell Hart,* then Professor of Sociology at Duke University in Durham, North Carolina.

Hornell Hart, hearing of Crookall's work, visited him and was immediately impressed. He described it as "the most promising pioneering now being done in psychical research."

"The method I used," Dr. Crookall told me, "was to divide the testimonies of these people into two groups—first, people who said they had left their bodies without being pushed out in any way, and secondly, people who had been pushed out of their bodies by drowning, a fall, or an anesthetic. I thus got two different stories—all the people who went out *naturally* told one and the same story, while all the people who were 'pushed out' told a different story. In other words, there were common factors in each group. Such consistencies cannot arise fortuitously and the correspondents had no contact with each other."

In an article written by Professor Hart just before he died (*Scientific Survival Research;* Parapsychology Foundation, 1967, p. 43), he described his own work and went on to pay tribute to the work of Dr. Crookall. The latter explained: "I had only tested statistically in a rough sort of way but Professor Hart used a stricter method and showed that one type of coincidence that I

*Hart was a world-famous authority on supernormal phenomena and author, among other works, of *The Enigma of Survival* (Rider & Company, Ltd., 1959). After corresponding with psychologists all over the world, Professor Hart produced a valuable report, *Six Theories of Apparitions,* published in Vol. L of *Proceedings of the Society for Psychical Research* in 1956.

had uncovered could not occur by chance in millions of cases. This was a good piece of evidence. Since then I have used still other methods of psychological analysis.

"In fossil plants I had to investigate a fossilized stem. Now, in order fully to understand the structure of this stem, I would take thin slices of 'sections' through it. The first would be across the stem, the next would be right down the middle, and the third would be tangential. These sections would be photographed through the microscope and they would reveal all the different kinds of tissues and the relationships between them. A model of the stem could then be made and exhibited in a museum.

"My psychological work on astral projection was similar but with psychological analysis instead of sections. The division of the cases into natural and enforced corresponded to one method of sectioning, say, the cross-section of a stem. Another psychological section consisted in dividing the deponents into two kinds of people, one, mediumistic people, the other, nonmediumistic people. Again I got two different stories, and the differences could be well explained in terms of the hypothesis I envisaged. That study was published in *Intimations of Immortality*."*

"What," I asked, "first got you interested in astral projection —convinced you, in other words, that this was a reality deserving serious study?"

"First of all," Crookall told me, "I was studying 'communications' which come from the supposed dead. I was trying to get some method of analyzing them. I divided them into natural deaths, people who died naturally, and people who had been forced out of the body by war, etc.

"In the course of doing this I also got into astral projection; death is a permanent stepping out of the body, projection a temporary excursion. There are gradations between the two. Very often a person who dies leaves his body and comes back to it more than once. . . ."

I asked Dr. Crookall about an experience I once had in Cornwall, when I was with my wife in an old farmhouse. My wife awakened in fright to see me standing by the bedside, a sort of luminous figure, *looking down at my sleeping body,* which was recumbent beside her. I was skeptical at the time, but she still holds to her story of what she saw.

*Published by James Clark & Co., Ltd., 1965.

"That," the doctor explained, "was the 'vehicle of vitality,' the vital body or etheric double, not the soul-body."

"What do you mean," I asked, "by 'vehicle of vitality'? It's not a term I have encountered before."

"The double, or form of body that detaches itself or moves away from a person's physical body, may be one of three things: the 'vehicle of vitality,' which is semiphysical; the 'soul-body,' which is superphysical, or an admixture of these two.

"I expect what your wife saw was the vehicle of vitality, because the figure looked pale. It was a ghost—your ghost. You didn't hear her. You didn't remember that you had been out of your body. If it had been the soul-body, you might have seen her, you might have seen outside the room, and you might have remembered the fact. The soul-body would be bright and highly colored, and look very young."

Dr. Crookall now postulates what he describes as "a hierarchy of bodies": the spiritual body—a formless radiation; the soul-body —superphysical, which has consciousness and powers of observation; the vehicle of vitality or vital body, which has no sense organs; and the dense physical body.

The manifestations of the vehicle of vitality include physical phenomena such as supernormal raps, direct voice manifestations, and materializations. When the soul-body is at work, says the doctor, the fact is shown by such phenomena as telepathy, clairvoyance, and foreknowledge.

"I digressed a little, Doctor, from my query as to what first convinced you that astral projection was a fact?"

"I began by examining communications from those who described how they died, and I divided these people into two groups —natural deaths, or sudden or enforced deaths, getting two different stories. I discovered, however, that there is no sharp break between permanently leaving the body and temporarily leaving the body. In fact, in many cases, as already said, a person leaves his body and comes back to it once or twice or even oftener again before death. Then again, the various things that were said by people who were supposed to have died—for instance, they said that they had a panoramic review of their past lives which had no emotional or responsible overtones; and then they claimed to have had a blackout in consciousness; and then they saw people who came to help and advise them.

166

"Now exactly the same things were said by astral projectors! If the projectors were telling the truth, and vice versa, we must then find some hypothesis which will explain the whole of these facts. The same type of analysis, or section through the material, was applicable to both, and therefore tended to substantiate both. I don't say it *proves* both. But if anyone rejects this, they should advance some other hypothesis which explains all these facts. In philosophy we have not got a 'knock-down,' a coercive proof, such as we have in chemistry. Water can be split into hydrogen and oxygen; this can be heated back into water. This is a 'knock-down' proof.

"In a philosophy the argument more nearly resembles a jigsaw puzzle than anything else. If all the pieces fit in and all the pieces are used up, then you know that the puzzle has been solved."

"What," I asked Dr. Crookall, "do you consider to be the significance of astral projection so far as human destiny is concerned?"

"It certainly indicates life after death."

"You're convinced of life after death?"

"Oh yes. I think the best answer to your question about destiny is in my appendix in *The Techniques of Astral Projection,* at the end—the object of life."

Here I will quote from that appendix:

Suppose that you were confronted with a machine that was swathed in tarpaulins. How would we decide its purpose? Having removed the coverings, we would note its components—wheels, levers, gears, etc., and their connections—and draw our deductions from the observed facts. Now physical science has, to a considerable extent, "taken the tarpaulin" off man, revealing his "components" (faculties such as telepathy, clairvoyance, and foreknowledge; abilities such as astral projection; and experiences such as those designated mystical or cosmic), and their "connections" in the various "selves," namely, the lesser, outer, or temporary self which uses the physical body, the psychic self or "Soul" which uses the Soul or Astral Body, and the Greater, Inner, or Eternal Self, the Over-Soul, which uses the Spiritual Body.

In a forthcoming book, *The Interpretation of Cosmic and Mystical Experiences* (James Clarke & Co., Ltd., 1970), Dr.

167

Crookall refers to the immense number of people whose testimony confirms the reality of astral travel:

> Hundreds of people, including quite young children and illiterate adults (obviating copying from the descriptions of others) have claimed that they have left their physical bodies temporarily, and many of them stated that they were in a second, nonphysical body which they variously called an "ethereal," "etheric," "astral," "soul," "psychical," "spiritual," etc., body.
> This was a replica or double of the physical body—but it could pass through walls and doors without hindrance, was unaffected by gravity and travelled instantly and automatically to any person or place, however distant, whereon the attention was directed.
> They claimed to have visited other localities on earth (or the "etheric doubles" thereof), localities in the relatively dim "Hades" world. . . . It is certain that those who claimed to visit different earth localities returned with information, later verified by others, which they would not have obtained by the use of physical senses.

If Dr. Crookall is right in his hypothesis that we all possess three bodies, then the idea of the nature of man is altered.

"As long," he told me, "as we are in this physical body, we are shut down to this physical world, using our instinct and our reason. Occasionally some of us get slightly out of the body—if it's the vehicle of vitality that gets out, then it's a pale ghost that sees nothing; if it's the soul-body that gets out, there are telepathic and clairvoyant experiences; if it's the spiritual body that gets out, there are experiences of God—mystical experiences. All these things can be had during our lifetime. The object and purpose of life can be illuminated by psychic research and mystical studies."

Will man ever develop the technique of astral projection to such an extent that he can send his soul-body—unaffected by gravity, capable of travel over immense distances, having consciousness and powers of observation—anywhere in space? Fantastic though it seems, if one accepts the reality of astral projection, then it may well have no measurable limits. We have learned already, from the fantastic Apollo projects, that distance is not the unbridgeable gulf we once supposed.

Astral projection, when it occurs, is certainly a highly significant experience. Many doubtless wish to experience it. But Dr. Crookall does not advise anybody to make a conscious "out-of-the-body" attempt.

It would seem that astral projection can happen spontaneously, without the sleeper's being aware of it. Within the context of an *Observer* profile of Olivia Manning, the distinguished novelist, and wife of the talented and hard-working BBC drama producer, R. L. Smith, appeared a passing mention of an astral projection. I took a taxi to Abbey Gardens in Hampstead and asked Olivia Manning to tell me more. She stroked her Siamese cat and spoke, reflectively and descriptively, of a strange experience one night in Alexandria:

"Toward the end of the war Reggie and I were staying in Alexandria before we left Egypt. We were staying in a *pension* and had a double room, rather high up, in one of these modern blocks. It had French windows that opened onto a balcony. I think we were on the ninth floor. It was one of those very brilliant Egyptian moonlight nights—the moonlight as pure and light and clear as it is possible for light to be. In some ways it is even more clear, if you like, than sunlight is in Egypt.

"I woke up at about two in the morning, and moonlight was shining directly into our room—a huge, silver block of light coming through the window and partly onto the bed. Standing by the open French window—leaning against one of the glass panels in the French window—was this man, this journalist, who lived in Cairo and was in Cairo at the time, a very distinct and solid figure, gazing at the pair of us in bed and smiling in a rather quizzical way. I think his arms were folded. He was just leaning against the window and gazing at us as though we were a bit of a joke, the pair of us, you know.

"I said to Reggie, 'Look!' When he looked up, he said, 'Good heavens! It's George Scott Watson.' The journalist wasn't a friend of mine. I didn't care for him really. He was a correspondent in Egypt."

It is not an experience that Olivia Manning would like to repeat. The supernatural frightens her. Three years later the journalist died under an anesthetic.

A curious and highly detailed account of what seems to me an instance of astral projection was related to me by Francis James Wydur, a thirty-four-year-old carpenter of 11 Oakland Avenue, Papatoetoe, Auckland, New Zealand. It happened when he was a baby:

> I was crawling across what was in that home the lounge. I was dressed in nappies and a singlet. I was aware of myself from within but could also in flashes see myself from about a foot away. All this happened very swiftly, as I had only crawled about half the lounge as it was happening.
>
> At this point I came across a small ball of something on the floor, and promptly picked it up, rolling it in my fingers as I did so. As all babies do, I put it in my mouth, but with a feeling of revulsion I spat it out as I realized what it was. At this point I became aware that someone was watching me and I looked up to see a very tall man standing at the front door, which was open, looking down at me.
>
> There then occurred the strangest event of my life to date. One second I was the baby on the floor looking up at the man at the door; the next I was that man looking down at the baby. A moment later I was the baby again and the man had gone.

Another similar experience occurred when he was being christened. At one moment he was howling over the font; at another moment he was with his parents and relatives actually witnessing the whole ceremony and watching the baby.

"These two events," he told me, "are as clear to me even now" (e.g., at the age of thirty-four years).

Impossible? A subjective, and not an objective, experience? A trick of the senses? A trick of memory? At this late stage, how can I say? What I can say is that Mr. Wydur expresses himself in a literate and coherent and explicit way and had absolutely nothing to gain by adducing this story about himself. Indeed, as early as the turn of the century the distinguished French psychical researcher Dr. Paul Joire had discovered that there was such a thing as the exteriorization of sensibility. He proved this by hypnotizing a subject and pricking, not his skin, but the area of air about an inch away. Whenever he touched the area around the body with a pin, he produced a localized reflex action and response of pain.

If sensibility can be exteriorized in this way, is there a complete inner self which can be exteriorized, too? The immense number of authenticated cases of phantasms of the living—people being seen at other places when they are active or asleep far away, suggests that it may be so. The term "astral projection" may be obscure and perhaps a little pretentious, but the phenomenon it is intended to describe is a real and a mysterious one.

☐ 10. "I Have Been Here Before"

I have been here before,
But when or how I cannot tell;
I know the grass beyond the door,
The sweet keen smell,
The sighing sound, the lights around the shore.
                                        —Dante Gabriel Rossetti

DR. Robert Crookall, like thousands of intelligent and educated men with a flair for scientific analysis and reasoned logic, believes in the survival of the human spirit. Sir Oliver Lodge, the Victorian scientist, was convinced beyond a doubt.

The literature of survival is vast. For thousands of years religions of one kind or another have taken the survival of the soul for granted. Even today countless millions of Christians, to name only one faith, accept in theory at least the doctrine of a life after death.

Doctrine is one thing, evidence another. The literature of spiritualism is rich in accounts of presences described as spirits who have, through a medium, told of life in the other world. I myself questioned H. Dennis Bradley, a famous spiritualist of the thirties, on what life was like after he had died. I did this through a medium in company with his two sons, who maintained that the voice was his, although coming through the mouth of a woman medium, and that the personal questions—which seemed to be trival, coming from a man who had only recently died and suddenly found himself able to speak to his two sons—were very evidential. One, I remember, was, "Why did you move the sponge?" I was told by one of the sons afterward that a sponge was habitually kept in the bathroom, but had for some reason I have forgotten, but for a reason exceptional at the time, been removed to another room. But Bradley's descriptions (if they were his) of the other world came in prompt and unhesitating reply to my considerable list of questions.

One American has claimed to be able to prove the existence of the human soul by scientific means. He is Professor Richard Carl Spurney, Instructor in Philosophy in Long Beach City College, Long Beach, California, who, in June, 1967, appeared in the James Kidd trial in Phoenix, Arizona. The purpose of the trial was to prove that man had a soul, for James Kidd, an eccentric and immensely wealthy miner, left a will providing that his fortune would go to anyone who could prove the existence of the human soul.

Professor Spurney's thesis and arguments, which he has been kind enough to send to me, are too well presented, and bear witness to too much hard work and deep-delving thought, to warrant any suspicion that he was actuated primarily by the desire to collect the late Mr. Kidd's fortune. He felt that the challenge was important enough to justify the immense labor involved, and I rather think that he enjoyed the battle even if, legally speaking, he did not win it.

I don't care what the law says about the existence of the soul. The truth interests me whether it is recognized or not. At any rate, Spurney's monograph *Philosophical Reflections, with 50 Scientific Proofs of the Human Soul* can be commended as a simple and logical argument in favor of survival.

The papers of Gardner Murphy in the *Journal of the American Society for Psychical Research,* and F. W. H. Myers' great work, *Human Personality and Its Survival of Bodily Death,* besides Hornell Hart's *The Debate About Survival,* are all attempts to justify the theory of survival on the basis of facts and reasoned argument as distinct from theological dogma.

One of the strangest, yet most ancient, and even today the most deep-rooted, theories of survival is that of reincarnation. Is it a romantic chimera or has it any historical or factual basis? For myself, there has always been a stumbling block to any acceptance of its basic premise—that on death the soul takes wings

173

and finds another home, like a butterfly leaving a dead flower for a live one. How can such a theory be equated with the continual increase in population? There wouldn't be enough souls to go around. For the farther back in history one goes, the smaller the total population was. Assuming that at one stage all the souls of the dead transmigrate, there would always be a great number left without a transmigrating soul. What happens then? Is the less-favored newborn left without a soul, or is there some emergency arrangement by which the Creator says, in effect, "There isn't a spare soul for this new infant; so he'd better have a new soul." That, at least, has been the obstacle for me. Nevertheless, there is considerable evidence that reincarnation does occur.

One indication that a person may have more than one life is the phenomenon of *déjà vu*—the feeling, when you arrive at a place that should be strange to you because it has never been described or visited, that it is nevertheless familiar in all its detail. If it is the place, the environment, a knowledge of the past associated with it, then it is either a retrogression—a case of retrocognition (a going back in time, due to some freak of time, or due to the place being charged or impregnated with some force that re-created the scene) or—if the scene was envisaged long before, together with action that subsequently is seen to take place—it is a case of precognition or seeing into the future.

If reincarnation is a fact, however, could it not mean that a memory of a previous life comes into operation?

Remember how Sir Walter Scott, the famous Scottish novelist, recorded in his diary on February 17, 1828: "At dinner I was strangely haunted by what I would call the sense of pre-existence —a confused idea that nothing that had passed was said for the first time, that the same topics had been discussed and that the same persons had expressed the same opinions on the same subjects."

A typical case was related to me by Mr. T. P. Greig of Sarsfield Road, London, S.W.12. The incident took place in 1898 when, as a lad of fifteen, he was recovering from a serious illness.

Mr. Greig had a vivid dream of being at Holyrood House, the ancient royal palace in Edinburgh. In this dream the boy saw reenacted the murder of Mary Stuart's supposed lover, David Rizzio. Lying on his sick-bed, Greig had a vivid imagery of Rizzio being dragged from her supper room, through the bedroom and

174

audience chamber to the head of the principal staircase, where the body was left.

Up to that time Greig had never been in Edinburgh or read anything about Mary Stuart's reign as Queen of Scotland. But when he was sent for convalescence to his grandmother's at Dundee, he told her of his dream and she arranged for a friend to take him to Holyrood.

When the boy arrived at Holyrood Palace every stone seemed familiar. So much so that he declined the guide's offer to show him around and instead led *him* through the building, directing him unerringly to the fatal supper room. He showed the guide the back staircase—which at the time of the murder lay concealed behind a tapestry—up which the conspirators had come into Queen Mary's bedroom, thence to the audience chamber, and on to the principal staircase where the Italian's body was left.

"That," the boy told the astonished guide, "is where Rizzio was killed!"

How could the boy have known? He was an old man when I spoke to him about it, and asked him what conclusion he had formed about it after all these years.

"I believe I must have been reincarnated," he told me. "I just don't see what else could explain it. But since I was undoubtedly at the scene of that murder the question is—*who* was I? Was I the victim, or one of the assassins?"

The interesting thing is that Mr. Greig had not read about Holyrood House, or heard about it from anyone who had visited it. I mention his case in passing as an example of a *déjà vu* experience which, in the opinion of the person concerned, was an indication of a previous life, or reincarnation. After so great a lapse of time any sort of "knock-down" proof is clearly impossible. One would need to confirm that none of his reading matter ever contained any reference to the place—and who can remember all he has read?

Belief in reincarnation (variously called transmigration of souls; pre-existence; palingenesis; and metempsychosis) presupposes two things: that the human soul exists, and that the soul survives the death of the human body.

Two of the world's great religions—Hinduism and Buddhism —teach the continual rebirth of the soul, the migration of the soul at bodily death to a new, live body of another person. Thus the psyche or soul is developing and expanding through the centuries, the respective bodies being mere vehicles or habitations. Bodies are discarded much as the snake sheds its skin.

One of the most outstanding, perhaps audacious, advocates of the theory of reincarnation is Joan Grant, who together with her husband Dr. Kelsey, a psychiatrist, insists she is now living her thirty-first life in Paris, and has recently embodied her ideas on reincarnation in a book she has written with him.

First let me make it clear that Joan Grant is a writer of unusual distinction. Her first book, *Winged Pharaoh,* was finely constructed, sensitively written, brilliantly descriptive and, so far as one can check, since some features of life in ancient Egypt are still a mystery, historically accurate. But ancient Egypt is still the best documented of all old civilizations, owing to the Egyptians' mania for incising hieroglyphics deeply and neatly into enduring objects such as stone and basalt, with the result that considerable records remain. The atmosphere and historical background of *Winged Pharaoh,* however, did not come, as is usually the case, from the examination of old records and visits to the places described, but from the mental storehouse of Miss Grant's own mind.

However, she would say the information stems from her memory. Her life in ancient Egypt, she maintains, was the first of her thirty-one incarnations. And they have been varied enough. She has, she believes, been an Egyptian Pharaoh, a Roman princess, a witch, a Red Indian, a Greek runner, a wandering minstrel in the sixteenth century, and a street-walking prostitute in ancient Paris.

Miss Grant claims to remember the agony of being born, a process which, she once told the BBC interviewer, was more painful than dying. If one accepts that a child being born has full consciousness (and the degree of its consciousness and awareness has never been fully established), then, presumably, there could be memory of it, although most psychologists and medical men are of the opinion that it is rare and difficult to remember clearly and in detail anything that happened before the age of three.

This contention, like so many medical claims, can be received with the greatest reserve. There are many levels of consciousness, and it is easy to prove by hypnotism that not a single

176

word, not even the most trival occurrence in human life, is truly forgotten. Stored, put away, relegated to the darkest corner of the mental junkshop, perhaps. But forgotten? Never.

The butterfly that fluttered past your sleepy eyes as you lay in a baby carriage; the harsh words spoken between parents when, as they imagined, they were out of your hearing; the disposition of clouds floating lazily across the horizon—a pattern varied millions of times at any point of the earth's atmosphere—are impressed indelibly upon the memory. The memories lie there dormant, yet given the appropriate stimulus they may be reactivated, or may condition future conduct by acting through what we call the sub-conscious mind.

Joan Grant's memory goes back, she claims, for thousands of years. For my own part, I would find such a capacity a disturbing facet of my existence. One cannot reshape the past. One cannot undo what has been done. If I had had former lifetimes, I would not wish to know anything about them.

Must one then relive all the frustrations, pains, fears, and sufferings of bygone centuries? Must one be reminded of the terrible injustices and cruelties that have shamed mankind and at times turned life into a nightmare? Must the wretched who, during the Inquisition, were impaled in an iron chair made of spikes, under which a fire was lit, relive their protracted agonies? Such reliving would of course be mental—but what memories!

But this is a philosophical question—whether oblivion may not be more merciful or desirable than everlasting life. Truth will not be affected by what people wish or do not wish. And what *is* the truth about reincarnation? Is there any factual substance for the extraordinary stories of multiple lives?

Joan Grant says, "Reincarnation automatically happens to everybody." But if this is so, it is hard to accept that only a small proportion of the millions who are reborn have any recollection of their previous lives. It is even more difficult to reconcile the "one-soul-one-body" idea inherent in reincarnation with the population explosion.

One interviewer asked Joan Grant, "Why can't we remember knowledge that we have learned in a previous existence. Even if it were only a language knowledge?"

Miss Grant thought it was because "language is only a matter of intellect but your character is the sum total of your previous experiences. Your character is the result of your previous incarnations, not your skills."

If one accepts reincarnation as a possibility, it is a little difficult to conceive of a spiritual entity having character but no inherent skills, the latter being a reflection or expression of the former. An artistic character would be more likely to produce paintings or poetry or esthetic works than, say, a person with a less visionary temperament. That must remain a matter for conjecture.

What is not a matter for conjecture is that many people have claimed to remember a former existence with a degree of detail that would appear to rule out the subconscious mind; that is to say, even if those details did emanate from the subconscious mind, it would remain a mystery how the details got there in the first place. I am thinking of specific cases in which the information could not have come from the usual range of resources—conversation with others; remarks and conversation overheard and remembered, though not, necessarily, remembered consciously; places seen or visited; books and records read.

What, for example, is one to make of the case of Vishala, a fifteen-year-old girl living in Bhopal, India? Ordinarily a happy and balanced child, she is given to manifestations of grief and tears, as though on the upsurge of some inner impulse. She tells of a past which has absolutely no relationship to her family or environment, describes London scenes, scenes of a city she has never visited, and maintains that she is a London doctor killed in a car crash at the age of twenty-two.

The strange case came to the notice of Professor Hemendra Banerjee, a scientist working at Rajasthan University, Jaipur. She was, says Vishala, Dr. Jaimini Watt, the daughter of a judge and attached to a London hospital. On the day of the accident that ended her life, she maintains, her father had left for Africa. She was in love with a man called Abraham, worked with a Dr. Walker, and had a friend named Sairiya.

Vishala often talks of returning "home"—to London. If all the facts she adduces can be checked, and Professor Banerjee is working hard to do so, her conviction could not be written off as neurosis or the workings of an overactive imagination.

An even more remarkable case is that of eleven-year-old

Mohini. She was sitting quietly with her family in the Punjab a few years ago (1966) when the subject of New York cropped up fortuitously. She at once regaled her astonished parents with detailed descriptions of the streets and sights and buildings.

Having recovered from their surprise, they decided it was a case of a child anxious to show off and using a young and fertile imagination. But Mohini went on to claim that she had lived in New York a hundred years ago. She had been brought up there by an uncle. She described the area in which she lived, the cobble-stoned streets, the game she played at Christmas, and even the family name. She had, she said, been drowned at the age of eighteen.

Professor Banerjee flew to New York to investigate. He traced the family (the descendants of the family described by Mohini) in the very spot she had claimed. Comparing the details of her conversations with him with the facts uncovered by his personal investigations, he found no fewer than ninety-four points of factual similarity.

In 1935 a nine-year-old girl, Shanti Devi, who was born in Delhi, began to worry her parents because of her strange behavior. She often mentioned a place called Muttra where she claimed to have lived in a former life. She had been married, she said, and was the mother of three children, describing their names and distinctive physical features. Her name had been Ludgi.

One day a knock came on the door of the Devi household and Shanti Devi rushed to open it. But instead of returning instantly to tell her parents who the caller was, or inviting him in, she stayed at the door conversing for so long that her mother went to investigate. She found the caller and her daughter in animated conversation. Excitedly, Shanti told her mother: "He's a cousin of my husband!"

The worried mother sent her daughter out of earshot and talked to the caller. He came from Muttra, he had a cousin living there, a cousin who had married a woman who had died in child-birth. Her name had been Ludgi.

Shanti was allowed to visit the scene of her "memories." Without guidance she found the home without difficulty, claimed to recognize different relatives, and spoke the Muttra dialect without having learned it. The "husband," not surprisingly, was not so happy about these claims, since if accepted at face value,

Shanti's story meant that his children had a mother who was younger than they were.

Shanti was subjected to some exacting tests. She was blind-folded, put into a carriage, and told to direct the driver to her old "home." This she did, describing on the way the streets, turnings, and buildings although she had never visited the town before. The "husband" solved the problem by suggesting that as the All-High had decreed that Ludgi should die and re-emerge as Shanti Devi, Shanti should accept his dispensation, live her new life, and not attempt to be two people at once.

A somewhat similar case, which occurred in the same year, was that of Iris Farczady, fifteen-year-old daughter of a Budapest engineer who astonished her parents by speaking a new language while she was ill with influenza. Puzzled and dismayed, they sent for a linguist, who identified her speech as fluent Spanish.

From that day Iris called her mother *señora*, spoke Spanish, sang Spanish songs, prepared Spanish dishes, and described scenes in her "native" Madrid. She told her parents—in Spanish—"I am Señora Lucia de Salvio." She asserted she had been married to a working man living in Madrid, and had died within a few days of her wedding. In actuality, she had never been out of Hungary.

It is easier to suspect reincarnation when there is a duplication of personality. So elusive is personality that the very arguments Dr. Julian Huxley once used against the fundamental idea of reincarnation could be used to support it. Dr. Huxley was satisfied that reincarnation was impossible. The combination of genes and chromosomes which he thought constituted personality run into so many countless billions that the odds against a personality being duplicated are astronomical—or, as he believed, impossible.

There is substance in Dr. Huxley's contention, and he is mathematically correct in his assessment of the possibility of a personality being duplicated. Twins often look similar, and have a number of personality traits in common, but all who have had close acquaintance with twins know that they are by no means identical and after a short familiarity become easily distinguishable. There are more than 3.42 billion people in the world and no two individuals are alike. Meet any one of them once, and even years afterward you would recognize him anywhere.

A mystery attaches to the famous "Mona Lisa," and the story of a possible reincarnation came to light following its sensational theft from the Louvre in Paris in 1911. It can only be understood within the context of the circumstances of the theft itself.

On the morning of August 22, 1911, Sergeant Poupardin was patrolling the Gallery of Apollo when he noticed that the "Mona Lisa" was missing from its place. Within minutes two hundred and fifty guards were searching frantically through the ancient palace that houses France's priceless art collection. At last, on a shelf in a little-used stairway, they discovered the frame and its glass cover. The picture itself was nowhere to be found.

There was, of course, a national outcry. The security precautions had been considered inviolable. How could the framed picture, weighing more than a hundred pounds, have been taken down under the noses of the numerous guards and the heavy sheet of walnut, four and one-half feet square, on which the actual portrait was painted, smuggled out of the building? It was not an easy thing to conceal. And what could be the possible motive for the theft? A picture known throughout the world could surely not be sold to anyone. Ever since Leonardo da Vinci had painted it (it had taken him four years to complete and music had been played at every sitting so that the elusive, rapt expression could be recaptured), the painting had been the best-known portrait in the world.

Alphonse Bertillon, famous for his now discredited "anthropometric" system of classifying the physical features of criminals, was called in. He pointed out, with heavy sarcasm, that the knob of the staircase door was missing, that the doorway led to an open courtyard leading, in turn, to the street. Jean Nicausse, the Sherlock Holmes of France, and police chief Hamaud of the Sûreté, reminded Bertillon that his wonderful system included the records of seven hundred thousand *right* thumbprints. Unfortunately, the thief had left the imprint of the other thumb.

The staff members were grilled. Various false trails were followed. The picture was variously reported to be in most of the world's capitals. There were theories by the dozen, including the hoary old "mad art collector who doesn't mind what he buys because nobody else will see it" legend. Nobody got anywhere. The hue and cry at last died down and the *cause célèbre* was forgotten.

In November, 1913, Alfredo Geri, an art dealer in Florence, received a letter from an unknown correspondent signing himself

Vincenzo Leonard—whose real name later proved to be Perrugia —offering to sell him the original "Mona Lisa" or, to give it its official title, "La Gioconda."

Obviously, said Geri, as he showed the letter to his friend Giovanni Poggi, curator of the Uffizi Gallery in Florence, the man was a crank. Even before the theft there had been hundreds of fakes in circulation, and this seemed clearly to be one of them. In any case, nobody but a lunatic would dream of offering so famous a painting in this way. Nevertheless, on his friend's advice, he replied, and on December 10 a haggard young man entered Geri's shop and announced that the painting was at his hotel, and that he wanted fifty thousand francs for it.

Together with his friend Poggi, the art dealer went to the hotel and watched as "Mr. Leonard" unwrapped the painting, weeping as he did so. He kissed the painting tenderly and then, almost distraught, said, "Take it—I can't starve any more!"

Poggi produced his powerful magnifying glass, and a sheaf of enlarged photographs showing every feature of the original. It took only a minute, and an examination of the walnut panel, for him to realize, that, incredibly, this *was* the genuine painting from the Louvre.

Perrugia was arrested, and the painting later borne in triumph to the Uffizi Gallery, where it had hung in honor centuries before. Crowds stormed the gallery to view it, and diplomatic relations between France and Italy were nearly ruptured because of France's sneaking suspicion that Italy might claim the painting as its own and refuse to return it. At last, with rejoicing and military pomp, it was restored to its rightful place in the Louvre.

The story that emerged at Perrugia's trial was as astonishing as the theft.

He had been a frequent visitor to the Louvre, and always the "Mona Lisa" had held a compelling attraction for him. In his own words, he had fallen in love with the painting. One day, while sitting in a Paris café, he was amazed to see the living replica of the painting sitting near him. The resemblance was so incredible that he caught his breath. She was a living reincarnation, the embodiment of the original in coloring and expression.

The girl was with an apache type. Then, as Perrugia watched, the warm, enigmatic expression that marked her as the living embodiment of the painting changed suddenly to consternation, then anger, then fear. She rose from the table, tried to leave, but as she did so her companion sprang after her and stabbed her with a knife. In the general melee the assailant fled, and Perrugia dashed to her aid. He tended her wound, then, picking her up bodily, carried her to his home. Spectators wondered what he could be talking about as he murmured, "Mona Lisa, Mona Lisa. . . ."

Perrugia was convinced that she was the Mona Lisa reincarnated, and that destiny had brought them together. An exchange of love letters followed. They fell desperately in love and when she died, not long after, Perrugia simply lived for the time he could spend looking at the picture. The desire to possess it became an obsession with him. He memorized the layout of the Louvre, discovered an easy outlet to the street, and chose his moment.

The trial was held in France, and some of the jurists wept openly as the story unfolded. Perrugia genuinely believed that the painting was rightfully his and photographs of his dead love—Mathilde—confirmed the uncanny likeness. He was given a light sentence of three hundred and eighty days' imprisonment, which was equivalent to immediate release because he had been in custody for nearly a year. But his life meant nothing to him after that.

"Without Mathilde or her picture I have nothing to live for," he told a friend.

He disappeared in 1916 and has never been heard of since.

☐ 11. The World of Witches

ONE of the strangest phenomena of the postwar world during the last quarter of a century has been the increase in interest in the "craft" of magic or witchcraft.

Nobody can say for certain exactly how many witches there are but reliable estimates suggest that there are nearly five hundred "covens" of witches in Britain alone and, as there are thirteen witches to a coven this would put the number at over six thousand.

What is witchcraft?

It is a cult worship of a horned god representing fertility and rebirth. The male priest, in the role of the horned god, presides at Halloween and the February Eve Sabbats while the priestess, acting as the moon goddess, conducts the May and August Eve Sabbats (or Sabbaths as they are sometimes called).

It is certain that the dates on which they hold their principal ceremonies predate Christianity. As the latter religion survived its own persecutions, it persecuted other sects and religions with a ferocity and theological sophistry that marks a black chapter in history.

Witchcraft, which incorporated the old pagan fertility cults, was singled out for special persecution because of its secrecy, but it also provided a handy excuse for the unleashing of the terror of the Inquisition by papal bull. For more than four centuries hundreds of thousands of people were arrested, tortured until they either died under the atrocious ill-treatment or "confessed" in delirium or desperation, and so died subsequently at the stake because their endurance and insistence on truth had finally been broken. Interestingly, the leaders of the Reformation shared the Catholic horror of witches and were equally as brutal in their treatment of suspects.

Although in most European countries vast numbers of people were killed, maimed, terrorized, and robbed who were not witches and had absolutely no interest in or knowledge of witchcraft, many of those who actually practiced the cult that had been handed down to them by word of mouth and by ritualistic example for generations also perished. But ideas and beliefs are notoriously the most difficult things to exterminate, and the cult of witchcraft, with numerous variations, has survived into the nuclear age.

The modern witch does not hobble back to her leaf-entwined cottage in the heart of the dark forest, trailing her besom behind her; she is more likely to drive home to a suburb and sit down to watch television. In Britain today the witches include priests, doctors, civil servants, film workers, actresses, and academics of all types.

Why are they drawn to it?

For some people, it is a means of protest against and escape from the monotony of urban and industrial life; for others, it constitutes a chance to work off sexual repressions within the secrecy of gathering which, in many ceremonies, involves completely nude participants and comprises six males and six females presided over by a male or female priest. For a few isolated individuals, witchcraft seems to be a bizarre and more esoteric edition of Rotary convocations, a means of meeting people in different walks of life under circumstances a little more interesting than eating lamb chops and frozen peas and listening to a Rotarian lecture in some provincial restaurant.

A small nucleus is genuinely interested in, and actively engaged in, the traditional magic of witchcraft—its historic stock-in-trade of herbal medicine, the mystical treatment of certain ailments, such as wart charming (one doctor told me that charming away warts certainly worked, but for the life of him he didn't know why), and its laying on and lifting of curses.

Dr. Gerald Gardner, who did more than any man in the twentieth century to re-establish witchcraft as a flourishing institution, really believed that "magic" could work. He founded and ran the Witchcraft Museum, which is still in existence in the Isle of Man, housed, appropriately enough, in an old mill used by generations of witches.

When I first met Gardner, he already looked like the embodiment of the traditional witch with his flowing white hair and piercing eyes. Gardner came from a comfortable, conventional, middle-class family in Lancashire. His father was in the timber business and well respected as a local citizen and magistrate, while his mother had literary tastes. As is the case with so many people who are subsequently drawn to mysticism in one or more of its branches, Gardner was plagued by poor health early in life. He was always a martyr to asthma, a disease that some neurologists have described as a "strangled cry for help"—an indication of emotional imbalance and inner psychological conflict.

Whatever the merits of their theories, Gardner was drawn to a study of magic and witchcraft through an initial interest in anthropology, which itself was the outcome of his asthma, because his parents took him everywhere in search of a cure for the ailment. From the Canary Islands he went to Africa, Ceylon, Singapore, and Borneo, all places in which superstition, esoteric religion, magic, and witchcraft are deeply rooted.

He did his early traveling under somewhat strange auspices; his companion-nurse was a hot-blooded Irish girl whose reckless, erratic, and erotic behavior made a lasting, if temporarily disturbing, impression upon his mind.

He became a rubber planter in Borneo and Malaya and studied comparative religions. Although lacking in any formal education, he sought out anyone who could throw light on the subjects that interested him. In Malaya he became interested in the legends attached to the *kris,* a Malay weapon which is said to kill anyone to whom it is pointed with magical intent. Gardner wrote a learned and interesting treatise on such weapons. He became a believer in the existence of spirits and in reincarnation, and on a visit to England just before World War II he met members of a Hampshire coven of witches. Their ceremonies seemed to him entirely familiar; in fact, he had the distinct feeling that he had always been a witch, and that some of the men and women in the coven had been part of his life for a long time.

Thereafter, he became a confirmed and practicing witch. He was also a nudist, during a period when nakedness as a cult was sufficiently unusual to be kept a secret, when a nude body was scarcely ever portrayed with any realism in a book illustration, let alone in films or upon the stage.

Gardner's nudism harmonized quite easily with his witchcraft, since so many of the ceremonies demand complete nakedness in the male and female participants. Until the end of his days, even when he was living and running his own coven from his Witchcraft Museum in the Isle of Man, Gardner attended a coven that met in a nudist camp near St. Albans.

It could be said that Dr. Gerald Gardner did for witchcraft in Britain what the late Aleister Crowley or the Rev. Montagu Somers did for magic and demonology—he revived interest in it, brought a certain discipline to many of its theories and contrived quite a few variations of his own.

Whatever else may be said of Gardner, he was not a dull man.

"Is witchcraft a good or an evil thing?" I asked him.

"Personally, I think witches and witchcraft are good, but everything can be good or evil, as you use it," was his answer.

"Have you practiced witchcraft and magic yourself?"

"I must have been at more than three hundred witchcraft ceremonies. More than half were simply religious ceremonies, where coven business was also discussed, and there was a feast and a dance. At about a quarter, instruction was given and possibly 'little magics' worked—not much more than asking the gods to grant a wish, or dancing out a rite. At less than a quarter I have actively helped in performing magic to influence events. . . ."

"But isn't witchcraft associated in most people's minds with paying off scores secretly and malevolently—putting curses on people and that sort of thing?"

"As I say, witchcraft can be used for good or evil. . . ."

The late Professor Margaret Murray, a tiny, white-haired woman who had both studied and practiced witchcraft, and was an explorer, anthropologist, and author of a controversial book, wrote an introduction to Gardner's *Witchcraft Today*. When I invited her and Dr. Gardner to take part in a television program on witchcraft, both accepted with alacrity.

I remember Dr. Murray's smiling expression when she told an interviewer that "some people join witchcraft because they just like dancing around in the nude"—and shot a half-humorous but highly perceptive glance at Dr. Gardner as she spoke. Dr. Murray once claimed that she knew a witch—a farmer's wife in Guernsey —who "could kill a pig by just looking at it." Similarly, she advised against being too facetious about sticking pins into wax images; the technique, she asserted, gave the witch something upon which to concentrate malevolent thoughts.

Is witchcraft to some degree, then, a matter of projecting thoughts, whether good or evil, in some manner similar to or involving what we call telepathy—mind-to-mind communication? Personally, I would not like to encourage this idea because it could give free rein to the superstitions and fears that bedevil the lives of otherwise normal people, and actually touch off certain types of psychotic or paranoid behavior. Extremities of fear have led in the past to extremities of cruelty, and a dark, dismal atmosphere of hate and counter-hate.

But there are many grades of witchcraft and the dividing line between white and black magic is not easily drawn. If we cannot decide the *effectiveness* of the magic (Aleister Crowley liked to call it "magick") practiced by members of covens, we can at least measure their intentions. Some magical ceremonies are enacted by witches to encompass good, to bring about a better state of health in somebody, to insure that they will find the love they seek, or enjoy good fortune; but there are many ceremonies performed with the sole purpose of producing evil, to bring about the death or illness of some person.

Can the malevolent impulses of certain witches be concentrated and projected to achieve particular results? Gardner believed this was entirely possible. Austin Osman Spare, the artist who was a mystic and hermit, who practiced a magic of his own and claimed to be a witch, agreed with Gardner.

In the course of an interview I recorded with Spare for a BBC program devoted to unusual beliefs, he once remarked, quite calmly, "I could kill a man with a curse." As we made the recording I wondered—having known Spare for nearly a quarter of a century—whether he had ever attempted to do so. I did not ask him. The remark, I remember, attracted to the BBC an anonymous letter accusing Spare of having been an associate of Aleister Crowley. This he vehemently denied.

Gardner claims in *Witchcraft Today* that "witches are taught and believe that a power resides within their bodies which they can release in various ways—the simplest being dancing around in a circle, singing or shouting, to induce a frenzy; this power they believe exudes from their bodies, clothes impeding its release. . . ."

Witchcraft being a fertility cult, it is not surprising that nakedness and the sexual instinct should figure prominently in its ceremonies. Sexual symbolism and, indeed, secret or open indulgence, have long been inherent features of many religious cults and in pre-Christian times were common enough. Yet Gardner may well have been right. At first it sounds like an alibi to assert that witchcraft ceremonies require the complete nakedness of their participants; but the claim that nakedness is essential to the generation of some type of force—a mental power which can be concentrated and projected—is not so inherently unlikely.

Is some type of telepathic force generated? Can a number of telepathic signals—if generated at the same time by a group of people thinking the same thoughts—thereby acquire extra force and potency, sufficient to travel over vast distances and affect the people concerned?

To admit that there may be "something in it" is not to be lost in a miasma of fear and superstition. It is simply to admit the *possibility* that in the mounting tension, frenzy, excitement, and visual eroticism of a secret witchcraft ceremony some force may be generated that in certain circumstances may achieve its desired effect.

It is common enough for human beings to discover, either by chance or by haphazard experiment, truths about forces they can use but do not fully understand. The ancients—the Egyptians especially—used hypnotism habitually, just as the Chinese, thousands of years ago, knew about electricity and used it without recognizing its nature or own presence; a piece of amber was used in the spinning wheel to make the silk thread stiff because it rubbed against the amber and produced static electricity.

The picture Margaret Murray and Gerald Gardner paint of witchcraft is, in my opinion, an oversimplification. The followers of all cults, including religions of all kinds, insist that their dogmas are the only fundamental and incontrovertible truths. While accepting the fact that the Christian church persecuted followers of rival religions, including witchcraft; while realizing that the vast majority of the victims were tortured until, in their agony, they "confessed" to anything—we need not assume that all historical "witches" were likeable people or that all modern witches wish merely to compound herbal remedies or pay noisy and drafty obeisance to the moon goddess.

Witchcraft does attract a good many psychotics. Psychosis may merely harm or limit the person concerned, but its rationalization into a dogmatic belief may stimulate psychotic behavior in others. The cruelty, amorality, and total lack of scruple that characterized Aleister Crowley have "inspired"—if one may use such a word in this context—a great many people.

It is a quarter of a century since, on the evening of St. Valentine's Day, the dead and mutilated body of Charles Walton was found under an oak tree not far from the village of Lower Quinton in Warwickshire. A pitchfork had been driven through his body. The whole thing bore the marks of a murder by witchcraft. Scotland Yard did, in fact, consult Professor Murray on the background of the witchcraft cult, in an attempt to assess the motives of the murderer and get a clue to his (or her) identity. But the murder of this seventy-four-year-old hedge-trimmer remains unsolved to this day.

Anybody can describe himself as a witch, formulate his own ceremonies, confer his own "degrees," and either use or adapt old ceremonies (of which there are a great number) to suit himself. The elements, however, remain—a sense of secrecy, a feeling of power, a real or imagined sense of wickedness, a catharsis of the emotions.

British witches rejoice in fanciful titles. Alex Sanders is described as "King of the Witches." Nickie Wilson, who inherited Gerald Gardner's Witches' Mill at Castletown, Isle of Man, enjoys the title of "Queen of the Witches." Sybil Leek, notable for her flowing cloak and the jackdaw which perches unprotestingly on her shoulders, has been described by others as "The High Priestess of Witchcraft."

Sanders states that he learned witchcraft at the age of seven, from his grandmother, who was certainly not a model of dignified old age. Mrs. Wilson, who is married to an ex-R.A.F. flight-lieutenant, claims to have been a witch most of her life and that both sides of her family "had the power."

The museum she inherited houses a collection that took Dr. Gardner more than forty years to amass. There are a number of objects belonging to a witch who died in 1951, a magician's study fully laid out, and a witch's cottage. The witch's objects include herbs required for charms and medicines (the herbs and plants had to be cut at the time when the moon or the planets were in a particular part of the zodiac, or under the right astrological aspects); a medieval magical ring belonging to the Earls of Lonsdale; large numbers of objects and amulets intended as a protection against the evil eye; relics of the notorious Matthew Hopkins, Her Majesty's Witchfinder General under Queen Elizabeth I; and instruments of torture used on witches.

There is mystery and perhaps, for some, a certain sinister glamor about many of the exhibits: the broomsticks on which witches of old are believed to have been borne aloft on their malevolent missions, the crystals in which they read the future, a black concave mirror consecrated at full moon in accordance with an ancient formula, a complete collection of the secret manuscripts of Aleister Crowley's magical fraternity—The Order of the Golden Dawn, the rubric used at his funeral, which was denounced as being a "Black Mass," books on magic and witchcraft, and instruments for magical killing, including the Australian "pointing bone" and the Malayan *kris,* used for the same purpose. On the more novel side, there is a modern instrument alleged to enable one to see the human "aura" and a charm devised in 1954 in Naples, to secure the acquittal of a guilty man during a trial.

The overall impression is of something unhealthy, depressing, and sadomasochistic. There is no standardized witchcraft ceremony in general use, although the basic ceremonies run much to a pattern and are often based on traditional observances.

The initiation of a witch is a complicated and sometimes uncomfortable ritual. The candidate, blindfolded and naked, is conducted to a witch's circle, at the edge of which he is challenged as to his determination to be initiated.

The naked coven members dance around him, chanting as they go; his hands are bound behind his back, and a high priestess presses the point of a sword against his breast in token challenge of his courage. She "draws" a circle with her witch's knife (athame) and then, with a series of kisses that start at his feet and end at his mouth, presses the whole length of her naked body against him.

The candidate is then forced to submit to a ritual scourging, a whipping of the buttocks—a common enough feature of initiation into many ancient and modern cults—an anointing, and an explanation of various tools such as the wand, sword, and pentacle. These activities are followed by a "feast" but they are not standardized. Those running covens have a natural tendency to modify or exaggerate the basic ceremony to suit themselves. But in many ceremonies—particularly the third degree—fully consummated sexual relations play a part.

It is easy to see why, especially in Britain and America, the cult of witchcraft is increasing. To young people it suggests what is called, rather absurdly, permissiveness (absurdly, because the young do not seek permission for their indulgences) with a dash of mysticism. Witchcraft is the opposite of commercial television, Main Street, the laundromat, the football field, the supermarket, and the organized social functions of urban boredom. It is a refuge from regimentation, a flight from logic, an escape from mundane civil obligations.

But what about magic? What is "black magic," "gray magic," or "white magic"? Who applies the color chart, and by what criteria? The rituals and observances often get mixed up. They vary from country to country, and even in a particular country the dividing line between witchcraft, magic, and sorcery cannot easily be drawn.

Broadly speaking, however, white magic is concerned with doing good; such ceremonies could include long rituals, invocations to the gods or spirits, and either real or simulated blood sacrifices. To bring rain, as a relief from drought, would come within this category.

Gray magic is a term applied to magical ceremonies or acts used for the purpose of personal advancement and pleasures, such as the compounding of love charms or the furtherance of business. Black magic, as its name implies, has a dark and sinister purpose; it is intended to do harm, and those who practice it believe that it does.

It is said that a coven of witches formed a "cone of power" in a long and elaborate ceremony at the time of the Armada and that, as a result of their magic, a storm blew up that brought disaster to the Spanish invaders. The claim has also been made that British witches concentrated on bringing about the fall of Hitler. If this is so, it is scarcely an advertisement for a witch's magic; Hitler survived numerous plots and assassination attempts, and continued to bring suffering and death to millions of people for many miserable years.

Witchcraft is rampant throughout the world. It has always had a hold upon the African peoples, and a few years ago a survey among *literate* adults in Ghana showed that 80 percent believed that a pregnant woman should be on guard against evil influences and 75 percent believed that witchcraft is often used because of envy of the success of others. More than half those questioned on the subject believed that witchcraft could cause illnesses that doctors and hospitals would be powerless to cure.

But it is not merely in African countries, or places where ancient folklore and superstition have not been eroded by the winds of psychology and materialism, that witchcraft flourishes. It has a considerable following in the United States. In their desire to repudiate by word and deed every convention and restriction of a society they consider decadent, many young Americans have turned to the mystical nihilism of black magic and witchcraft.

The shocking tragedy in the luxurious mansion in Bel-Air, California, on August 9, 1969, when five people, including the lovely young actress Sharon Tate, were found murdered, is a reminder of the extremes to which an obsession with evil rituals can lead. For there was every evidence that the horrible sequence of events represented a ritual killing. In that house of carnage the pregnant twenty-six-year-old star—nude except for a bikini—was hanging by a rope from a beam in the ceiling. Outside was the body of Abigail Folger, a twenty-six-year-old heiress. Sharon Tate's former fiancé, his body black-hooded, was hanging on the other end of the rope that strangled her.

In New York, as in many other American cities, the impedimenta of witchcraft ceremonies are much in demand, the stock of some shops and stalls including such unlikely items as graveyard dust and bats' blood. Anthony Pacetta, the former Commissioner of Markets for the city, caused quite a few curses to be invoked against him by his efforts to prevent the sale of such stuff to people who practice voodoo. There are do-it-yourself cursing outfits and "hexing" candles whose use, the buyers believe, will carry their barbed messages of hate to their intended victims. It is improbable that the graveyard dust comes from graveyards, or that the dried bats' blood is correctly described. But the intent and purpose are there, just the same.

Witchcraft is not the monopoly of any special ethnic group in America. But it was perhaps inevitable, with the enormous intake of African slaves, that they brought with them various forms of fetishism, sorcery, and magic, and these have evolved into a wide variety of bizarre cults. These, in turn, have been followed, copied, or modified by succeeding generations and by other groups.

Throughout Europe, including the Iron Curtain countries, belief in magic and witchcraft is still widespread. In Italy it permeates all classes, and the belief in the darker forms of superstition often has horrifying results.

A few years ago a Sicilian peasant was sentenced to fifteen years' imprisonment by an Agrigento court for murdering his wife by a cruel and protracted process, tearing her face with fingernails, scissors, and a knife—in an effort, he claimed, to release the evil spirits by which she was possessed. He was a modern example of the truth made evident by the persecution of the Middle Ages—that superstition breeds fear and fear breeds cruelty.

It came as a surprise to many people, who had assumed that Communist indoctrination must eradicate superstition, to learn, in May, 1969, that some gypsies in Hungary had tried to burn an old woman at the stake because they believed her to be a witch. A member of their tribe had been knocked off her bicycle by a large black dog. The dog took to its heels, disappeared around a corner, and, a few seconds later, an old woman came around the same corner, carrying a stick.

The gypsies decided she was a witch who had turned herself into a dog. Late that night they seized the old woman in her home, bound and gagged her, and tried to burn her at the stake. If her son and some friends had not spotted the flames and reached her in time, she would certainly have died; even so, she was very seriously burned. The six gypsies were tried by a court at Szeged and sentenced to five years' imprisonment each, a rather mild sentence considering the cruel and cowardly offense.

A few weeks afterward, another witchcraft trial was held in the same town. A whole family tried to kill old Mrs. Csupics, a fellow villager, and burn her house down, because they suspected her of casting spells on men and animals, and of transforming herself into a cat, which—according to the traditional superstitions still rife in the country district of Asotthalma—is the usual way witches go about their evil work.

194

Mrs. Hebok, one of the accused, told the court that she became convinced Mrs. Csupics was a witch after her brother, who was courting the old woman's granddaughter, was pushed off his bicycle by a big white cat. This happened a second time to the youth, Janos Halacz. When the family consulted a local seer, he attempted to break the spell by touching the lad with tobacco and a waistband—both supposed to have anti-witch properties—and advising the family to keep watch at the spot to see what happened when the lad rode by on his bicycle.

Keeping vigil, the family asserted that, as the youth rode by, a big white cat with a human face appeared out of the earth and shoved him off his bicycle. Finally convinced that poor old Mrs. Csupics had put a spell on the lad, they visited her home. She told the court of the terror of working in a small village beset with such superstitious fear—how the most harmless, fortuitous happening would be interpreted as evidence of witchcraft; how she had feared attack from children; how people came to her home threatening to burn it down with her inside it; how she had slipped in terror from her home, in a flimsy nightdress, and sought refuge in the pigsty. She decided to leave the village, with her husband, for good.

In 1966 Italian police were called to the tiny village of Melito, Irpino, in Southern Italy, to protect a girl of nine who was accused by her neighbors of being a witch. The stories about her gained circulation when Nicolina Mustone went to stay with her aunt and uncle in their three-room cottage. Hens stopped laying, rabbits started killing each other, water turned bad, jars in the house seemed to be pushed off the mantelpiece by an unseen hand, and a table overturned unaccountably.

When Nicolina went home, the troubles stopped. But the moment she returned to her uncle and aunt the disturbances resumed. Poor Nicolina was chased out of fields by farmers with pitchforks, and children threw stones at her. In this case there seems merely to have been a poltergeist in the house. For, after the bishop of the area had blessed Nicolina, a local seer sealed the house at the doors and windows and commanded the "spirit" to depart. It was taken for granted that the spirit, if there was one, would not require either windows or doors for the purposes of egress. When the house was reopened, all the furniture had been disarranged.

Whatever the causes of the disturbances in that house, the fact remains that local belief in witchcraft was strong enough to put the young girl's life in danger.

A few years ago a prison sentence was passed on a young man in Germany for the attempted murder by burning of a "witch," Elisabeth Hahn, aged sixty-four. He had set fire to her cottage in the village of Mailach in Hesse. All her property was totally destroyed, but she was lucky enough to escape—to meet a natural death shortly afterward.

What is so disturbing about this particular trial—one of many similar trials in Germany—is the evidence it provides of the extent and intensity of belief in witchcraft, a proof of paranoia that can be contagious and can jeopardize the lives of innocent people. Poor Elisabeth Hahn was ostracized and hated by her neighbors. Villagers placed their garden forks in front of their cottages with the prongs turned outward to keep spells at bay, and they paid a local "wizard" to counteract the spells Elisabeth Hahn was supposed to be concocting.

It was said at the trial that thousands of people throughout Germany still believe in witchcraft, and that many hundreds of so-called witch doctors (or de-witchers) made a lucrative living by protecting the fearful against the witches' spells.

In Britain, there has been ample evidence of black magic rites going far beyond gallivanting around bonfires and nude dancing. Many years ago James Gardner, owner of the deep caves at Eastrey, Kent, had the fright of his life when he found some candles guttering on a rough-hewn altar in a natural "chapel" at the end of a great labyrinth of tunnels.

The discovery was made at 6 A.M. and it was thought that the low, guttering candles must have been lighted at about 2 A.M. Nobody but Mr. Gardner had the key to the entrance and, although he made a thorough search of the tunnels, he found nobody. Two months previously he had come upon a crude stone statue and an urn on the altar. The general disposition of these objects lent color to the assumption that a black magic ceremony had been held there.

Shocking evidence that some black magicians will go to any lengths to indulge their weird and perverted tastes was provided in 1963. A black mass was believed to have been held in the lonely ruins of a tenth-century church—St. Mary's, Clophill, Bedfordshire. One Sunday it was discovered that the bones of a woman —Jenny Humberstone, who died in 1770—had been removed from her tomb in the churchyard and laid out in symbolic fashion around an improvised iron stake near the southwest door. The skull was impaled on the spike. Both these things pointed to a black magic ceremony. The altar had been cleared of dust and rubble. A cock's feathers were found nearby—another indication of a magical ceremony, in which the sacrifice of a cock frequently figures.

The ruined church stands on top of a hill, so that the celebrants would have been in a good strategic position to observe the approach of strangers. There must have been several of them for, after trying to violate the graves of six women buried in the churchyard, they managed to prise open a stone cover weighing five hundredweight. Since four policemen were unable to lift it, they believed it took at least six strong men to move it. It must have been a macabre scene: the ruined church, illumined by the full moon; the hooded figures enacting their hideous and secret ritual; a member skilled in the black arts incising and coloring in red paint a strange geometric rounded cross on the wall.

An interesting feature was the fact that many of the cabalistic figures painted on the walls of the church were found to be of different periods, indicating that earlier ceremonies of a similar kind must have been held there.

A crude death charm was found five years ago on the land Queen Elizabeth II owns at Sandringham. Black magic death symbols, including a naked female effigy, were found nailed to the wall of a ruined church at Babingley, Norfolk. They included also a sheep's heart pierced with thorns and the stub of a black candle. The six-inch nude effigy had a thorn stuck through its heart and was nailed to the wall of the old bell tower. Similar symbols have been found in a castle at Castle Rising and in a ruined church at Bawsey, less than ten miles from Sandringham.

Behind these unseemly disturbances there is some type of organized movement. Great care is taken to guarantee the absolute secrecy of the arrangements, and if disturbed in their activities, the culprits offer fierce resistance.

A few years ago Mr. Walter Binsted, bell-ringer at the nine-hundred-year-old country church of St. Mary the Virgin at West Ham, near Pevensey, Sussex, saw four men arrive. Later he entered the church to switch on the lights for the visitors, only to observe that they had lit four candles from the altar and placed them on the floor to form a cross. They were standing there while their leader chanted in some strange tongue. Mr. Binsted quickly sought out the vicar and his churchwarden. They hurried to the scene only to meet stiff resistance from the intruders, who broke free and got away in their car. Police who searched the church discovered that the altar cross had been spat upon.

When St. Giles Church in Camberwell, London, was desecrated by black-magic followers who broke in through the vestry window, Dr. Mervyn Stockwood, the Bishop of Southwark, conducted a service of rededication. The intruders had forced aside two-inch iron bars protecting the church safe, burst the locks, and removed holy water and consecrated bread.

One rector took the unusual course of cursing those who desecrated his churchyard. He was the Rev. Ernest Streete of Bramber, West Sussex, who, to the astonishment of his parishioners stretched out his arms over the altar and declared:

> I pronounce a curse on those who touch God's acre in this churchyard. May their days be of anguish and sorrow and may God have mercy on their souls.

The wording of the curse was his own, for the Anglican prayer book contains no curses for any occasions.

However unorthodox the rector's reaction, his anger and revulsion were easily understood. A stone cross had been torn from a grave and propped against the front door of the church, heads were smashed off stone angels, and a black mass sign marred the church's porch.

What is called the black mass is a bowdlerized version of Communion or Mass—a mixture of profanity and obscenity and a repudiation of the morals and ethics implied in Christianity. Its main appeal to the perverted is that it defies beliefs which they previously held or were taught to honor. The ceremony would have little significance to anyone unfamiliar with Christian teachings.

The menace of black magic has no relationship to the alleged effectiveness of the "magic" itself. Its effect upon those who practice it must inevitably be baneful and dangerous. Its keynote is

198

hate and destruction. It induces a fanaticism and obsession that can take a fatal hold upon the imagination, unbalancing a normal mind and pushing toward paranoia those who have a latent predisposition to it.

There is a good deal of interest in black magic in British universities. In fact, a few years ago a theology professor denounced a plan to form a black magic group in Exeter University. In August, 1969, Jacqueline Batters, aged eighteen, of Castle Bromwich, Birmingham, gained a General Certificate of Education "O-level" certificate for a thesis on witchcraft and black magic. But this was done merely as a piece of social anthropology, an exercise in research, and the personal assessment of collated facts; in short, it was useful intellectual exercise.

The growth of interest in witchcraft and black magic (I am not equating the two and have no wish to offend respectable witches) is, as I said, indicative of the boredom inherent in much suburban and urban life, an index of the decline in religion and a symptom of the "try-anything-once" syndrome of people searching for kicks. To the latter one might say, "If you dabble in black magic for kicks you may find the kicks harder and more dangerous than you ever imagined."

☐ 12. From Other Worlds?

IN 1961 I was having a pleasant, leisurely dinner with an officer of the Middle East Command in the Officers' Club on the outskirts of Tripoli. I should explain that it was in no sense like the traditional officers' club. It was a cross between a luxury hotel and a pleasure resort—a handsomely spaced complex of buildings facing the Mediterranean, the dining room in which we sat being decorated in a completely contemporary style. Outside there were terrace gardens, leading down to the bedrooms which faced the sea.

It was about 11 P.M. when I asked the major to come to my room to look at some papers. We went out on to the terrace and, as we walked down some shallow steps, I stopped in my tracks. It was almost pitch dark. The Mediterranean sky was as black as a blackboard. My eyes were directed toward a red glow in the sky.

"The moon looks very odd," I said. "I've never seen it look like that."

"It isn't the moon," he said laconically.

"Then what on earth *is* it?" I said. Then I added excitedly, "But it's moving—and moving steadily, at an even speed."

We peered intently at the sky. At a distance of approximately a mile, at a height of a thousand feet, was what I had taken at first glance, to be a round, red, luminous outline. Closer observation showed it to be more like some flat, saucerlike object, glowing red yet decidedly brighter and almost orange in color toward the base. Over it was a hazy superstructure, a vague outline of luminous haze such as might be made by smoke trapping a light from beneath. But this last observation was not accurate; the indeterminate shape kept its outline. It did not dissipate like cigar smoke catching the light.

"I suppose you notice," I said, "that it is traveling at an even speed."

"Yes," he said thoughtfully, "it is. And it's keeping the same height."

"It's manned all right. But what *is* it? It isn't an airplane. It isn't a helicopter. It's not a balloon."

Our excitement grew as, keeping the same speed and height, it came nearer to the shores of Libya. I was thankful that I had slung over my shoulder a sturdy and mechanically dependable tape recorder that I had bought in Aden. Quickly I plugged the microphone in and recorded what we were watching, for I know how fallible memory can be. I was also glad that I had a witness to this strange affair. To admit to any sighting of this kind is an invitation to people to speculate about your mental balance.

Another strange aspect of the occurrence was that I had a distinct feeling *we* were being observed. Of course, I fully realized that even if this were some experimental craft being tried out by one or other of the major powers, such observation would be simple enough. Infrared telescopes that see in the dark are common enough; so are infrared cameras; and certain beams permit the picking up of conversations from considerable distances. It has even been alleged that the space satellites thrown into orbit by the Russians and Americans can, from a height of several miles, read with ease the headlines in a newspaper being read by a man sitting on a park bench. But I cannot explain, and even find it difficult to define precisely, the *feeling* I had at the time, that we were being watched.

Our excitement mounted as the object or craft continued its steady journey toward the coast. Now the contrast between its body and its base became more marked. The base was far brighter than the superstructure, appearing to be yellow-orange in color. The rest was a definite crimson, while the strange "smoke" attachment remained constant and in place. At last it receded from our line of vision, at the same height, but at a much faster speed. Soon the sky was as black as the night.

Neither of us could decide what we had seen, but we were convinced of the validity of our senses. Our observations tallied.

Subsequently I asked a diplomat resident in Tripoli if he had witnessed anything similar. His description tallied with ours. Two other people to whom I spoke had also seen the strange object.

I was very grateful to have had this experience. It was, of course, by no means the first such sighting. Unidentified flying objects have been reported in many countries long before the beginning of this century. The Des Moines *Register* of October 8, 1869 reported an unidentified flying object over St. Paul's Junction, Iowa. It was seen at the time of a solar eclipse. A few weeks earlier Alvin G. Clark, a grinder of telescopic lenses, saw twenty unexplained objects moving swiftly across his lens's field of vision as he watched from Shelbyville, Kentucky.

However, although reports of unexplained flying objects have been with us for a long time, it is significant that in number, detail, and dramatic manifestation, such occurrences increased enormously since the first atomic bombs were dropped upon Hiroshima and Nagasaki toward the end of World War II.

Did those tremendous, explosive flashes attract the attention of some extraterrestrial form of life? Is there life on other planets, anyhow? And if such life exists, what form might it take? This will be matter for the next chapter. For the moment I want to examine the general case for what used to be called, loosely, "flying saucers" and which by general consent are now described as Unidentified Flying Objects (UFO's).

Are all these reports a mass neurosis? Anyone who has read Charles MacKay's *Memoirs of Extraordinary Popular Delusions, Or the Madness of Crowds* will know that, however crazy a mania may be, it will spread like wildfire if circumstances favor it.

But the reports of UFO's are too numerous, too documented, too corroborated, and too consistent when related by people having no contact with each other, to justify a sweeping rejection of them all. Would not so many of the things we now accept as commonplace have been considered magic if they had happened years ago? And if people had no cognizance of them, could they have believed any of these things? Could they have accepted such miraculous modern phenomena as a voice's being heard by millions at the same moment, capable of traveling several times around the

202

world in a second; metal machines that fly; astronauts being rocketed to the moon and walking upon its eons-old surface?

Similarly, if you had never seen a chrysalis or a butterfly, would you find it possible to believe that a dirty-looking grub could go to sleep, change its form, discard its outer body, and emerge as a winged creature of glorious coloring?

The years 1954 and 1955 were extraordinarily full of reports of unidentified flying objects. The American Army, in 1955, was receiving several hundred reports a week. One remembers the skepticism—and interest—with which George Adamski's *Flying Saucers Have Landed* was received in 1953. He even photographed the spaceship which he alleged he had seen. Some cynics declared that it resembled an electric lamp. But within weeks a similar object was viewed in the skies over Norwich in Norfolk, by members of the British Astronomical Association.

The flying saucer photographed by Mr. Adamski looked, some alleged, like three electric bulbs set in a sort of metal "hat" —a broad-brimmed, hollow saucer on top of which was a round superstructure with holes (or portholes, as Adamski would have it) set into it. A sketch made by one of the Norwich party was almost identical with the photograph taken by Adamski. A photograph by two boys aged thirteen and eight, of an object which they maintained emerged from the clouds over Coniston, Lancashire, on February 15, 1954, shows features similar to Adamski's photograph and the sketch made by the Norwich astronomer.

I remember thinking to myself, when reading Adamski's book years ago, that it all sounded too facile. How convenient, I reflected moodily, that there were no witnesses. But since then there have been far too many reports of this kind, from people who had absolutely nothing to gain (and often much to lose) by the publicity, to justify any sweeping assertion that it is all nonsense.

The Americans did not consider the whole thing apocryphal. The United States Air Force actually commissioned a team at the University of Colorado, working under the supervision of Dr. Edward U. Condon, to investigate reports of unidentified flying objects, and for years the Air Force kept a high-ranking officer, based in London, to watch for and evaluate all UFO reports.

All countries are ambivalent in their attitude toward UFO's. There is an initial disinclination to accept any report whose facts do not make sense in the light of current scientific knowledge, an irritation born of popular credulity. There is also a natural desire to be able to explain any new happening that *might* be of significance.

In 1969, the Colorado team produced a massive and highly technical report whose main thesis was that such UFO sightings are largely imagination or a misinterpretation of natural phenomena. In effect, some of the Condon Report's compilers felt that the subject was not worth pursuing further and in December, 1969, the Air Force's Project Blue Book was abandoned.

Some critics felt that the Air Force had bungled the whole thing, had made themselves look foolish by adducing explanations of UFO phenomena that were too facile, suggesting that they were glad to be shut of the whole thing. It does not automatically follow, of course, that if the American Air Force abandons a particular line of inquiry, the subject will also be ignored by other official agencies such as the FBI or CIA. But whether or not American government agencies, public or secret, remain interested in UFO phenomena, private and public organizations and individuals in the United States continue to investigate these matters.

The American Association for the Advancement of Science, during a symposium held in Boston, Massachusetts, December 26–31, 1969, devoted the best part of two days to the subject of UFO's, and sent a letter to the Air Force asking that the documentation that has accumulated should be made available to independent scientists and others who wish to continue their research into the subject. I append the text of their letter, which includes the signatures of many who were associated with Project Blue Book. It makes clear that the decision of the United States Air Force to abandon UFO research is not generally endorsed, and that a considerable number of people want to carry on with it:

The Hon. Robert Seamans, Jr.
Secretary of the Air Force
Washington, D.C.
Dear Mr. Secretary:

The scientists listed below, convened at a General Symposium during the Annual Meeting of the Association, understand that USAF Project BLUE BOOK has been discontinued in accordance with Dr. E. U. Condon's recommendation in the Colorado Study of Unidentified Flying Objects. We know that Project BLUE BOOK accumulated, over the past two decades, irreplaceable data of great historical interest and potential value to physical and (particularly) behavioral scientists.

After two days' discussion of the data involved, the Colorado Study, and several proposed studies by sociologists and psychologists, we formally request that you, Mr. Secretary

(1) Ensure that *all* of the material, both classified and un-classified, be preserved without alteration or loss.
(2) Declassify promptly all documents filed by the Aerial Phenomena Section of the Wright-Patterson Air Force Base which are classified by virtue of AFR 200-17 and AFR 80-17.
(3) Make all the unclassified documents available to quali-fied scientific investigators at a more suitable location than the USAF Archives (we recommend a major uni-versity in the Midwest), and
(4) Order an annual review of the remaining classified docu-ments in the present file to determine when they can be declassified without alteration in accordance with current USAF security procedure.

My twelve colleagues, who receive copies of this letter, would appreciate your favoring us with a reply. I can dis-tribute it to the others if you address it to Dr. Page, 18639 Point Lookout Drive, Houston, Texas 77058.

Sincerely,
Thornton Page (Wesleyan University)
Chairman, AAAS Special Committee, for

Walter Orr Roberts,
  Retiring President, AAAS
Franklin E. Roach,
  University of Hawaii
William Hartmann,
  University of Arizona
Lester Grinspoon,
  Harvard University
Robert Hall,
  University of Illinois
Philip Morrison,
  Mass. Inst. of Technology

Douglass Price-Williams,
  Rice University
J. Allen Hynek,
  Northwestern University
James McDonald,
  University of Arizona
Carl Sagan,
  Cornell University
Walter Sullivan,
  The New York Times
George Kocher,
  University of S. California

The Soviet Union, whose ideology commits its scientists to a materialistic interpretation of everything, has also been interested in the phenomenon of flying saucers. Although the government officially maintains a skeptical posture, reports of these alleged happenings are collected from all over the world. Furthermore, *Soviet Life* recently printed a highly factual report by Dr. Felix Zigel of Moscow's Aviation Institute, which included several specific accounts of UFO's having been seen (often by several people at the same time) over Soviet territory or by various groups of Soviet citizens.

One such account describes how eight members of a geophysical expedition from the Leningrad Research Institute were in their field camp about eleven miles from "the nearest populated locality," Koktal in Kazakhstan, at 11 P.M. local time on August 16, 1960. Nikolai Sachevanov, the camp's chief, who held a master's degree in geology and mineralogy, observed an unusual luminous object appear over the mountains on the eastern slope of the valley. It was moving from north to south and its diameter was two and a half times that of the moon. "A few seconds later the body disappeared behind a mountain top, reappeared and headed southeast, *keeping constant speed and height above the earth*." (The italics are mine.)

On July 26, 1965, three Latvian astronomers were studying cloud formations at an observation station at Ogra. At about 9:35 P.M. they saw what they at first assumed to be an unusually bright star moving slowly in a westerly direction. A more detailed study through powerful binoculars disclosed an amazing spectacle. They were observing an object more than three hundred feet across—a sort of disk. At its heart was a kind of globe. Around its perimeter, at a distance of about two diameters, three identical globes rotated, like satellites around a planet. After an interval of from fifteen to twenty minutes the spheres moved farther and farther away from their "parent" disk, finally disappearing (as did the disk, too) altogether from view. This extraordinary occurrence apparently took place about fifty or sixty miles above the surface of the earth.

In July, 1967, Soviet astronomers observing from a mountain station near Kislovodsk in the Caucasus received numerous letters concerning the flight of what was described as a kind of reddish crescent moving across the sky at about 9:20 P.M. on the

206

night of July 17. The following morning the Soviet astronomer on duty noticed a kind of white cloud that appeared in the northeast. It was dense and milky-white but appeared to have a rosy-red nucleus that remained suspended when the surrounding white mass dispersed.

At 8:40 P.M. on August 8, 1967, at the same mountain station, the Soviet astronomer observed a completely unfamiliar flying object.

"It was shaped like a crescent, and luminous ribbons reminiscent of the condensation trail of a jet plane followed the horns of the crescent," he later stated.

It was yellow with a reddish tinge. Then as it moved away from the observers it dwindled, turned into a small disk, and completely disappeared. In many respects this object resembled that which my friend and I had glimpsed off the coast of Tripolitania. The only exception was that, whereas the Russians described their object as "yellow with a reddish tinge," that disk I observed was mainly red, but turning orange or almost yellow (and much brighter) toward the base. It will, of course, be realized that since my UFO was a mile away and a thousand feet up, my view was oblique. What the color scheme might have seemed had I been immediately below it, or flying in an airplane at the same level, it is difficult to say.

In his article, Dr. Zigel declares that the usual natural explanations cited by so many people when confronted with stories of unidentified flying objects—rainbows, refraction of light, mirages, haloes, and so on—do not begin to explain the cases that he quoted.

Another fact militating against the "it's all a natural phenomenon" approach is that so many of these objects have been photographed in circumstances that have been proved to preclude fake. UFO's have frequently been viewed on radar screens.

Major Baidukov of the Soviet Air Force reported a strange object on his radar screen while on a night patrol April 4, 1966, in the Odessa region. The renowned Soviet pilot, Valentin Akkuratov, while reconnoitering the area of Cape Jesup, Greenland, in 1956, suddenly spotted an unknown craft flying on a parallel course on his port side. It was a craft of completely unknown type and design, "like a large pearl-colored lens with wavy, pulsating edges."

Believing himself to be under observation by some secret invention of the Americans, Akkuratov tried to shake off his unwanted companion. He took cover in a huge bank of cloud, flying in its concealment for forty minutes before coming into clear sky again. But the weird craft was still with him—on the port side and at the same distance.

Although no occupants were seen, the craft seemed to be capably controlled. It could not be shaken off despite the most adroit maneuvers and avoiding actions. The craft performed extraordinary somersaults, using bursts of speed that would be impossible for any known flying vehicle. It emitted no exhaust vapor, left no trail. There were no wings or portholes or aerials.

Suddenly the craft rose and disappeared into the blue sky at incredible speed.

Insofar as the Soviet Union is concerned, UFO's are a subject that warrants careful surveillance. Thus, in 1967, a UFO section of the All-Union Cosmonautics Committee was established, with headquarters at the Central House of Aviation and Cosmonautics in Moscow, and with Air Force Major-General Porfiri Stolyarov serving as its first Chairman.

That the curtain of secrecy should thus far have been lifted delighted UFO investigators throughout the world, for information must be collected from everywhere, irrespective of national boundaries or aspirations, if the common factors in these phenomena are to be isolated and the basic truths established. But the committee was short-lived. It came under violent attack in the Soviet press, and was shortly afterward abandoned. UFO enthusiasts in the USSR find it wiser to keep their enthusiasm to themselves.

Dr. Zigel, in his article in *Soviet Life,* makes it clear that even if these accounts compiled by Soviet scientists were the only ones, they would constitute impressive evidence that UFO's exist. However, he adds, "Many thousands of such observations have been documented in the last twenty years . . . a growing number of scientists are not satisfied with explanations characterizing the sightings as visual aberrations." He goes on to say that, if all these thousands of factual and specific accounts—many of them corroborated by a dozen or more people—are due to mass hallucination, such "global psychic illness" would be as difficult to justify as the existence of UFO's themselves.

One factor, coincidental or not, is worth noting. Sightings of UFO's increase as the planet Mars approaches the earth. Mars has an eccentric orbit as a result of which its distance from the earth varies from 35 million miles to more than 60 million miles.

I asked Charles Bowen, Editor of *The Flying Saucer Review**—an international publication with scientific advisers and correspondents in most countries of the world—which he considered one of the most unassailable flying saucer reports in the long list of sightings.

I should mention here that Bowen is not a fanatic or visionary of any kind, but a practical man with the training of an accountant, and sufficient stability to be employed in a responsible job as a London civil servant. He is a family man, and by temperament objective and observant. Certainly he brings to the whole subject an enthusiasm that I do not consider out of place.

His independent stature is of particular importance. Governments and government departments merely say what suits them when it suits them. It is no use looking to any government, Western, Eastern, Iron Curtain or non-Iron Curtain, for any objective assessment of the UFO mystery. If UFO's exist—and I personally believe they do—they are of manifest interest to the various defense departments involved, and each government will approach the subject from the restrictive and exclusive standpoint of its own national interest. It will be seen, therefore, that Mr. Bowen's neutral and independent situation is of special value on a subject of this kind. Editing *The Flying Saucer Review,* despite the extensive correspondence it involves, the evaluation of material, and the production problems, is for him a labor of love, entirely conducted in his own personal time.

Returning to the matter of which case Bowen considered particularly impressive, he immediately mentioned the McMinnville, Oregon, case, one of two cases which the Condon Report admitted were beyond explanation.

The Report, published by *The New York Times* in January, 1969, runs to more than a quarter of a million words and the project itself cost twice as many dollars to execute. The motives underlying the expensive project, and the wide publicity given to it (no armed service is under any obligation to make the subject

*21 Cecil Court, Charing Cross Road, London, W.C. 2. Annual subscription: £ 1.10s.0; £ 1.12s.0 overseas; U.S. $4.20.

of its research projects generally available), lend some color to the claim that in 1953 the Central Intelligence Agency tried to "debunk" the whole idea of flying saucers. What motive would a secret service have in debunking reports having world-wide circulation?

If people *are* credulous, naive, romantic, misinformed, illogical, superstitious, or unbalanced (and millions of people are on record as having seen flying saucers), why should it worry the CIA? It surely leaves the agency more at liberty to pursue its special aims if the mass of people are too unintelligent to either take note of their activities or actively obstruct them.

The general tenor of the Condon Report is skeptical. However, as Mr. Bowen pointed out to me, it could not dismiss the McMinnville case, of which it concludes: "This is one of the few UFO reports in which all factors investigated, geometric, psychological, and physical appear to be consistent with the assertion that an extraordinary flying object, silvery, metallic, disk-shaped, tens of meters in diameter, and evidently artificial, flew within sight of two witnesses. It cannot be said that the evidence positively rules out fabrication, although there are some physical factors such as the accuracy of certain photometric measures of the original negatives which argue against a fabrication."

Mr. Bowen's comment on that is: "This was one of sixty-odd cases which were selected. One gets the impression that many of these cases were selected because they would give an easy answer. Here is one where they could not show that there is fabrication; indeed, the case remained unidentified. And yet we get this damning conclusion by Dr. Condon saying that they're all meteorites, all balloons, all temperature inversions, and so on. And in the conclusions and recommendations with which he opens the report, he says, 'Careful consideration of the record as it is available to us leads us to conclude that further extensive study of UFO's probably cannot be justified in the expectation that science will be advanced thereby.'

"Later—on page two—he says, 'Scientists are no respecters of authority. Our conclusion that study of UFO reports is not likely to advance science will not be uncritically accepted by them. Nor should it be, nor do we wish it to be.' Then he goes on, after downgrading the subject generally, 'It seems to us that only such attention to the subject should be given as the Department of

Defense deems necessary strictly from a defense point of view. The level of effort should not be raised because of arguments that the subject has scientific importance so far as present indications go. It is our impression that the defense function could be performed within the framework established for intelligence and surveillance operations without the continuance of a special unit such as Project Blue Book, but this is a question for defense specialists rather than research scientists.'

"So," continued Mr. Bowen, "the subject of UFO's is considered to be of no value to science yet still important enough to be relegated to the intelligence services, which, of course, is where the interest has always been taken in this subject. One gets the impression that this project was put on to keep public interest at a minimum. But there is one big fear in all this: that if they stop public interest you're going to run short of cases, which I'm sure they're interested in having reported."

Let us go back two decades and look again at the extraordinary experience of the farmer Paul Trent of McMinnville, Oregon.

Farmer Trent is no camera buff. Although he liked taking photographs occasionally—if there was a subject that particularly appealed to him—he made a reel last a long time. Thus in the winter of 1950 he photographed a snow scene. A month later, using the same roll of film, he took picture number two, a weeping willow in his front yard. Weeks passed, then months. Then on the evening of May 11 Mr. Trent took two more photographs, this time in a state of high excitement.

I note with some amusement that the Condon Report states rather plaintively that when its investigator went to find the negatives of the flying saucer that Trent and his wife saw that evening, he found a baby playing with the negatives on the floor. But if an investigator waits for nearly twenty years before checking on the facts of an occurrence of this nature, he need hardly be surprised if some of the evidence has become dispersed.

Fortunately, we need not turn to the Condon Report for its belated description of what happened on the Trent farm all those years ago, because the facts were recorded with equal care by the local paper, immediately after the event.

After taking the photographs on May 11, Trent waited a few

211

more weeks, used up the remainder of the spool, and had it developed. Later, a friend to whom he showed the pictures told him he ought to show them to the McMinnville *Telephone Register,* a local weekly newspaper. Its editor was impressed and printed the pictures, together with Trent's account.

"It was late in the evening when we saw the object in the sky," Mrs. Evelyn May Trent, who was then twenty-eight years old, told the *Telephone Register.* "The camera! Paul raced for it and took the first picture. The object was coming in toward us and seemed to be tipped up a bit."

To the Oregon *Journal* Paul Trent, her husband, said, "It was about twenty or thirty feet in diameter and was moving fairly slowly. After I had snapped the first picture, it moved a little to the left and I prepared to take another picture. Then it seemed to pick up speed suddenly and in no time at all it vanished."

He did not tell anybody about it at the time because "I was kinda scared. You know you hear so much about those things— and the government. . . . I didn't believe all that talk about flying saucers before, but now I have an idea the Army knows what they are."

In a radio interview Mrs. Trent said that the object looked "like a good-sized parachute canopy without the strings, only silvery bright mixed with bronze." It was not rotating.

In the Condon Report Paul Trent is referred to somewhat coyly as "Witness II" and the author of that section of the report was impressed by Trent's casual attitude to the whole thing. When interviewed, he did not even get off his tractor—which again is not so surprising considering that he is a farmer with plenty of work to do, and the authorities were questioning him about something that had happened nearly twenty years before!

Another extraordinary UFO case, spectacularly well documented, technically unchallengeable in its evidence, and attested by innumerable witnesses highly trained in the art of observation, is the Lakenheath case. Until publication of the Condon Report nothing was known publicly of the sightings, which took place over East Anglia on the night of August 13–14, 1956. It is extraordinary that the facts could have been suppressed for so long; it is equally remarkable that the Condon Report should devote so little space to a case which, the authors admit, "is the most puzzling and unusual case in the radar-visual files. The apparent rational, intelligent

212

behavior of the UFO suggests a mechanical device of unknown origin as the most probable explanation of this sighting." Having advanced absolutely no explanation for a phenomenon which was observed by ground and air radar, the Condon Report observes that "in view of the inevitable fallibility of witnesses, more conventional explanations of this report cannot be entirely ruled out." It does not say what "conventional explanations" it has in mind. As to the fallibility of witnesses, they have no monopoly of it. Compilers of reports can be fallible too.

A detailed paper on this case was submitted by Dr. James E. McDonald, Professor of Atmospheric Sciences at the University of Arizona in Tucson, at the 1969 meeting of the American Association for the Advancement of Science in Boston, to which earlier reference has been made. The initial reports centered around the Royal Air Force stations at Bentwaters (six miles east of Ipswich), Lakenheath, about twenty miles northeast of Cambridge, and Sculthorpe, near Fakenham, in the vicinity of the Wash. G.C.A. (Ground Control Approach) radars at two of these three stations were involved in the ground radar sightings, as was the Radar Traffic Control Center unit at Lakenheath.

Briefly, the UFO "was tracked by air traffic control radar at two U.S.A.F.-R.A.F. stations, with apparently corresponding visual sightings of round, white rapidly moving objects which changed directions abruptly. Interception by R.A.F. fighter aircraft was attempted; one aircraft was vectored to the UFO by G.C.A. radar and radar 'gunlock.' The UFO appeared to circle around behind the aircraft and followed it in spite of the pilot's evasive maneuvers. Contact was broken when the aircraft returned to base, low on fuel. The preponderance of the evidence indicates the possibility of a genuine UFO in this case. The weather was generally clear with good visibility."

Professor McDonald's report runs to nearly ten thousand words, is extremely detailed, and forms a landmark in UFO history. One is only left to speculate why the facts were kept quiet for so long, and why it was thought necessary, when loaning Dr. McDonald the case history, to delete the names of all witnesses. The suppression of the names of witnesses appears almost a mania with the compilers of the Condon Report, who seem determined that their word should be the last, and that others should be discouraged from carrying on investigations where they chose to leave off.

213

To return to my most informative meeting with Charles Bowen. I then put to him this simple question: "Are you satisfied that there have been a number of UFO's appearing in different parts of the world?"

"Yes."

"And you don't think they can all be accounted for by illusion?"

"No."

"Do you think—speaking for yourself, and so far as you can judge—they might be or could be extraterrestrial?"

"It's possible."

"If they are not extraterrestrial, what could they be?"

"There have been suggestions, of course (this is really stretching it to the limit), that there are other worlds around and within us; a parallel universe business. This is a bit of a myth, possibly. It seems incomprehensible, anyway."

(But Aimé Michel, the French UFO expert, has said that even an extraterrestrial visitation by a superior technology would appear like magic to us. And this is most important. Let us look at this planet a thousand years, ten thousand years ago. What we do now would seem like magic to people living then.)

"Can you think of another mysterious and dramatic case of an unidentified flying object that has been reported to you?" was my next question.

"Oh, without doubt the BOAC North Atlantic sighting off the coast of Labrador," Bowen answered quickly.

The facts of what is now known as the Goose Bay case are worth recounting because the phenomenon was witnessed by so many people, including Captain Howard, his copilot, ground control, the pilot of a fighter plane sent up to investigate, and thirty-nine out of forty passengers.

The sighting occurred in June, 1954. Captain Howard was in command of a BOAC Boeing Stratocruiser en route from New York to London via Goose Bay, Labrador, a refueling stop. The plane was flying at a height of nineteen thousand feet over Seven Island when Captain Howard and his copilot became aware of something moving along on their port side at a lower altitude about five miles away, in and out of a broken layer of stratocumulus cloud.

"As we watched," Captain Howard said, "these objects

214

climbed above the cloud and we could now clearly see one large and six small. As we flew on toward Goose Bay, the large object began to change shape and the smaller to move relative to the larger.

"We informed Goose Bay that we had something odd in sight, and they made arrangements to vector a fighter on us. Later I changed the radio frequency to contact this fighter; the fighter told me he had me in sight on radar closing me head-on at twenty miles. At that the small objects seemed to enter the larger, and then the big one shrank. I gave a description to the fighter and a bearing of the objects from me."

On a BBC program on May 9, 1968, Captain Howard provided further details not mentioned in the Condon Report. The objects, he said, "stayed with us for about six minutes in all." The six small objects were roughly globular in shape but the large one "slowly but continually changed its shape. On one occasion it looked rather like a dumbbell or upturned telephone receiver lying on its side. At another time it looked rather like an arrowhead and then it shifted back into a globular shape again."

Captain Howard added the following facts: "It was dark in color and, although silhouetted against a fairly bright sky, it was absolutely opaque. People have often asked me whether we were in any sense afraid of them. The answer is exactly the opposite. I talked with my crew later about this, and all of them agreed that they felt some sort of bond of affection between us and them."

Them. The inference is that the captain and his copilot sensed that they were in touch with some kind of active intelligence. If these were "visitors" from another planet, if these strange objects were a probe from an extraterrestrial source, the occupants could have been representatives of some far older evolutionary species, in which case some faculties we are only beginning to develop might be commonplace with them and in constant use—telepathy, for example. The feelings of affection Captain Howard experienced may well have been projected.

This dramatic and well-corroborated account is attributed by the Condon Report to Venus: "It is more probable that the image of Venus was distorted by some optical effect. . . ."

Charles Bowen had an interesting epilogue to the Goose Bay case for me: "The most amazing thing, though, was that within seventeen hours of that sighting an incredible film was taken by Swedish and other scientists who had chartered three aircraft to fly toward the North Pole to photograph the eclipse of the sun which was seen that day. They saw two objects rolling away in the distance, which they estimated to be about fifteen miles. They were seen at this distance, yet the explanation given by others of that experience was that they were watching seagulls or seeing reflections in the windows of the aircraft, regardless of the fact that the team had said that the windows were taken out of the aircraft so that they would have no reflections. The third explanation advanced was that the scientists were watching a Russian secret weapon."

I asked Bowen about the aircraft in which they flew. "I suppose they must have had the windows taken out? Obviously the cabin wasn't pressurized."

"No, it wasn't," he told me. "It was open so that they could aim cameras through and get their photographs. They were flying at fifteen thousand feet and were properly clothed for the rigors of an open plane."

The secret weapon theory is, admittedly, interesting, but who is to say how much validity it carries? I recall an unusual sighting involving a flaming red cone that trailed a green mist and looked to be "half the size of the moon" reported over Ohio, Kentucky, and Tennessee in January, 1948, at a height of twenty-two thousand feet. It was seen by thousands of people. And it was observed by men in the control tower at Clinton County Army Air Base, Ohio, for thirty-five minutes.

Colonel Guy Hix, an airfield commander, saw the object and radioed three National Guard pilots who were flying to Louisville, Kentucky. Two pilots who went up to fifteen thousand feet could not approach the cone because of its speed. The third pilot, twenty-five-year-old Thomas F. Mantell, got nearer to it. There was a tremendous explosion, and Captain Mantell's plane crashed near a farmhouse near Franklin, Kentucky. Mantell, who had sent no message through his radio, was killed instantly.

Was the UFO in this case a secret weapon, and did Mantell die because his plane ventured too close to the strange object? To this day no one can answer that question.

What about the flying saucer that landed in fields behind the

Bentilee Estate, Stoke-on-Trent, on the evening of Saturday, September 2, 1967? It was a glowing, yellow-orange disk with a red dome, whose appearance greatly frightened two adults and six children. Somebody dialed the police, who came rushing to the scene, to be told by one excited adult that the saucer was now airborne. And so it was. Police and onlookers saw it rise over low hills, hang stationary for a few seconds, then vanish. Five children playing football in a nearby field also saw it.

Police tried to account for the phenomenon by attributing it to some trick of automobile headlights. However, two astronomers —Roger Stanway and Anthony Pace—are convinced after numerous inquiries that more than a dozen people, in no position to influence each other and separated by distance, would hardly experience the same optical illusion at the same time. They *did* see something. They agree on the main features of what they saw. And what they saw frightened them badly.

And what about the "thing" in North Devon, seen in October, 1967, by Constables Roger Willey and Clifford Waycott of the local police? They were on patrol near Holsworthy when they saw "what looked like a star-spangled cross radiating points of light from all angles." They chased it in their car, at times reaching speeds of ninety miles per hour, but it eluded them. The two constables later told a press conference that it first appeared to the left of them, then went in an arc and dipped down, so that they thought it had landed.

"It seemed to be watching us and wouldn't let us catch up," they said. It was at various altitudes but for most of the time at a level just above the trees. "It had terrific acceleration. It seemed to know we were chasing it."

Constable Waycott described how at one moment it stopped in a field. But when the policemen left their vehicle to observe it more closely, it moved away again. It was neither a helicopter nor an airplane, though it was about the size of an orthodox airplane. The closest they could get to it was four hundred yards. They radioed their police headquarters, and their unlikely reports evoked some very strange responses from the men at the desk.

Determined to secure some confirmation of what they were watching, the two policemen found a car parked in a turnout and awakened the driver, Mr. Christopher Garner of Luton, who could scarcely believe his eyes as he looked at the strange flashing object. It disappeared into the distance, being joined in the process by a second such object, glistening and brilliant.

The number of sightings in Britain, of which those quoted are typical, cannot be written off casually as visual aberration or natural phenomena. The British Ministry of Defence figures show that about fifty sightings were reported in 1965, ninety-five in 1966, and one hundred and fifty-three in 1967.

In 1969, strange lights in regular formation were seen streaming across the skies over London, and the official explanation was that they were scraps of a Russian Sputnik re-entering the earth's atmosphere and getting burned out in the process. Perhaps. The lights were seen by thousands of Londoners, and their regular formation was certainly curious.

But as far back as 1954 defense experts were puzzled (it is always tactless to suggest that they might be worried) by strange sky formations that persistently appeared from nowhere at about midday at a height of twelve thousand feet. They were first spotted by a civilian radar scientist and were subsequently plotted by radar sites throughout Britain. The "blips" would first appear in an irregular "U" pattern, later disengage and redeploy in two parallel lines, then reassemble in a "Z" formation. They were invisible to the naked eye, but on the radar screens appeared as innumerable dots formed by between forty and fifty echoes. The area covered amounted to many miles.

Now is all this a new kind of folklore, a science-age fairy story? It is estimated that between 1 million and 5 million people in the United States alone have seen UFO's. Their stories are too factual, and come from too many people of probity and social position to support the "mass hallucination" theory. As the Editor of *The Flying Saucer Review* put it to me:

"If all these things were secret weapons of a foreign power whether hostile or not hostile, then what are they doing flying them over all manner of territories, all over the world, and landing them, and taking off again? I can't imagine that anyone with a secret weapon would operate in this fashion. And these sightings are reported from every corner of the globe, even from places as remote as New Guinea or Antarctica, or in lavender fields in France. . . ."

"Lavender fields?" I asked, a little startled.

"Yes. We call it the Lavender Field case. It happened on July 1, 1965. It was a lavender farm, and the farmer spotted an object standing in the middle of the lavender field. He was preparing to work at about a quarter to six in the morning and heard a whistling sound. He saw a thing which at first he thought must be a helicopter. It looked like a car standing on six legs with a central pivot under it. He saw two little 'boys' nearby. There had been instances in the weeks preceding this event of lavender plants being tampered with by unknown persons; and he approached stealthily through a vineyard, keeping down because the vines were very low, and came to the nearest point, at the edge of the vineyard, to the object.

"As he was about to emerge from the vineyard, he realized that they were not little boys but the oddest sort of things he'd ever seen—small creatures about three feet six inches in height. And this is the first instance we have of these creatures being completely covered from head to foot. They had, apparently, grayish-colored uniforms covering the rest of their bodies but their heads were bare. They had strange pointed chins, lipless mouths, large eyes which tapered off and went around the sides of their heads, puffy cheeks, and dome-shaped craniums.

"He was advancing toward them when suddenly one of them turned and pointed at him what appeared to be a stick, and he stopped dead in his tracks because he couldn't move. It was described loosely as paralysis; of course, it could not have been muscular paralysis, or he would have died. It could not have been nerve paralysis, or he would have fallen over. It sounds like some form of hypnotic suggestion.

"We have never been able to establish what went on between the onset of this sighting and the departure of the entities. They returned to the machine—as he described it, 'bubbling up' into the machine almost, and there they were sitting in it, facing him. There was a thump from its central pivot, which rose out of the ground; the six legs whirled; the whole thing hovered and then moved away slowly for about twenty meters and then just disappeared. This occurrence was at Valensole."

"You went to see the percipient?" I inquired.

"Yes, I went with Aimé Michel."

219

"And you're satisfied as to his integrity?"

"Oh, yes. He's a typical peasant farmer, about fifty years of age; he was a Maquis fighter during the war."

"Not the sort of person, you would say, to engage in fantasies or be easily misled in practical matters?"

"No. A straight, practical man not given to dreaming."

"You will gather that I myself have no closed mind on this subject. To me, there is nothing inherently unlikely in the thought of there being life on other planets, or of others sending probes to the earth to see what's going on. . . ."

As I said this I was comforted by the thought of how, twenty years ago, when I was editing the BBC's *Focus* series of weekly radio documentaries, I initiated a thirty-minute documentary on interplanetary travel. I remember that the planners were somewhat skeptical about my including such a "way-out" topic and devoting so much broadcasting time to a subject so remote from daily life and even more remote, in their opinion, from probability.

However, the program did go on the air, as a realistic and detailed assessment of the likelihood of space travel becoming a reality, and with the cooperation of the British Interplanetary Society and of writers whose faith and foresight have made them deservedly famous in this field—Kenneth Gatland and Arthur C. Clarke. Nevertheless, it is amusing to recall the skepticism of the BBC's hierarchy then and their current acceptance (in color) of direct television broadcasts from the moon. Today's impossible event is tomorrow's commonplace occurrence.

With respect to the persistence of UFO phenomena Charles Bowen told me: "Flying saucers and UFO's continue to be seen despite all the ridicule that has been heaped upon reports of sightings. And the reports, as I've said before, come from people who have no ax to grind at all. They don't go away on lecture tours; they don't write books about the phenomenon. All they do is to say, in the surprise which hits them, that they had this experience."

"It's like people who have experiences of ghosts," I commented. "There may be individuals who are predisposed to see ghosts, or who accept too readily some story about their homes being haunted. However, most people with ghost stories—and I have hundreds of them in my files—are quite ordinary people, with nothing to gain by it and indeed often something to lose, because they are likely, if they make their experiences known, to be regarded as cranks."

It is believed that governments generally are clamping down on the subject of UFO's. This is especially the case in such countries as Brazil, Argentina, and France. In these countries, as in the U.S.A. and in Britain, the authorities share a common tendency to discount the validity of any sightings.

"France," states Bowen, "insists that UFO's don't exist, yet whenever there's a report, immediately the place is cordoned off and truckloads of Air Force and Army personnel and gendarmes descend on the place."

It may be argued that because members of the Apollo missions did not see flying saucers on their journeys to and from the moon, flying saucers cannot exist. Such a premise ignores the vastness of space and the extreme unlikelihood of such craft ever being seen unless the human travelers were sought out deliberately. If such an easy premise were accepted, one would also have to agree with the Russian astronaut who said that there cannot be a God because no God was seen.

Since millions of people throughout the world have seen UFO's and since the Condon Report attributes most cases (but certainly not all) to freak conditions or faulty perception, let us consider briefly what factors might produce hallucinations. What ordinary circumstances—or extraordinary, for that matter—could be visually deceptive?

For one thing, there is the element of movement—which is often related to observation of a stationary object. If you are traveling in a car, you can imagine that the telegraph pole is moving toward you. If you regard the moon from a moving vehicle in relation to a stationary object such as a telegraph pole, the moon will appear to be moving through the heavens. If you look out of a railroad car window when the train is traveling at high speed, and is passed by a train going in the same direction on a parallel track at only slightly greater speed, your own train will appear stationary while the other will seem to be crawling along at a snail's pace.

Incidentally, it would not be out of order to inquire if some nation has really made a flying saucer and kept it on the secret list. It isn't so inherently unlikely in these days of miraculous engineering achievements. During World War II some weird and wonderful flying contraptions, some looking almost like flying crabs, reached the drawing board and silhouettes were issued to aircraft spotters in case they ever became a reality. In April, 1953, there were reports that aircraft designers at the Avro Canada Works at Malton, near Toronto, Canada, had made a flying saucer. It was supposed to be capable of a speed of fifteen hundred miles per hour and to be independent of prepared runways. It could take off vertically from a launching chassis with booster rockets to supplement the gas turbine.

It may be that such a prototype exists somewhere, and has been tested without any official announcement being made. But even if this were the case, it would only account for a few of the thousands of UFO reports. Many of the UFO's change form, enlarge, shrink in size, move at incredible speeds, or vanish. They vary in color—orange, green, red, yellow—as well as in shape.

What other scope is there for illusion?

Well, our old friend the meteorological balloon is often blamed. Britain and many other countries release these into the upper atmosphere. In fact, in the United States more than a hundred of these radio-sonde balloons are sent up. At forty thousand feet, and fully inflated, such balloons can reach a diameter greater than twenty feet.

The nature of the balloon and its appendages gives plenty of scope for visual effect, if one remembers the varying lighting conditions and the continual interplay of atmosphere, cloud, sunshine, and moonlight. Add to this the varying force of the wind and its ability to move objects, and you have a very dramatic backcloth indeed. The balloon has attached to it a parachute for bringing the instruments down undamaged when the balloon bursts. A short distance down its dangling cable it has a reflector that enables the balloon to be tracked by radar. Farther down is its radio-sonde by which meteorological recordings are transmitted to the ground.

Freak atmospheric conditions produce mirages. Nonexistent lakes have been seen in arid deserts. The images of ships and icebergs have loomed up in the mists and fogs of the polar regions. The refractive index varies continuously through the atmosphere. A ray of light, traveling through one medium, is bent or made to deviate from its path when it reaches some medium with a different refractive index. If this happens often enough, the path of the light becomes curvilinear. This brings about all kinds of queer phenomena, of which the mirages of the Sahara and Turkestan deserts are only one example.

Over large, built-up cities another optical illusion may occur. A warm layer of air rides on top of a cold layer, due to the fact that the earth below cools more rapidly than the atmosphere. In these conditions, if the sky happens to be dark, the reflections of the lights of a distant city may be seen.

The upper atmosphere often includes formations of icy droplets. As they ice up, they can reflect the sun's rays with a dazzling effect. The sun's rays are so bright that any true mirror will transmit them with amazing fidelity. Some people notice how, on a hot sunny day, diminutive scraps of mica or crystal in paving stones reflect sunlight with the brilliance of miniature searchlights.

Meteor trails, the light reflected by an airplane's fuselage, and lenticular clouds have all possibly been mistaken at different times for flying saucers. But neither singly nor collectively do these natural explanations account for all the phenomena recorded—and in the case of some reports, none of them could. For example, the two "humanoids" or human-type creatures seen by the French farmer Maurice Masse on his lavender field at Valensole.

The description of the creatures seen by Masse is certainly extraordinary, and by human standards such forms of life—lipless, large-eyed, puffy-cheeked, dome-headed—do not sound very attractive or credible. Nor do the odd entities seen by three children in the garden of Rua Conselheiro Gualberto, Belo Horizonte, capital of the Brazilian state of Minas Gerais.

The children, one aged twelve and the others seven at the time the report was made, on August 28, 1963, had gone into the garden to wash a coffee percolator when the garden was suddenly illuminated by a brilliant light. They observed a spherical, transparent vehicle containing four "people" who, on emerging, proved to be wearing a sort of diving suit surmounted by a transparent dome. The creatures descended from the craft between two beams of light, as though floating.

Predictably, neighbors received the accounts with disbelief; they were dismissed as the fantasies of children. Yet the children, questioned at length by a skilled investigator, were consistent in their respective accounts. One of them had come into the house terrified and thrown himself under one of the beds. Señora Gualberto had noticed nothing amiss while the craft was landing, except for a brilliant light shining through the shutters, which puzzled her, as automobiles with headlights do not come that way; but her curiosity was not so great as to lead her to inspect and find the cause for this strange illumination.

In a translation of a detailed report by Gordon Creighton, an international expert on UFO's and a consultant to *The Flying Saucer Review,* Fernandez, the oldest of the children, declared: "They don't want to believe it, eh? Well one day *they'll see what we saw,* and then it will be proved that we aren't telling lies."

Was this a childish conspiracy to make themselves the center of attention? A practical joke to demonstrate how credulous adults can be, how easily deceived? The result of a surfeit of comics and childish fantasy?

There is nothing in the children's background to encourage any such speculation. Furthermore, while it is not unknown for children to be good actors, I know of no actor who can simulate pallor at will. One of the children was so scared he became as pale as a ghost—or as pale as a ghost is alleged to be.

According to a survey of UFO landings, covering the century from 1868 to 1968 and first published in the French monthly *Lumières dans la Nuit,* the three areas in which sightings were most frequent were the United States, France, and Latin America. From 1868 onward (with the exception of 1880 when two were reported) there was merely one UFO sighting a year. In 1897 there were twenty-one such cases. Thereafter, the number remained at one or two until the end of World War II.

Since the War there has been a consistent sharp rise in sightings and reported landings until in 1954 there were two hundred and thirty-six of them.

I find this rise after the end of World War II of immense significance. I do not have to ask myself, or anyone else, *"Is there life on other planets?"* I cannot prove that there is, but the odds against there *not* being life on other planets are so overwhelming that the existence of life elsewhere is for me axiomatic. The case for there not being life outside the earth is more wildly improbable, in fact, than the thought of there being life in very many other places in the universe. I will give the logical and statistical basis for this assertion presently.

The fact that UFO manifestations have been so numerous since 1945 implies to me that, just as we are sending probes into space to uncover secrets of the universe, so somebody somewhere is doing just the same thing to the earth. If the Russians and Americans can send rockets hurtling toward the moon, or Mars, or Venus, why could this not happen in reverse?

My own opinion is that the various atomic explosions, including the annihilation of Nagasaki and Hiroshima in 1945, may have attracted the attention of living creatures on another planet, who decided to investigate. We must never forget that the earth is not the oldest planet by any means. Let us look at a few basic facts about the universe and see if man, conceited as he is, can get his own role into proper perspective.

☐ 13. The Mysterious Universe

IT is forty years since Sir James Jeans in his trail-blazing book, *The Mysterious Universe,* told, in his wonderfully expressive opening paragraph, of the immensity of the universe we live in:

> A few stars are known which are hardly bigger than the earth, but the majority are so large that hundreds of thousands of earths could be packed inside each and leave room to spare; here and there we come upon a giant star large enough to contain millions and millions of earths. *And the number of stars in the universe is probably something like the total number of grains of sand on all the beaches of the world.* Such is the littleness of our home in space when measured up against the total substance of the universe.

To take our own galaxy first. The sun is not its center— it lies toward the edge of our galaxy, whose diameter is about 100,000 light-years. The distances involved in the universe are so vast that ordinary measurements are useless. A light-year is the distance that light would travel in a year, namely, *nearly 6 million million miles.* In other words, even if we could travel at this incredible speed of light (186,300 miles per second in a vacuum) it would take 4.3 light-years to get to the nearest star, other than the sun. If you had a rocket capable of speeds of up to 10,000 miles an hour and enough fuel to last the journey, it would take you 75,000 years to reach the nearest star.

There are a vast number of stars in our galaxy, sometimes

called the galactic system, at other times the Milky Way. There are in our own little cluster about 100,000 million stars. The galaxy forms a sort of disk. If we take its diameter as 100,000 light-years (the distance across), we can say that its depth is about 20,000 light-years. The galaxy includes an enormous variety of solar bodies, from the raging furnace of the sun, whose solar flares often reach a height of 500,000 miles, to "red dwarfs"—cooling suns. But there are also "red giants," such as Betelgeuse in the constellation of Orion, whose diameter is about 250 million miles or three hundred times that of the sun. There are "white dwarfs," smaller in size than the earth, but containing a far greater mass— so much greater that a few cubic inches of their material would weigh many tons.

To look through a powerful telescope at the Andromeda nebula, the nearest galaxy to ours (yet still *2 million light-years* away), is to be filled with a tremendous sense of awe. As Sir Bernard Lovell, Professor of Radio Astronomy in the University of Manchester and Director of the Jodrell Bank Experimental Station in Cheshire (home of the famous Jodrell Bank telescope), has put it: "May I remind you that in astronomy we have no knowledge of the present time: as we penetrate into space, so we penetrate back in time. Our knowledge of the Andromeda nebula is as it was 2 million years ago, not as it is now, because the light from it started out on its journey 2 million years ago."

Andromeda has, according to Sir Bernard Lovell, between 10,000 and 100,000 million suns. But the vast range of galaxies brought into view by the great telescopes of Mount Palomar and Jodrell Bank shows the universe to be illimitable. The 200-inch reflector of the largest optical telescope currently operating, at Mount Palomar in California, can photograph as many as 1,000 million galaxies.

So there you have it. Within our own limited range of tele-scopic vision there are 1,000 million galaxies each with about 100,000 million stars. The Russians are at the moment completing a 236-inch telescope that will bring still more galaxies into view.

The sun controls a planetary system, yet it is an ordinary star. On the basis of present astronomical knowledge it is estimated there are 100,000 million multiplied by 1,000 million suns in the universe. At least some of these suns must control planetary systems of their own. *Can we really entertain, even for a second, the notion that this earth—a mere speck of dust in the universe—is the only planetary body that can support living creatures?* Even in our own solar system there are two planets that might possibly sustain life of some kind—Mars and Venus.

The planet Mars has white polar caps that may well consist of ice or frost. These suggest that it may have an atmosphere, as they grow during the Martian winter and decrease at other times, which may be analogous to our spring or summer. These seasonal variations are on quite a large scale, while a dark band around the polar caps, which follows the outline of the diminishing caps, suggests a belt of country exposed by the retreating ice. There are dark regions, sometimes thought to be seas, whose color never changes. And there are light areas whose color is variable.

The series of American space probes Mariners IV, VI, and VII have revealed, in photographs, numerous craters but no mountain ranges. There appear to be white, blue, or yellow clouds whose precise composition has yet to be determined. There appears to be a minute amount of water vapor, but little oxygen. On available evidence it would not seem likely that the planet could support higher forms of life, yet we cannot be certain.

And Venus? It is the second planet from the sun in our solar system, and almost the earth's twin in size. Venus appears to be covered with thick clouds, but there is no evidence of oxygen in its atmosphere.

There is a disagreement as to whether there is any significant amount of water vapor on Venus, or even any at all. A series of Soviet and American probes have revealed that the planet's surface temperature is 800 degrees Fahrenheit, and that its unusually dense atmosphere is chiefly composed of carbon dioxide.

So high a surface temperature and so great a concentration of carbon dioxide in Venus' atmosphere could scarcely favor life in any form that we know it. It would, however, be arrogant, as well as totally without evidence, to assume that life *as we know it* is the only sort of life that could exist.

These two planets, therefore, are no criteria by which to attempt to assess the possibilities of life on what must be thousands of millions of other planets, many of which may be millions of years old. What proportion of such planets might support life? I put this question to Mr. Maxwell Cade, a Fellow of the Royal Astronomical Society who is also a distinguished scientist with medical, electronic, and physical knowledge. Here is what he told me:

"It is probable that practically all stars do have planetary systems, but on the basis of present knowledge it is estimated that not more than 4 percent could have planetary systems capable of supporting life, not only as we know it, but in any form that we can think of. This is because stars which are very hot have a large ecosphere—that is, they warm up a large area of space to a temperature in which such life as could exist would be short-lived, too short-lived for evolution as we know it to occur.

"Stars which have adequate time for evolution very often warm up only a small area of space, so that many of their planets would be too cold. Others, of course, may be too near the star and thus too hot. And then, about two thirds of stars are not single, but double or multiple stars, so that any planets around them will have very complex orbits and will be exposed to the extremes of heat and cold.

"On this basis you have to reduce the number of stars carrying planets to about 4 percent of that value to get the number that will probably have life."

I asked Mr. Cade: "What do you feel about my assertion that the proposition that there is not life elsewhere in the universe is more incredible, more an affront to reason and known facts, than the proposition that there *is* life on the planets elsewhere?"

"I agree with every word of your assertion," he replied, promptly.

"But you have postulated, have you not, that there are many odds against life—you said only 4 percent will probably have life?"

"The universe is large, and 4 percent would be large too. There have been a number of astronomers who have quoted the simile that the number of stars in the universe is comparable to the number of grains of sand on all the beaches of the earth. It is also now well established that many of the observable stars are accompanied by dark bodies; and modern theories of the formation of stars from local accumulations of galactic dust lead one to suspect that *all* stars are accompanied by such bodies. Considerations of gravitational force, atmosphere, and the complexity of orbits in the vicinity of multiple stars reduce the total which it seems could support life—in any form that we consider probable,

229

not merely life as we know it—to about 4 percent of the number of stars observable. *This still means that there is an overwhelming probability that milliards of stars throughout all the galaxies are accompanied by planets supporting some kind of life* [my italics]."

An overwhelming probability. Milliards of stars. But then, if this should be so, many of those stars would have histories of development far longer than ours. Life might have been evolving many more millions of years! Is this question tied up with the UFO mystery?

I asked Charles Gibbs-Smith, the well-known aviation historian, whether the thought of UFO's coming from other planets was outlandish or crazy. "Of course not," he replied. "Look at the immensity of space! And our civilization is a baby to some that might exist. It's childish, it's conceited, to think we could possibly be the only intelligent beings in the universe."

I asked him: "You have gone on record as saying that the stuff of the universe is more or less the same, and that there may be thousands or millions of inhabited planets in space. You also said that they might be immensely more advanced than we are, their civilizations having existed longer. Do you still feel there is life on other planets?"

His reply came pat. "I'm absolutely sure of it."

How did life begin on earth? There is the Biblical version, of course. There are numerous theories. However, life might have commenced by the transmission here of live organisms by meteorites rushing in from outer space. Most meteorites entering the earth's atmosphere are completely vaporized far above the earth's surface. This is just as well. One meteorite that fell in the Krasnoiarsk region of Siberia on June 30, 1908, caused a series of explosions heard more than six hundred miles away and blew over horses and men at distances of more than one hundred miles.

The meteorite must have weighed at least forty thousand tons, and it is a mercy indeed that it fell in an uninhabited wilderness and not upon a city. As it was, the impact devastated sixty miles of forest, the huge trees being flattened like corn in a storm. (One Russian scientist, Alexander Kazantsev, has advanced the extraordinary theory that it was not a meteorite at all but an intelligently directed craft, which exploded.)

There have, of course, been more recent cases of meteorites that have reached the earth before being vaporized. One fell in the scrub desert north of Mount Kenya in East Africa in 1946, flattening villages within a perimeter of sixty miles. A report in *Nature* of November 18, 1961, suggested that the famous Orgeuil meteorite might contain organic materials or fossilized algae.

We do not need to turn to meteorites, however, for conviction that forms of life exist on other planets. Just as our sun illumines and enlivens our earth, so millions of other suns may be the centers of innumerable planetary systems. Or, as Patrick Moore, Fellow of the Royal Astronomical Society, has said:

"There is no reason to suppose that the sun's family is unique. . . . *It follows that many of these planets are habitable, and that life in the universe may be widespread* [my italics]."*

A revolutionary theory on UFO's is propounded by Professor Giuseppe Bonfante in an article in the *Journal* of Centro Richerche Biopsichiche,† a translation of which appeared in the *Journal of Paraphysics,* Vol. 3, No. 5, of 1969. If the earth *is* being visited or observed by extraterrestrial forms of life, how could they have traveled such vast distances?

The answer, says Professor Bonfante, is that there may be "parallel universes." UFO's, he thinks, may be from "a galactic civilization," which, having reached a stage of development millions—or thousands of millions of years—in advance of our own, "exploiting a form of energy unknown to us, has succeeded in producing a force field which modifies the fundamental constants of matter of any object (that is, gravitational constant, speed of light, Planck's constant) *by means of which the same object suddenly disappears from the visible universe, entering another dimension beyond time and space* [my italics]."

This possibility of access to another "parallel universe" would explain the ability of UFO's to cover vast distances in a short time, and dispose of the question of how UFO's could bridge the millions-of-years gap inevitable for them to reach the earth from the more distant stars.

"An advanced civilization," declares Professor Bonfante, "could thus have resolved the problem of space and time and passed beyond the barrier of time."

The theory of parallel universes is a complex one and I do not propose to attempt either its elucidation or expansion here.

Geographical Magazine, December, 1963.
†Address: via Dante 13/a, 35100 Padova, Italy.

Broadly, it suggests that our space and time is not the only space and time. We do not, indeed, know if our universe is the only one. Is there an infinity of *universes?* It would not surprise me in the least if there proved to be.

As Maxwell Cade has reminded me, it is useful to remember in connection with the size of the universe that, at a distance of 2,000 million light-years, stars are thought to recede at a speed close to the velocity of light. That is the maximum size that the *observable* universe can have, because at that distance stars are receding as fast as their light is emitted and the light consequently doesn't reach us.

But that is merely a reminder of the ultimate impossibility of ever observing the universe wholly. The question of parallel universes is a dramatic and important one. If there are other universes, might they not have other dimensions of time and space altogether?

I believe it to be highly probable that the earth *is* being observed by forms of life, intelligent life, in other parts of the universe or other universes. It does not follow that only one planet is involved. If they have sent out probes, as we have done, to see what is going on, they would have every reason to fear man and wish to limit his excursions into the universe.

If man can be so barbaric to man as he has been throughout the ages—even in the last few decades millions of beings have deliberately killed one another—if he can pollute the atmosphere, poison the oceans and rivers with chemical effluents, massacre all forms of animal and bird life, defoliate forests, raze cities to the ground by the touch of a button, one can imagine any visitor from outer space returning in a hurry and reporting: "On that planet live some dangerous creatures indeed. They're so unpleasant and cruel to each other that it would be a poor outlook if they ever landed here."

A civilization in advance of ours would certainly have mastered the art of telepathy, of conveying thoughts to each other, and implanting thoughts in the minds of others at will. If there is anything in the "parallel universe" idea, it would be easy to understand why some UFO's simply vanish from our sight.

The possibility that the world may be under observation implies a certain irony. So far, nothing has united mankind. Nations have cooperated only on such international business as banking arrangements and postal services, and day-to-day matters such as health controls, where the benefits are mutual. Otherwise, each pursues its own national prosperity and power, each holding that the end justifies the means and that the state is entitled to do anything for its own advancement.

A threat from outer space might constitute a threat to all humanity. Xenophobic invaders could easily view all earthly men as "foreigners." And so, too late probably, men might abandon their nationalisms, and racial and religious differences would be forgotten as they braced themselves for the last desperate struggle.

It might be *the* last desperate struggle, and a losing one. In the hierarchy of planets our earth is very small and very young. If invaders ever came from outer space they could, as Professor Bonfante has said, be millions of years in advance of us, possessing weapons, techniques, and powers not even suspected by ourselves and against which there might be no remedy.

I can almost hear somebody say, as the clouds of flying saucers hove into view: "If only we'd never fired that atom bomb! Then we might never have been noticed. The earth to them would have been a mere twinkling dot in their telescopes, indistinguishable from millions of other dots."

Whatever may happen, this much is sure: that of all mysterious worlds, using "world" in the figurative sense, the universe is the most mysterious of all.

Index

Henry III, 74
Henshaw, Mrs. Joyce, 129, 130
Hess, Rudolph, 113
Heywood, Rosalind, 55, 56
Hill, Charles, 116-120
Hilprecht, H. V., 43, 44, 45
Hinduism, 175
Hitler, Adolf, 60, 192, 193
Hockenhull, Leslie, 88, 89
Holly, Buddy, 94
Holsworthy, Devon, case (UFO), 217, 218
Holyrood House, Edinburgh, 174, 175
Home, William Douglas, 74
Hopkins, Matthew, 191
Horton, Johnny, 95
House of Bewley, Chester, 127, 128
Howard, Richard, 118
Hughes, Stanley, 130
Humanoids, 219, 223
Hutchinson, Norman, 113
Huxley, Dr. Julian, 180
Hypnagogic state, 127
Hypnotism, 17, 18, 20, 58

Ibbott, Thomas, 75
Ingham, David, 138, 139
Institute for Brain Research, Leningrad, 20
Institute of Dream Research, Miami, 50-51
Institute of Higher Nervous Activity, Moscow, 21
International Space Conference, 24
Isaiah, 73, 74
Ivanov-Smolensky, A. G., 19

Jackson, Robert, 95
Jacob, 41
Jacubson, Dr. Hirsch Gregory, 63-65
James, William, 72
Jeans, Sir James, 226
Jodrell Bank Experimental Station, 227
Joire, Dr. Paul, 16, 170
Jones, Dr. J. C., 93
Jonson, Ben, 4
Joseph, 42

Kakkezai, Altaf Husain, 32, 33
Kane, Eden, 94
Kazantsev, Alexander, 230
Kazhinsky, Bernard, 19
Kekule, Friedrich von, 58
Kennedy, John F., 74
Kennedy, Robert, 86
Kidd, James, 173
King, Dr. Martin Luther, Jr., 86
Kleitman, Dr. Nathaniel, 49
Knulst, Mrs. H. M., 31, 32
Konecci, Dr. Eugene, 24
Krippner, Dr. Stanley, 52

Lakenheath case (UFO), 212-213
Lannoy, Richard, 98, 99
Lavender field case (UFO), 219, 220, 223
Leek, Sybil, 190
Leonard, Vincenzo. See Perrugia
Leontovitch, Alexander, 19
Lewis, C. S., 131-134
Light-year, 226
Ligonier, Jean Louis (Field-Marshal), 108
Liguori, Alphonse de, 144, 145
Lincoln, Abraham, 74
Lissauer, Mrs. Janice, 84, 85
Littlecote Manor, 109, 110
Lodge, Sir Oliver, 72, 74, 172
Longleat, 110
Louvre Museum, Paris, 181
Lovell, Sir Bernard, 227

Magic
  Black, 192, 196-199
  Gray, 192
  White, 192
  See also Witchcraft
Maimonides Dream Laboratory, 52
Mann, James F. A., 135-136
Manning, Olivia, 169
Mantell, Thomas F., 216
Mars (planet), 209, 228
Marshall, Jack, 79
Martin, Mrs. Klaire L., 29
Mary Stuart, Queen of Scotland, 174, 175

Sanders, Alex, 190
Sanders, Dudley N., 126
Satterlee, Mrs. Katherine, 80
Schrenck-Notzing, Dr. Albert von, 17, 18
Scott, Sir Walter, 174
Second All-Russian Congress on Psychoneurology (1924), 20
Second sight. *See* Telepathy
Sidgwick, Henry, 2, 17, 71
Sinclair, Upton, 18, 25
Sleep, 35, 36, 49
Sleeplessness, 49
Sleepwalking, 59
Society for Psychical Research, 2, 3, 13, 14, 17, 66, 71, 72, 73, 76, 77, 137, 138
Somers, Rev. Montagu, 187
Soul, human, 173
Space, outer, 24, 226-233
Spanish Armada, 192
Spiritualism, 172-183
Spurney, Richard Carl, 173
Stars, 226, 227
Stevens, William Oliver, 8, 9
Stevenson, Robert Louis, 57, 58
Stewart, Balfour, 72
Stockwood, Dr. Mervyn, 198
Stoke-on-Trent case (UFO), 216-217
Stolyarov, Maj. Gen. Porfiri, 208
Stoney, Mrs. W. M., 27
Streete, Rev. Ernest, 198
Subconscious mind, 58

Talmud, 43
Tartini, Giuseppe, 57
Tate, Sharon, 193
Taylor, Edwina, 91
Telekinetic energy, 122
Telepathic thought. *See* Telepathy
Telepathy, 1-11, 12-25, 215
    Experimental, 3, 12-25, 104
    Military uses, 25

Spontaneous, 3-11
    See also Astral projection; **Dreams**
Telescopes, 227
Thomsett, Roy, 129
Titanic (ship), 79, 80
Toynbee, Mrs. Arnold, 14-15
Trent, Paul, 211, 212
Tyrrell, G. N. M., 18

UFO. *See* Unidentified flying objects
Ullman, Dr. Montague, 52
Underwood, Peter, 118-120
Unidentified flying objects, 200-225, 230-233
United States, 22, 24, 48, 49
United States Air Force, 25, 203-206
Universe, 226-233

Vasiliev, Leonid, 19-23
Venus (planet), 228
VERITAC, 25
Vestigial faculties, 127

Walther, Dr. Gerda, 18
Walton, Charles, 190
Westinghouse Electric Corporation of America, 22
Whittacker, Alan, 125
Wills, David Seton, 109, 110
Wilmot, S. R., 149-150
Wilson, Nickie, 190
Wiltse, A. S., 81, 82
Witchcraft, 184-199
Witchcraft Museum, Isle of Man, 186, 190, 191
Witches, 184-199
Wydur, Francis James, 169, 170

Xavier, Father, 145, 146

Zener cards, 18, 24, 104
Zigel, Dr. Felix, 206-208